T0313975

# Demystifying Deep Learning

**IEEE Press**
445 Hoes Lane
Piscataway, NJ 08854

**IEEE Press Editorial Board**
Sarah Spurgeon, *Editor in Chief*

| | | |
|---|---|---|
| Jón Atli Benediktsson | Behzad Razavi | Jeffrey Reed |
| Anjan Bose | Jim Lyke | Diomidis Spinellis |
| James Duncan | Hai Li | Adam Drobot |
| Amin Moeness | Brian Johnson | Tom Robertazzi |
| Desineni Subbaram Naidu | | Ahmet Murat Tekalp |

# Demystifying Deep Learning

An Introduction to the Mathematics of Neural Networks

*Douglas J. Santry*
University of Kent, United Kingdom

IEEE PRESS

WILEY

Copyright © 2024 by The Institute of Electrical and Electronics Engineers, Inc.
All rights reserved.

Published by John Wiley & Sons, Inc., Hoboken, New Jersey.
Published simultaneously in Canada.

No part of this publication may be reproduced, stored in a retrieval system, or transmitted in any form or by any means, electronic, mechanical, photocopying, recording, scanning, or otherwise, except as permitted under Section 107 or 108 of the 1976 United States Copyright Act, without either the prior written permission of the Publisher, or authorization through payment of the appropriate per-copy fee to the Copyright Clearance Center, Inc., 222 Rosewood Drive, Danvers, MA 01923, (978) 750-8400, fax (978) 750-4470, or on the web at www.copyright.com. Requests to the Publisher for permission should be addressed to the Permissions Department, John Wiley & Sons, Inc., 111 River Street, Hoboken, NJ 07030, (201) 748-6011, fax (201) 748-6008, or online at http://www.wiley.com/go/permission.

Trademarks: Wiley and the Wiley logo are trademarks or registered trademarks of John Wiley & Sons, Inc. and/or its affiliates in the United States and other countries and may not be used without written permission. All other trademarks are the property of their respective owners. John Wiley & Sons, Inc. is not associated with any product or vendor mentioned in this book.

Limit of Liability/Disclaimer of Warranty: While the publisher and author have used their best efforts in preparing this book, they make no representations or warranties with respect to the accuracy or completeness of the contents of this book and specifically disclaim any implied warranties of merchantability or fitness for a particular purpose. No warranty may be created or extended by sales representatives or written sales materials. The advice and strategies contained herein may not be suitable for your situation. You should consult with a professional where appropriate. Further, readers should be aware that websites listed in this work may have changed or disappeared between when this work was written and when it is read. Neither the publisher nor authors shall be liable for any loss of profit or any other commercial damages, including but not limited to special, incidental, consequential, or other damages.

For general information on our other products and services or for technical support, please contact our Customer Care Department within the United States at (800) 762-2974, outside the United States at (317) 572-3993 or fax (317) 572-4002.

Wiley also publishes its books in a variety of electronic formats. Some content that appears in print may not be available in electronic formats. For more information about Wiley products, visit our web site at www.wiley.com.

*Library of Congress Cataloging-in-Publication Data Applied for:*

Hardback ISBN: 9781394205608

Cover Design: Wiley
Cover Image: © Yuichiro Chino/Getty Images

Set in 9.5/12.5pt STIXTwoText by Straive, Chennai, India

# Contents

## About the Author

**Douglas J. Santry**, PhD, MSc, is a Lecturer in Computer Science at the University of Kent, UK. Prior to his current position, he worked extensively as an important figure in the industry with Apple Computer Corp, NetApp, and Goldman Sachs. At NetApp, he conducted research into embedded and real-time machine learning techniques.

## Acronyms

| | |
|---|---|
| AI | artificial intelligence |
| ANN | artificial neural network |
| BERT | bidirectional encoder representation for transformers |
| BN | Bayesian network |
| BPG | backpropagation |
| CNN | convolutional neural network |
| CNN | classifying neural network |
| DL | deep learning |
| FFFC | feed forward fully connected |
| GAN | generative adversarial network |
| GANN | generative artificial neural network |
| GPT | generative pre-trained |
| LLM | large language model |
| LSTM | long short term memory |
| ML | machine learning |
| MLE | minimum likelihood estimator |
| MSE | mean squared error |
| NLP | natural language processing |
| RL | reinforcement learning |
| RNN | recurrent neural network |
| SGD | stochastic gradient descent |

# 1

# Introduction

Interest in deep learning (DL) is increasing every day. It has escaped from the research laboratories and become a daily fact of life. The achievements and potential of DL are reported in the lay news and form the subject of discussion at dinner tables, cafes, and pubs across the world. This is an astonishing change of fortune considering the technology upon which it is founded was pronounced a research dead end in 1969 (131) and largely abandoned.

The universe of DL is a veritable alphabet soup of bewildering acronyms. There are artificial neural networks (ANN)s, RNNs, LSTMs, CNNs, Generative Adversarial Networks (GAN)s, and more are introduced every day. The types and applications of DL are proliferating rapidly, and the acronyms grow in number with them. As DL is successfully applied to new problem domains this trend will continue. Since 2015 the number of artificial intelligence (AI) patents filed per annum has been growing at a rate of 76.6% and shows no signs of slowing down (169). The growth rate speaks to the increasing investment in DL and suggests that it is still accelerating.

DL is based on ANN. Often only neural networks is written and the artificial is implied. ANNs attempt to mathematically model biological assemblies of neurons. The initial goal of research into ANNs was to realize AI in a computer. The motivation and means were to mimic the biological mechanisms of cognitive processes in animal brains. This led to the idea of modeling the networks of neurons in brains. If biological neural networks could be modeled accurately with mathematics, then computers could be programmed with the models. Computers would then be able to perform tasks that were previously thought only possible by humans; the dream of the electronic brain was born (151). Two problem domains were of particular interest: natural language processing (NLP), and image recognition. These were areas where brains were thought to be the only viable instrument; today, these applications are only the tip of the iceberg.

*Demystifying Deep Learning: An Introduction to the Mathematics of Neural Networks,*
First Edition. Douglas J. Santry.
© 2024 The Institute of Electrical and Electronics Engineers, Inc. Published 2024 by John Wiley & Sons, Inc.

In the field of image recognition, DL has achieved spectacular results and, by some metrics, is out-performing humans. Image recognition is the task of finding and identifying objects in an image. DL has a better record than humans (13; 63) recognizing the ImageNet (32) test suite, an important database of millions of photographs. Computer vision has become so reliable for some tasks that it is common for motor cars to offer features based on reliable computer vision, and in some cases, cars can even drive themselves. In airports and shopping malls, we are continually monitored by CCTV, but often it is a computer, not a human, performing the monitoring (39). Some CCTV monitors look for known thieves and automatically alert the staff, or even the local police, when they are spotted in a shop (165). This can lead to problems. When courts and the police do not understand how to interpret the results of the software great injustices can follow.

One such example is that of Robert Julian-Borchak Williams (66). Mr. Williams' case is a cautionary tale. AI image recognition software is not evidence and does not claim to be. It is meant to point law enforcement in a promising direction of investigation; it is a complement to investigation, not a substitute. But too often the police assume the computer's hint is a formal allegation and treat it as such. Mr. Williams was accused of a crime by the police that he did not commit. The police were acting on information from AI image recognition software, but the police were convinced because they did not understand what the computer was telling them. A computer suggested that the video of a shoplifter in a shop could be Mr. Williams. As a result, a warrant was obtained on the basis of the computer's identification. All the "safeguards," such as corroborating evidence, despite being formal policy of the police department, were ignored, and Mr. Williams had a nightmare visited upon him. He was arrested, processed, and charged with no effort on the part of the police to confirm the computer's suggestion. This scenario has grown so frequent that there are real concerns with the police and the courts using AI technology as an aid to their work. Subsequently, Amazon, IBM, and Microsoft withdrew their facial recognition software from police use pending federal regulation (59). DL, like any tool, must be used responsibly to provide the greatest benefit and mitigate harm.

DL ANNs have also made tremendous progress in the field of NLP. Natural language is how people communicate, such as English or Japanese. Computers are just elaborate calculators, and they have no capacity for inference or context; hence, people use programming languages to talk to computers. The current state-of-the-art NLP is based on transformers (155) (see Section 9.4 for details). Transformers have led to recent rapid progress in language models and NLP tools since 2017. Moreover, progress in NLP systems is outstripping the test suites. A popular language comprehension benchmark, the General Language Understanding Benchmark (GLUE) (158), was quickly mastered by research systems, leading to its replacement by SuperGLUE in the space of a year (159).

SuperGlue will soon be upgraded. Another important benchmark, the Stanford Question Answering Dataset 2.0 (SQUAD) (121) has also been mastered[1] and is anticipating an update to increase the challenge. The test suites are currently too easy for modern NLP systems. This is impressive as the bar was not set low per se. DL ANNs are, on average, outperforming humans in both test suites. Therefore, it can be argued that the test suites are genuinely challenging.

Of particular note is OpenAI's ChatGPT; it has dazzled the world (128). The author recently had to change the questions for his university course assignments because the students were using ChatGPT to produce complete answers. Because ChatGPT can understand English, some students were cutting and pasting the question, in plain English, into the ChatGPT prompt and doing the reverse with the response. ChatGPT is able to produce Python code that is correct. The irony of students using DL to cheat on AI course work was not lost on him.

A lot of the debate surrounding ChatGPT has centered on its abilities, what it can and cannot do reliably, but to do so is to miss the point. The true import of ChatGPT is not what it can do today. ChatGPT is not perfect, and its creators never claimed it was far from it. The free version used by most of the world was made available to aid in identifying and fixing problems. ChatGPT is a point in a *trend*. The capabilities of ChatGPT, today, are not important. The real point is the implication of what language models will be capable of in five to ten years. The coming language models will clearly be extremely powerful. Businesses and professions that think they are safe because ChatGPT is not perfect are taking terrible risks. There is a misconception that it is low-skilled jobs that will experience the most change, that the professions will remain untouched as they have been for decades. This is a mistake. The real application of DL is not in low-skilled jobs. Factories and manufacturing were already disrupted starting in the 1970s with the introduction of automation. DL is going to make the professions more productive, such as medicine and law. It is the high-skilled jobs that are going to experience the most disruption. A study by OpenAI examining the potential of its language models suggested that up to 80% of the US workforce would experience some form of change resulting from language models (38). This may be a conservative estimate.

Perhaps one of the most interesting advances of DL is the emergence of systems that produce meaningful content. The systems mentioned so far either classify, inflect (e.g. translate), or "comprehend" input data. Systems that produce material instead of consuming it are known as *generative*. When produced with DL, they are known as a Generative Artificial Neural Network (GANN). ChatGPT is an

---

1 The leaderboard shows 90% is now a common score: https://rajpurkar.github.io/SQuAD-explorer. The human score is 89%.

**Figure 1.1** Examples of GAN-generated cats. The matrix on the left contains examples from the training set. The matrix on the right are GAN-generated cats. The cats on the right do not exist. They were generated by the GAN. Source: Karras et al. (81).

example of a generative language model. Images and videos can also be generated. A GANN can draw an image this is very different from learning to recognize an image. A powerful means of building GANNs is with GAN (50); again, very much an alphabet soup. As an example, a GAN can be taught impressionist painting by training it with pictures by the impressionist masters. The GAN will then produce a novel painting very much in the genre of impressionism. The quality of the images generated is remarkable. Figure 1.1 displays an example of cats produced by a GAN (81). The GAN was trained to learn what cats look like and produce examples. The object is to produce photorealistic synthetic cats. Products such as Adobe Photoshop have included this facility for general use by the public (90). In the sphere of video and audio, GANs are producing the so-called "deep fake" videos that are of very high quality. Deep fakes are becoming increasingly difficult for humans to detect. In the age of information war and disinformation, the ramifications are serious. GANs, are performing tasks at levels undreamt of a few decades ago, the quality can be striking, and even troubling. As new applications are identified for GANs the resources dedicated to improving them will continue to grow and produce ever more spectacular results.

## 1.1 AI/ML – Deep Learning?

It is all too common to see the acronym AI/ML, which stands for artificial intelligence/machine learning, and worse to see the terms used interchangeably. AI, as the name implies, is the study of simulating or creating intelligence, and even defining intelligence. It is a field of study encompassing many areas including, but not limited to, machine learning. AI researchers can also be biologists (histology and neurology), psychologists, mathematicians, computer scientists, and philosophers. What is intelligence? What are the criteria for certifying something as intelligent? These are philosophical questions as much as technical challenges. How can AI be defined without an understanding of "natural" intelligence? That is a question that lies more in the biological realm than that of technology. Machine Learning is a subfield of AI. DL and ANNs are a subfield of machine learning.

The polymath, Alan Turing, suggested what has come to be known as the Turing Test[2] in 1950 (153). He argued that if a machine could fool a human by convincing the human that it is human too, then the computer is "intelligent." He proposed concealing a human and a computer and linking them over a teletype to a third party, a human evaluator. If the human evaluator could not distinguish between the human and the computer, then, effectively, the computer could be deemed "intelligent." It is an extremely controversial assertion, but a useful one in 1950. It has formed an invaluable basis for discussion ever since. An influential argument forwarded in 1980 by the philosopher, John Searle, asserts that a machine can never realize real intelligence in a digital computer. Searle argued that a machine that could pass the Turing test was not necessarily intelligent. He proposed a thought experiment called the Chinese Room (135). The Turing test was constrained to be performed in Chinese, and it was accepted that a machine could be programmed to pass the test. Searle argued that there is an important distinction between simulating Chinese and understanding Chinese. The latter is the true mark of intelligence. He characterized the difference as "weak AI" and "strong AI". A computer executing a program of instructions is not thinking, and Searle argued that is all a computer could ever do. There is a large body of literature, some of which predates Turing's contribution and dates back to Leibniz (96; 98), debating the point. OpenAI's recent offering, ChatGPT, is a perfect example of this dichotomy. The lay press speculates (128) on whether it is intelligent, but clearly it is an example of "weak AI." The product can pass the Turing test, but it is not intelligent.

To understand what machine learning is, one must place it in relation to AI. It is a means of realizing some aspect of AI in a digital computer; it is a subfield of AI. Tom Mitchell, who wrote a seminal text on machine learning (105), provides a

---

2  Alan Turing called it the "imitation game."

useful definition of machine learning: "A computer program is said to **learn**[3] from experience, E, with respect to some class of tasks, T, and performance measure, P, if its performance at tasks in T, as measured by P, improves with experience E." [Page 2]. Despite first appearances, this really is a very concise definition. So while it is clear that machine learning is related to AI, the reverse is not necessarily true. DL and ANN are, in turn, specializations of machine learning. Thus, while DL is a specialization of AI, not all AI topics are necessarily connected to DL.

The object of this book is to present a canonical mathematical basis for DL concisely and directly with an emphasis on practical implementation, and as such, the reference approach is consciously eschewed. It is not an attempt to cover everything as it cannot. The field DL has advanced to the point where both its depth and breadth call for a series of books. But a brief history of DL is clearly indicated. DL evolved from ANNs, and so the history begins with them. The interested reader is directed to (31) for a more thorough history and to (57; 127) for a stronger biological motivation.

## 1.2 A Brief History

ANNs are inspired by, and originally attempted to simulate, biological neural networks. Naturally, research into biological neural networks predated ANNs. During the nineteenth century, great strides were taken, and it was an interdisciplinary effort. As physicists began to explain electricity and scientists placed chemistry on a firm scientific footing, the basis was created for a proper understanding of the biological phenomena that depended on them. Advances in grinding lenses combined with a better appreciation of the light condenser led to a dramatic increase in the quality microscopes. The stage was set for histologists, biologists, and anatomists to make progress in identifying and understanding tissues and cell differentiation. Putting all those pieces together yielded new breakthroughs in understanding the biology of living things in every sphere.

Alexander Bain and William James made independent seminal contributions (8; 76). They postulated that physical action, the movement of muscles, was directed and controlled by neurons in the brain and communicated with electrical signals. Santiago Ramón y Cajal (167) and Sir Charles Sherrington (136) put the study of neurology on a firm footing with their descriptions of neurons and synapses; both would go on to win Nobel prizes for their contributions in 1906 and 1932, respectively.

By the 1940s, a firm understanding of biological neurons had been developed. Computer science was nascent, but fundamental results were developed. In the

---

3 The word, learn, is in bold in Mitchell's text. The author clearly wished to emphasize the nature of the exercise.

1930s, Alonzo Church had described his Lambda Calculus model of computation (21), and his student, Alan Turing, had defined his Turing Machine[4] (152), both formal models of computation. The age of modern computation was dawning. Warren McCulloch and Walter Pitts wrote a number of papers that proposed artificial neurons to simulate Turing machines (164). Their first paper was published in 1943. They showed that artificial neurons could implement logic and arithmetic functions. Their work hypothesized networks of artificial neurons cooperating to implement higher-level logic. They did not implement or evaluate their ideas, but researchers had now begun thinking about artificial neurons.

Daniel Hebb, an eminent psychologist, wrote a book in 1949 postulating a learning rule for artificial neurons (65). It is a supervised learning rule. While the rule itself is numerically unstable, the rule contains many of the ingredients of modern ANNs. Hebb's neurons computed state based on the scaler product and weighted the connections between the individual neurons. Connections between neurons were reinforced based on use. While modern learning rules and network topologies are different, Hebb's work was prescient. Many of the elements of modern ANNs are recognizable such as a neuron's state computation, response propagation, and a general network of weighted connections.

The next step to modern ANNs was Frank Rosenblatt's perceptron (130). Rosenblatt published his first paper in 1958. Building on Hebb's neuron, he proposed an updated supervised learning rule called the perceptron rule. Rosenblatt was interested in computer vision. His first implementation was in software on an IBM 704 mainframe (it had 18 k of memory!). Perceptrons were eventually implemented in hardware. The machine was a contemporary marvel fitted with an array of $20 \times 20$ cadmium sulfide photocells used to create a 400 pixel input image. The New York Times reported it with the headline, "Electronic Brain Teaches Itself." Hebb's neuron state was improved with the introduction of a bias, an innovation still very important today. Perceptrons were capable of learning linear decision boundaries, that is, the categories of classification had to be linearly separable.

The next milestone was a paper by Widrow and Hoff in 1960 that proposed a new learning rule, the delta rule. It was more numerically stable than the perceptron learning rule. Their research system was called ADALINE (15) and used least squares to train the network. Like Rosenblatt's early work, ADALINE was implemented in hardware with memristors. The follow-up system, MADALINE (163), included multiple layers of perceptrons, another step toward modern ANNs. It suffered from a similar limitation as Rosenblatt's perceptrons in that it could only address linearly separable problems; it was a composition of linear classifiers.

In 1969, Minksy and Papert published a book that set a pall on ANN research (106). They demonstrated that ANNs, as they were understood at that

---

4 It was Church who coined the term, Turing Machine.

point, suffer from an inherent limitation. It was argued that ANNs could never solve "interesting" problems; but the assertion was based on the assumption that ANNs could never practically handle nonlinear decision boundaries. They famously used the example of the XOR logic gate. As the XOR truth table could not be learnt by an ANN, and XOR is trivial concept when compared to image recognition and other applications, they concluded that the latter applications were not appropriate. As most interesting problems are nonlinear, including vision and NLP, they concluded that the ANN was a research dead end. Their book had the effect of chilling research in ANNs for many years as the AI community accepted their conclusion. It coincided with a general reassessment of the practicality of AI research in general and the beginning of the first "AI Winter."

The fundamental problem facing ANN researchers was how to train multiple layers of an ANN to solve nonlinear problems. While there were multiple independent developments, Rumelhart, Hinton, and Williams are generally credited with the work that described the backpropagation of error algorithm in the context of training ANNs (34). This was published in 1986. It is still the basis of training today. Backpropagation of error is the basis of the majority of modern ANN training algorithms. Their method provided a means of training ANNs to learn nonlinear problems reliably.

It was also in 1986 that Rina Dechter coined the term, "Deep Learning" (30). The usage was not what is meant by DL today. She was describing a backtracking algorithm for theorem proving with Prolog programs.

The confluence of two trends, the dissemination of the backpropagation algorithm and the advent of widely available workstations, led to unprecedented experimentation and advances in ANNs. By 1989, in a space of just 3 years, ANNs had been successfully trained to recognize hand-written digits in the form of postal codes from the United States Postal Service. This feat was achieved by a team led by Yann Lecun at AT&T Labs (91). The work had all the recognizable features of DL, but the term had not yet been applied to neural networks in that sense. The system would evolve into LeNet-5, a classic DL model. The renewed interest in ANN research has continued unbroken down to this day. In 2006, Hinton et al. described a multi-layered belief network that was described as a "Deep Belief Network," (67). The usage arguably led to referring to deep neural networks as DL. The introduction of AlexNet in 2012 demonstrated how to efficiently use GPUs to train DL models (89). AlexNet set records in image recognition benchmarks. Since AlexNet DL models have dominated most machine learning applications; it has heralded the DL Age of machine learning.

We leave our abridged history here and conclude with a few thoughts. As the computing power required to train ANNs grows ever cheaper, access to the resources required for research becomes more widely available. The IBM Supercomputer, ASCI White, cost US$110 million in 2001 and occupied a special purpose room. It had 8192 processors for a total of 123 billion transistors with a peak performance of 12.3 TFLOPS.[5] In 2023, an Apple Mac Studio costs US$4000, contains 114 billion transistors, and offers peak performance of 20 TFLOPS. It sits quietly and discreetly on a desk. In conjunction with improvements in hardware, there is a change in the culture of disseminating results. The results of research are proliferating in an ever more timely fashion.[6] The papers themselves are also recognizing that describing the algorithms is not the only point of interest. Papers are including experimental methodology and setup more frequently, making it easier to reproduce results. This is made possible by ever cheaper and more powerful hardware. Clearly, the DL boom has just begun.

## 1.3 The Genesis of Models

A model is an attempt to mimic some phenomenon. It can take the form of a sculpture, a painting or a mathematical explanation of observations of the natural world. People have been modeling the world since the dawn of civilization. The models of interest in this book are quantitative mathematical models. People build quantitative models to understand the world and use the models to make *predictions*. With accurate predictions come the capacity to exploit and manipulate natural phenomena. Humans walked on the moon because accurate models of gravity, among many other things, were possible. Building quantitative models requires many technologies. Writing, the invention of numbers and a means of operating on them, arithmetic, and finally mathematics. In its simplest form, a model is a mathematical function. In essence, building a model means developing a mathematical function that makes accurate predictions; the scientific method is an extraordinarily successful example of this. DL ANNs are forms of models, but before we examine them let us examine how models have traditionally been developed.

### 1.3.1 Rise of the Empirical Functions

People have been building models for millennia. The traditional means of doing so is to write down a constrained set of equations and then solve them. For millennia, the constraints have been in the form of natural laws or similar phenomena. The laws are often discovered scientifically. Ibn al-Haytham and Galileo Galilei (45) independently invented the scientific method, which when combined with the

---

5  TFLOP (teraflops), trillions of floating point operations per second.
6  For example, sites such as https://arxiv.org/list/cs.LG/recent offer researchers and the community early peer review and uncopyrighted access to research. The time frames are convenient for research, not journal deadlines.

calculus (invented independently by Newton and Leibniz in 1660s), a century later led to an explosion of understanding of the natural world. The scientist gathers data, interprets it, and composes a law in the form of an equation that explains it. For example, Newton's law of gravity is

$$Force\,of\,Gravity = \frac{Gm_1m_2}{r^2}, \tag{1.1}$$

where $G = 6.674 \cdot 10^{11} \text{ m}^3 \cdot \text{kg}^{-1}\text{s}^{-2}$ in SI units, r is the distance between two objects, and $m_i$ are the masses of the objects.

Using the equation for gravity, one can build models by writing an equation and then solving it. The law of gravity acts as the constraint. Natural laws are discovered by scientists collecting, analyzing, and interpreting the data to discern the relationships between the variables, and the result is an interpretable model. Once natural laws have been published, such as the conservation of mass, scientists, and engineers can use them to build models of systems of interest. This is done for exciting things like the equations of motion for rockets and dull things like designing the plumbing for an apartment building; mathematical models are everywhere.

The process of building a model begins with writing down a set of constraints in the form of a system of differential equations and then solving them. To illustrate, consider the trivial problem of producing a model that computes the time to fall for an object from a height, $h$, near the surface of the Earth. The object's motion is constrained by gravity. The classical means of proceeding is to use Newton's laws and writing down a constraint. Acceleration near the surface of the Earth can be approximated with the constant, g (9.80665 m/s$^2$). Employing Newton's notation for derivatives, we obtain the following equation of motion (acceleration in this case) based on the physical constraint:

$$\ddot{x} = g. \tag{1.2}$$

The equation can be integrated to obtain the velocity (ignoring friction),

$$\dot{x} = \int g \cdot dt = gt, \tag{1.3}$$

which in turn can be integrated to produce the desired model, $t = f(h)$,

$$h \equiv x = \frac{g}{2}t^2 \implies t = \sqrt{\frac{2h}{g}} = f(h). \tag{1.4}$$

This yields an analytical solution obtained from the constraint, which was obtained from a natural law. Of course this is a very trivial example, and often an analytical solution is not available. Under those circumstances, the modeler must resort to numerical methods to solve the equations, but it illustrates the historical approach.

With modern computers another approach to obtaining a function, $\hat{f}(h)$, is possible; an ANN can be used. Instead of constraining the system with a natural law, it is constrained empirically, with a dataset. ANNs are trained with supervised learning techniques. They can be thought of as functions that start as raw clay. Supervised training moulds the clay into the desired shape (an accurate model), and the desired model is specified with a dataset, that is, the dataset defines the model, not a natural law. To demonstrate, the example of $f(h)$ is revisited.

Training the ANN is done with supervised learning techniques. The raw clay of the untrained ANN function needs to be defined by data, so the first step is to collect data. This is done by measuring the time to fall from a number of different heights. This would result in a dataset of the form, $\{(h_1, t_1), \ldots, (h_N, t_N)\}$, where each tuple consists of the height and the time to fall to the ground. Using the data, the ANN can be trained and we obtain,

$$t = \mathrm{ANN}(h) \equiv \hat{f}(h). \tag{1.5}$$

Once trained, the ANN model approximates $\hat{f}(h) \approx f(h)$, the analytical solution.

There are now two models, hopefully producing the same results, but arrived at with completely different techniques. The results of both are depicted in Figure 1.2. There are, however, some meaningful differences. First, the ANN is a black box, it may be correct, but nothing can really be said about it. The final model does not admit of interpretability. The analytical result can be used to predict asymptotic behavior or the rearrangement of variables for further insights. Moreover, the analytical solution was obtained by rearranging the solution to the differential Eq. (1.4). Second, the training of the ANN uses far more compute resources, memory, and CPU, than the analytical solution. And finally, assembling the dataset is a great deal of trouble. In this trivial example, someone already did that and arrived at the gravitational constant, g. Comparing the two methods, the ANN approach seems like a great deal more trouble.

This begs the question, given the seeming disadvantage of ANNs, why would anyone ever use them? The answer lies in the differences between the approaches, the seeming "disadvantages." The ANN approach, training with raw data, did not require any understanding or insight of the underlying process that produced the data to build an accurate model, *none*. The model was constrained empirically – the data, and no constraint in the form of a natural law or principle was required. This is extremely useful for many modern problems of interest.

Consider the problem of classifying black-and-white digital images as one of either a cat, a dog, or a giraffe; we need a function. The function is $f : \mathbb{R}^M \rightarrow \mathbb{K}$, where $\mathbb{K}$ is the set, $\mathbb{K} = \{\,\mathtt{cat},\ \mathtt{dog},\ \mathtt{giraffe}\,\}$, and $M$ is the resolution of the image. For such applications, empirically specifying the function is the only means of obtaining the model. There are no other constraints available, Einstein cannot help with a natural law, the Black Scholes equation is of no use, nor can a

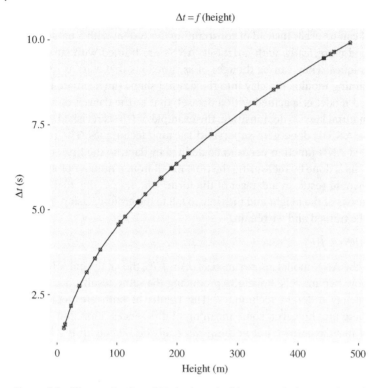

$\Delta t = f\,(\text{height})$

**Figure 1.2** The graph of $t = f(h)$, is plotted with empty circles as points. The *ANN(h)*'s predictions are crosses plotted over them. The points are from training dataset. The ANN seems to have learnt the function.

principle such as "no arbitrage" be invoked. There is no natural starting point. The underlying process is unknown, and probably unknowable. The fact that we have no insight into the process producing the data is no hinderance at all. There is a drawback in that the resulting model is not interpretable, but never the less the approach has been immensely successful. Using supervised learning techniques for this application imposes the requirement to collect a set of images and labeling them with the correct answer (one of the three possible answers). Thus, ignoring the need for interpretability or an understanding of the generating process, it is possible to accurately model a whole new set of applications.

Even for applications where natural laws exist leading to a system of constraints, ANNs are beginning to enjoy some success. Combinatoric problems such as protein folding have been successfully addressed with ANNs (16). ANNs are better at predicting the shapes of proteins than approaches solving the differential equations and quantum mechanical constraints. Large problems lacking an analytical solution, such as predicting the paths of hurricanes, are investing in the use of ANNs to make predictions that are more accurate (22). There are many more examples.

### 1.3.2 The Biological Phenomenon and the Analogue

Finally, it is worth bearing in mind the inherent differences between the DL models composed of ANNs and animal brains. ANNs were motivated by, and attempted to simulate, biological neuron assemblies (Hebb and Rosenblatt were psychologists). Owing to the success of DL, the nature of the simulation is often lost while retaining the connection; this can be unfortunate.

It must not be forgotten that biological neural networks are physical; they are cells, "hardware." Biological neurons operate independently, asynchronously, and concurrently; they are the unit of computation. In this sense, a brain is a biological parallel computer. ANNs are software simulating biological hardware on a completely different computer architecture. There are inherent differences between the biological instance and the simulation that render the ANN inefficient. A simulated neuron must wait to have its state updated when a signal "arrives." The delay is owing to waiting in a queue for its turn on a CPU core – the simulation's unit of computation. Biological neurons are the "CPU"s and continually update themselves. A human brain has approximately 100 billion neurons with an average of 10,000 synapses (connections) each (79), and they do not need to wait their turn to compute state – they are the state. The ANN simulation must queue all its virtual neurons serially for a chance on a CPU to update their state. To do this efficiently, DL models typically impose strong restrictions on the topology of the network of virtual neuron connections. ANN software is simulating a parallel computer on a serial computer. Even allowing for the parallelism of GPUs, the simulation is still $O$(number of neurons). The characteristics are different too: a biological neural network is an analog computer and modern computers are digital.

The nature of a computer is also very much at variance with an animal brain. A human brain uses around 20 W of energy (79). An Intel Xeon CPU consumes between 200 and 300 W, as do GPUs. The power usage of the GPU farms used to train Google's BERT or NVIDIA's GANN is measured in kilowatts. Training language models can cost US\$8,000,000 just for the electricity (19). It is also common to compare biological neurons to transistors. It is a really fine example of an apple to orange comparison. Transistors have switching times in the order of $10^{-9}$ seconds. Biological neuron switching times are in the order of $10^{-3}$ seconds. Transistors typically have 3 static connections, while neurons can have thousands of connections. A neuron's set of connections, synapses, can be dynamically adapting to changing circumstances. Neurons perform very different functions, and a great many transistors would be required to implement the functionality of a single neuron.

None of this is to say that DL software is inappropriate for use or not fit for purpose, quite the contrary, but it is important to have some perspective on the nature of the simulation and the fundamental differences.

## 1.4   Numerical Computation – Computer Numbers Are Not ℝeal

Before presenting DL algorithms, it should be emphasized that ANNs are mathematical algorithms implemented on digital computers. When reading this text, it is important to understand that naïve computer implementations of mathematical methods can lead to surprising [7] results. Blindly typing equations into a computer is often a recipe for trouble, and DL is no exception. Arithmetic is different on a computer and varies in unexpected ways, as will be seen. Unlike the normal arithmetical operations of addition and subtraction, most computer implementations of them are not associative, distributive, or commutative. The reader is encouraged to peruse this section with a computer and experiment to aid understanding the pitfalls.

Consider the interval, $S = [1,2] \subset \mathbb{Z}$, a subset of the natural numbers. The cardinality of $S$, $|S|$, is two. Intervals of the natural numbers are *countable*. Now consider $S = [1,2] \subset \mathbb{R}$. The real number line is *continuous*, a characteristic relied upon by the calculus. So, in this case, $|S| = \infty$. Indeed, $S = [1, 1.0000001] \subset \mathbb{R}$ also has a cardinality of infinity. Equations are generally derived assuming that $\mathbb{R}$ is available, but the real number line does not exist in a computer. Computers simulate $\mathbb{R}$ with a necessarily discrete (finite) set called floating point numbers. This has profound implications when programming. Two mathematically equivalent algorithms can behave completely differently when implemented on the same digital computer.

By far, the most common implementation of floating point numbers on modern digital computers is the IEEE-754 standard for floating point values (25). First agreed in 1985, it has been continually updated ever since. Intel's x86 family of processors implement it as well as Apple's ARM chips, such as the Mx family of SoCs. It is often misunderstood as simply a format for representing floating point numbers, but it is actually a complete system defining behavior and operations, including the handling of errors. This is extremely important as running a program on different CPU architectures that are IEEE-754 compliant will yield the same numerical results. The most common IEEE-754 floating point types are the

---

7 "Surprising" is an engineering and scientific euphemism for unwelcome.

32-bit ("single-precision") and the 64-bit ("double-precision") formats.[8] Computer languages usually expose them as native types and the programmer uses them without realizing it. It is immediately clear that, by their very nature of being finite, an IEEE representation can only represent a finite subset of real numbers. A 32 bit format for floating point numbers can, at most, represent $2^{32}$ values; that is a long way from infinity.

To illustrate the pitfalls of floating point arithmetic, we present a simple computer experiment following the presentation of Forsythe (41) and the classic Linear Algebra text, Matrix Computations (49). Consider the polynomial, $ax^2 + bx + c$. The quadratic equation, a seemingly innocuous equation known by all school children, computes the roots with the following:

$$root = \frac{-b \pm \sqrt{b^2 - 4ac}}{2a}. \qquad (1.6)$$

There are two roots. At first glance, this appears to be a trivial equation to implement. For the smallest root of the quadratic ($a = 1$, $b = -2p$, and $c = -q$):

$$root_- = p - \sqrt{p^2 + q}, \qquad (1.7)$$

or, alternatively,

$$root_- = \frac{-q}{p + \sqrt{p^2 + q}}. \qquad (1.8)$$

Both of these forms are *mathematically* equivalent, but they are very different when implemented in a computer. Letting $p = 12,345,678$ and $q = 1$, and trying both methods, two different answers are obtained (assuming an IEEE 754 double precision implementation): $-4.097819\text{e-}08$ and $-4.05\text{e-}08$, respectively. Only the latter root is correct despite both equations being mathematically equivalent (verify this!). To understand what has occurred, and how to avoid it, we must examine how floating point numbers are represented in a computer.

### 1.4.1  The IEEE 754 Floating Point System

Digital computers represent quantities in binary form, that is, base 2 (base is also known as the radix). Modern humans think in decimal.[9] People write numbers with an implied radix of 10, but there is nothing special about decimal numbers. For example, $2_{10} = 10_2$ and $10_{10} = 1010_2$. In everyday life, people drop the subscript as the base of 10 is assumed.

---

8 The "C" language types float and double often correspond with the 32-bit and 64-bit types respectively, but it is not a language requirement. Python's float is the double-precision type (64-bit).

9 The oldest number system that we know about, Sumerian (c. 3,000 BC), was sexagesimal, base 60, and survives to this day in the form of minutes and seconds.

| ± | Exponent (8 bits) | Mantissa (23 bits) |
|---|---|---|

| 1 | 0 | 1 | 1 | 0 | 0 | 1 | 1 | 0 | 0 | 1 | 0 | 1 | 1 | 0 | 1 | 1 | 1 | 1 | 1 | 0 | 0 | 1 | 0 | 0 | 0 | 1 | 1 | 1 | 0 | 0 | 1 |

**Figure 1.3** IEEE-754 representation for the value of $4.050000 \cdot 10^{-8}$. The exponent is biased and centered about 127, and the mantissa is assumed to have a leading "1."

The integers are straight forward, but representing real numbers requires more elaboration. The correct root was written in scientific notation, $-4.050000 \cdot 10^{-8}$. There are three distinct elements in this form of a number. The mantissa, or significand, is the sequence of significant digits, and its length is the precision, 8 in this case. It is written with a single digit to the left of the decimal point and multiplied to obtain the correct order of magnitude. This is done by raising the radix, 10 in this case, to the power of the exponent, $-8$. The IEEE-754 format for 32-bit floating point values encodes these values to represent a number, see Figure 1.3. So what can be represented with this system?

Consider a decimal number, abc.def, each position represents an order of magnitude. For decimal numbers, the positions represent:

$$100 + 10 + 1 \cdot \frac{1}{10} + \frac{1}{100} + \frac{1}{1000},$$

while binary numbers look like:

$$4 + 2 + 1 \cdot \frac{1}{2} + \frac{1}{4} + \frac{1}{8}$$

Some floating point examples are $0.5_{10} = 0.1_2$ and $0.125_{10} = 0.001_2$. So far so good, but what of something "simple" such as $0.1_{10}$? Decimal 0.1 is represented as $0.0\overline{0011}_2$, where the bar denotes the sequence is repeated ad infinitum. This can be written in scientific notation as $\overline{1.100} \cdot 2^{-4}$. Using the 32-bit IEEE encoding its representation is 00111101110011001100110011001101. The first bit is the sign bit. The following 8 bits form the exponent and the remaining 23 bits comprise the mantissa. There are two seeming mistakes. First, the exponent is 123. For efficiently representing normal numbers, the IEEE exponent is biased, that is, centered about $127 : 127 - 4 = 123$. The second odd point is in the mantissa. As the first digit is always one it is implied, so the encoding of the mantissa starts at the first digit to the right of the first 1 of the binary representation, so effectively there can be 24 bits of precision. The programmer does not need to be aware of this – it all happens automatically in the implementation and the computer language (such as C++ and Python). Converting IEEE 754 back to decimal, we get, $0.100000001$.[10]

---

10 What is 10% of a billion dollars? This is a sufficiently serious problem for financial software that banks often use specialized routines to ensure that the money is correct.

Observe that even a simple number like 1/10 cannot be represented in the IEEE 32-bit values, just as 1/3 is difficult for decimal, $0.\overline{3}_{10}$.

Let $\mathbb{F} \subset \mathbb{R}$ be the set of IEEE single-precision floating point numbers. Being finite $\mathbb{F}$ will have minimum and maximum elements. They are 1.17549435E-38 and 3.40282347E+38, respectively. Any operation that strays outside of that range will not have a result. Values less than the minimum are said to *underflow*, and values that exceed the maximum are said to *overflow*. Values within the supported range are known as normal numbers. Even within the allowed range, the set is not continuous and a means of mapping values from $\mathbb{R}$ onto $\mathbb{F}$ is required, that is, we need a function, $\mathbf{fl}(x) : \mathbb{R} \rightarrow \mathbb{F}$, and the means prescribed by the IEEE 754 standard is rounding.

All IEEE arithmetical operations are performed with extra bits of precision. This ensures that a computation will produce a value that is superior to the bounds. The result is rounded to the nearest element of $\mathbb{F}$, with ties going to the even value. Specifying ties may appear to be overly prescriptive, but deterministic computational results are very important. IEEE offers 4 rounding modes,[11] but rounding to nearest value in $\mathbb{F}$ is usually the default. Rounding error is subject to precision. Given a real number, 1.0, what is the next largest number? There is no answer. There is an answer for floating point numbers, and this gap is the machine epsilon, or unit roundoff. For the double precision, IEEE-754 standard the machine epsilon is 2.2204460492503131e-16. The width of a proton is 8.83e-16 m, so this is quite small (computation at that scale would choose a more appropriate unit than meters, such as Angstroms, but this does demonstrate that double precision is very useful). The machine epsilon gives the programmer an idea of the error when results are rounded. Denote the machine epsilon as $\mathbf{u}$. The rounding error is $|\mathbf{fl}(x) - x| \leq \frac{1}{2}\mathbf{u}$. This quantity can be used to calculate rigorous bounds on the accuracy of computations and algorithms when required.

Let us revisit our computation of the smallest root, which was done in double precision. $p$ was *very* close to the result of the square root. For our values of $p$ and $q$, $p \approx \sqrt{p^2 + q}$, and so performing $p- \approx p$ ($p$ minus almost $p$) canceled out all of the information in the result. This effect is known as *catastrophic cancellation*, but it is widely misunderstood. A common misconception is that it is a bad practice to subtract floating point numbers that are close together, or add floating point numbers that are far apart, but that is not necessarily true. In this case, the subtraction has merely exposed an earlier problem that no longer has anywhere to hide. The square root is 12,345,678.000000040500003, but it was rounded to

---

11 In C, the mode is specified with FLT_EVAL_METHOD, the default is defined in float.h. Python does not have a standard means of specifying the IEEE rounding mode.

12,345,678.000000041 so that the result can fit in a double-precision value. In a large number like that the *relative* error is manageable, but when subtracted from a nearby number the rounding error is completely exposed; the relative error explodes. The correct rule of thumb is to be careful with results that are contaminated with rounding error. The relative error needs to be minimized. In this case, producing the final result with a division was much safer. Theoretically, both methods should produce the same result, they do on paper, but in practice the minutia of computer arithmetic is important.

The properties of addition and subtraction of $\mathbb{F}$ are also different, for example, associativity does not always hold: $(x + y) + z \neq x + (y + z)$. Consider a machine with 3 digits of precision, it is easy to show that on a computer the rules of arithmetic do not necessarily apply. Setting $x, y$, and $z$ to 1.24, −1.23, and 0.001, respectively, two different results are obtained. The result on the left is 0.011, and the result on the right is 0.01. $\mathbf{fl}(-1.23 + 0.001)$ loses the precision required to contain the answer; the order mattered. Performing the operations in the reverse order, turning two large numbers into a smaller number prior to an operation with another smaller number increased the chances of obtaining the correct answer. Planning the sequence of operations can be very important.

### 1.4.2 Numerical Coding Tip: Think in Floating Point

A common algorithmic activity is to loop waiting for some value to reach 0.0, such as a residual error. A terrible mistake is to code something like:

```
while (error != 0.0) {
        // some code
}
```

The error may never reach 0.0 or potentially pass through it. A better way is to test with the operator, $\geq$. Even if it is "mathematically impossible" for the error in question to be less than zero, when working with $\mathbb{F}$ instead of $\mathbb{R}$ there are always nasty surprises. Paranoia is the only means of reducing the chance of terrible and undebuggable errors.

In general, the same caution should be exercised when testing the result of any computation. For example, when verifying that a matrix inversion is correct, an obvious test is to compute $A^{-1}A = I$. A simple test for correctness might look like Algorithm 1.1.

Algorithm 1.1 will almost certainly fail, even though the implementation of the algorithm that computed it is correct. The expected 1s and 0s are rarely so precise and have tiny residuals. In general, it is best to use a tolerance when testing for a desired value. A better way of verifying the result is Algorithm 1.2.

---

**Algorithm 1.1** Unsafe verification of an identify matrix

---

1: **for** $i \in$ *rows* **do**
2:     **for** $j \in$ *columns*j **do**
3:         **if** i == j **then**
4:             assert (I[i,j] == 1.0)         $\triangleright$ I[i,j] more likely to be 1.000021
5:         **else**
6:             assert (I[i,j] == 0.0)         $\triangleright$ I[i,j] more likely to be -0.0000309
7:         **end if**
8:     **end for**
9: **end for**

---

---

**Algorithm 1.2** The use of a tolerance to verify a matrix

---

1: **for** $i \in$ *rows* **do**
2:     **for** $j \in$ *columns*j **do**
3:         **if** i == j **then**
4:             assert (abs(1 - I[i,j]) $\leq \epsilon$)     $\triangleright$ Subtract the expected 1 to get 0
5:         **else**
6:             assert (I[i,j] $\leq \epsilon$)
7:         **end if**
8:     **end for**
9: **end for**

---

The choice of $\epsilon$ will be a suitably small value that the application can tolerate. In general, comparison of a computed floating point value should be done as abs($\alpha - x$), where $x$ is the computed quantity and $\alpha$ is the quantity that is being tested for. Note that printing the contents of $I$ to the screen may appear to produce the exact values of zero and one, but print format routines, the routines whose jobs is to convert IEEE variables to a printable decimal string, do all kinds of things and often mislead.

A great contribution of the IEEE system is its quality as a progressive system. Many computer architectures used to treat floating point errors, such as division by zero, as terminal. The program would be aborted. IEEE systems continue to make progress following division by zero and simply record the error condition in the result. Division by zero and $\sqrt{-1}$ results in the special nonnormal value "not a number" recorded in the result (NaN). Overflow and underflow are also recorded as the two special values, $\pm\infty$ (if used they will produce an NaN). These error values need to be detected because if they are used, then the error will contaminate all further use of the tainted value. Often there is a semantic course of action that can be adopted to fix the error before proceeding. They are notoriously difficult to debug so it is critical to catch numerical problems early. At key points in a program, it can be useful to check for unwanted errors. Many languages offer facilities to test for the special values. POSIX C implements `isnan` and `isinf` to test for errors, and Python's `math` package implements both as well.

We conclude with some rules of thumb to bear in mind when writing floating point code:

- Avoid subtracting quantities when one of them is contaminated with error (such as round off) – this is the root of catastrophic cancelation.
- Avoid computing quantities with much larger intermediate values than the result. Such computations need to be designed carefully if unavoidable. The canonical example is computing the variance with $\sigma^2 = \mathbb{E}(x^2) - \mathbb{E}(x)^2$.
- Consider the ramifications when implementing a mathematical expression and anticipate problems. Expanding or simplifying an expression may have consequences. Prefer division to subtraction. Plan the sequence of operations carefully.
- Overflow and underflow should be monitored when possible.
- Check for IEEE error conditions when they are possible.

These are rules of thumb. Thinking in floating point improves the chances of getting things right. ANNs can require trillions of floating point operations to train or millions to compute so when things go wrong the debugging can be extremely challenging. A single NaN, which at least makes it clear that something went wrong, will void all progress; but at least the problem is visible. More pernicious are the silent problems such as the inaccuracies resulting from catastrophic cancelation – so plan well.

## 1.5 Summary

While DL has become synonymous with AI in the public's imagination, it is a subfield of machine learning, which in turn is a specialization of AI. ANNs are models produced by constraining a system empirically with a dataset. They are of use when there is no other convenient constraint available, such as a law of nature. The resultant model is usually not interpretable. The real number line does not exist in a digital computer. When dealing with any kind of computer model, care must be taken that the arithmetic has not gone wrong. Appendix I provides a brief review of the mathematics required to understand the text. It also includes references to further reading.

## 1.6  Projects

1. Formulate a definition of intelligence. Complement it with a set of testable criteria. If the criteria are empirical, compose a single score that summarizes the "intelligence" of a system that was tested.
2. Contrive a formula that exhibits catastrophic cancelation. How did you verify that it does indeed produce the wrong answer?
3. In your favorite computer language initialize a variable $x$ to 0.0. Write a loop that accumulates 0.1 in $x$ 10 times. The test, $x = 1.0$, results in a false (do not just print the result). What went wrong?

# 2

# Deep Learning and Neural Networks

In Chapter 1, it was stated that deep learning (DL) models are based on artificial neural networks (ANNs). In this chapter, deep learning will be defined more precisely, which is still quite loose. This will be done by connecting deep learning to ANNs more concretely. It was also claimed that ANNs can be interpreted as programmable functions. In this chapter, we describe what those functions look and how ANNs compute values. Like a function, an ANN accepts inputs and computes an output. How an ANN turns the input into the output is detailed. We also introduce the notation and abstractions that we use in the rest of the text.

A deep learning model is a model built with an artificial neural network, that is, a network of artificial neurons. The neurons are perceptrons. Networks require a topology. The topology is specified as a *hyperparameter* to the model. This includes the number of neurons and how they are connected. The topology determines how information flows in the resulting ANN configuration and some of the properties of the ANN. In broad terms, ANNs have many possible topologies, and indeed there are an infinite number of possibilities. Determining good topologies for a particular problem can be challenging; what works in one problem domain may not (probably will not) work in a different domain. ANNs have many applications and come in many types and sizes. They can be used for classification, regression, and even generative purposes such as producing a picture. The different domains often have different topologies dictated by the application. Most ANN applications employ domain-specific techniques and adopt trade-offs to produce the desired result. For every application, there are a myriad of ANN configurations and parameters, and what works well for one application may not work for others. If this seems confusing – it is (107; 161). A good rule of thumb is to keep it as simple as possible (93).

*Demystifying Deep Learning: An Introduction to the Mathematics of Neural Networks,*
First Edition. Douglas J. Santry.
© 2024 The Institute of Electrical and Electronics Engineers, Inc. Published 2024 by John Wiley & Sons, Inc.

## 2.1 Feed-Forward and Fully-Connected Artificial Neural Networks

This section presents the rudiments of ANN topology. One topology in particular, the feed-forward and fully-connected (FFFC), topology is adopted. There is no loss of generality as all the principles and concepts presented still apply to other topologies. The focus on a simple topology lends itself to clearer explanations. To make matters more concrete, we begin with a simple example presented in Figure 2.1. We can see that an ANN is comprised of neurons (nodes), connections, and many numbers. Observing the figure, it is clear that we can interpret an ANN as a directed graph, $G(N, E)$. The nodes, or vertices, of the graph are neurons. Neurons that communicate immediately are connected with a directed edge. The direction of the edge determines the flow of the signal.

The nodes in the graph are neurons. The neuron abstraction is at the heart of the ANN. Neurons in ANNs are generally perceptrons. Information, that is, signals, flow through the network along the directed edges through the neurons. The arrow indicates that a signal is coming from a source neuron and going to a target

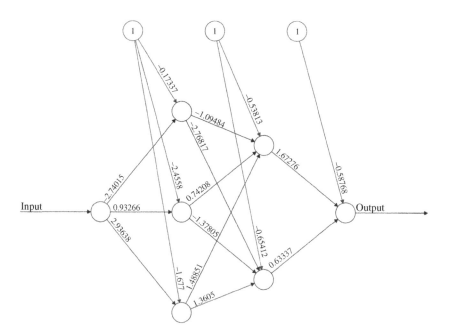

**Figure 2.1** A trained ANN that has learnt the `sine` function. The circles, graph nodes, are neurons. The arrows on the edges determine which direction the communication flows.

neuron. There are no rules respecting the number of edges. Most neurons in an ANN are both a source and a target. Any neuron that is not a source is an *output* neuron. Any neuron that is not a target is an *input* neuron. Input neurons are the entry point to the graph, and the arguments to the ANN are supplied there. Output neurons provide the final result of the computation. Thus, given $\hat{y} = \text{ANN}(x)$, $x$ goes to the input neurons and $\hat{y}$ is read from the output neurons. In the example, $x$ is the angle, and $\hat{y}$ is the sine of $x$.

Each neuron has an independent internal state. A neuron's state is computed from the input signals from connected source neurons. The neuron computes its internal state to build its own signal, also known as a *response*. This internal state is then propagated in turn through the directed edges to its target neurons. The inceptive stage for the computation is the provision of the input arguments to the input neurons of the ANN. The input neurons compute their states and propagate them to their target neurons. This is the first signal that triggers the rest of the activity. The signals propagate through the network, forcing neurons to update state along the way, until the signal reaches the output neurons, and then the computation is finished. Only the state in the output neurons, that is, the output neurons' responses, matter to an application as they comprise the "answer," $\hat{y}$.

Neurons are connected with edges. The edges are weighted by a real number. The weights determine the behavior of the signals as received by the target neuron – they are the crux of an ANN. It is the values of the weights that determine whether an ANN is sine, cosine, $e^x$ – whatever the desired function. The weights in Figure 2.1 make the ANN sine. The ANN in Figure 2.2 is a cosine. The graphs in Figure 2.3 present their respective plots for 32 random points. Both ANNs have the same topologies, but they have very different weights. It is the weights that the determine what an ANN computes. The topology can be thought of as supporting the weights by ensuring that there is a sufficient number of them to solve a problem; this is called the learning capacity of an ANN.

The weights of an ANN are the parameters of the model. The task of training a neural network is determining the weights, $w$. This is reflected in the notation $\hat{y} = \text{ANN}(x; w)$ or $\hat{y} = \text{ANN}(x|w)$ where $\hat{y}$ is conditioned on the vector of parameters, $w$. Given a training set, the act of training an ANN is reconciling the weights in a model with the examples in the training set. The fitted weights should then produce a model that emits the correct output for a given input. Training sets consisting of sine and cosine produced the ANNs in the trigonometric examples, respectively. Both sine and cosine are continuous functions. As such building models for them are examples of *regression*, we are explaining observed data from the past to make predictions in the future.

The graph of an ANN can take many forms. Without loss of generality, but for clarity of exposition, we choose a particular topology, the fully-connected

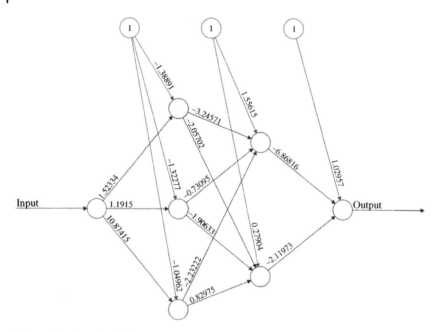

**Figure 2.2** A trained ANN that has learnt the `cosine` function. The only differences with the `sine` model are the weights. Both ANNs have the same topologies.

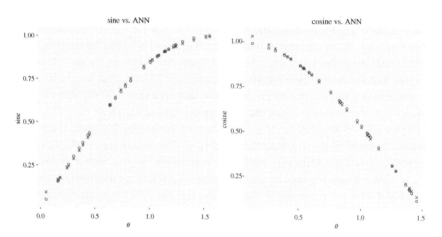

**Figure 2.3** The output of two ANNs is superimposed on the ground truth for the trained `sine` and `cosine` ANN models. The ANN predictions are plotted as crosses. The empty circles are taken from the training set and comprise the ground truth.

feed-forward architecture, as the basis for all the ANNs that we will discuss. The principles are the same for all ANNs, but the simplicity of the feed-forward topology is pedagogically attractive.

Information in the feed-forward ANN flows acyclically from a single input layer, through a number of *hidden* layers, and finally to a single output layer; the signals are always moving forward through the graph. The ANN is specified as a set of layers. Layers are sets of related, peer, neurons. A layer is specified as the number of neurons that it contains, the layer's *width*. The number of layers in an ANN is referred to as its *depth*. All the neurons in a layer share source neurons, specified as a layer, and target neurons, again, specified as a layer. All of a layer's source neurons form a layer as do its target neurons. There are no intralayer connections. In the language of graph theory, isolating a layer produces a tripartite graph. Thus, a layer is sandwiched between a shallower, source neuron layer, and a deeper target layer.

The set of layers can be viewed as a stack. Consider topology in Figure 2.1, with respect to the stack analogy, the input layer is the top, or the shallowest layer, and the output layer is the bottom, or the deepest layer. The argument is supplied to the input layer and the answer read from the output layer. The layers between the input and output layers are known as hidden layers.

It is the presence of hidden layers that characterizes an ANN as a deep learning ANN. There is no consensus on how many hidden layers are required to qualify as deep learning, but the loosest definition is at least 1 hidden layer. A single hidden layer does not intuitively seem very deep, but its existence in an ANN does put it in a different generation of model. Rosenblatt's original implementations were single layers of perceptrons, but he speculated on deeper arrangements in his book (130). It was not clear what value multiple layers of perceptrons had given his linear training methods. Modern deep learning models of 20+ hidden layers are common, and they continue to grow deeper and wider.

The process of computing the result of an ANN begins with supplying the argument to the function at the input layer. Every input neuron in the input layer receives a copy of the full ANN argument. Once every neuron in the input layer has computed its state with the arguments to the ANN, the input layer is ready to propagate the result to next layer. As the signals percolate through the ANN, each layer accepts its source signals from the previous layer, computes the new state, and then propagates the result to the next layer. This continues until the final layer is reached; the output layer. The output layer contains the result of the ANN.

To further simplify our task, we specify that the feed-forward ANN is fully connected, sometimes also called dense. At any given layer, every neuron is connected to every source neuron in the shallower layer; recursively, this implies that every neuron in a given layer is a source neuron for the next layer.

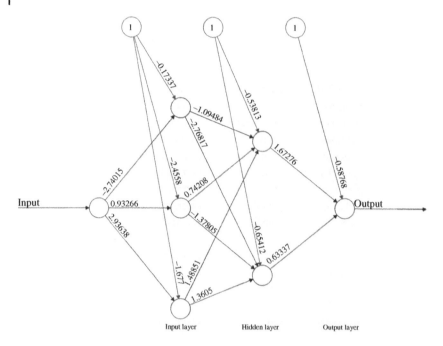

**Figure 2.4** The sine model in more detail. The layers are labeled. The left is shallowest and the right is the deepest. Every neuron in a layer is fully connected with its shallower neighbor. This ANN is specified by the widths of it layers, 3, 2, 1, so the ANN has a depth of 3.

Let us now reexamine the ANN implementing sine in Figure 2.4 in terms of layers. We see that there are 3 layers. The first layer, the input layer, has 3 neurons. The input layer accepts the *predictors*, the inputs of the model. The hidden layer has 2 neurons, and the output layer has one neuron. There can be as many hidden layers as desired, and they can also be as wide as needed. The depths and the widths are the hyperparameters of the model. The number of layers and their widths should be kept as limited as possible (93). As the number of weights grows, that is, trainable parameters, the size of the ANN increases exponentially. Too many weights also leads to other problems that will be examined in later chapters.

As sine is a scaler function, there can only be one output neuron in the ANN's output layer; that is, where the answer (sine) can be found. Notice, however, that the number of input neurons is not similarly constrained. Sine has only one predictor (argument), but observe that there can be any number of neurons in the input layer. They will each receive a copy of the arguments.

The mechanics of signal propagation form the basis of how ANNs compute. Having seen how the signals flow in a feed-forward ANN, it remains to examine what those signals are and how they are computed. This will lead to a recurrence equation that we will use to succinctly describe the computation. This is the topic of the Section 2.2.

## 2.2 Computing Neuron State

The signals percolating through the graph of the ANN are the states of the neurons. The state of an individual neuron is computed from the signals received from its source neurons; the immediately shallower layer. The signals are weighted on a per edge basis. Perceptrons are used as neurons and so their state is computed as follows. Each neuron, $n_j$, in a layer, $\ell$, computes the following dot product with independent weights:

$$\forall n_j \in \ell \;:\; u_j = \sum_{i}^{M_{\ell-1}} z_i w_{j,i} + w_{j,b}, \tag{2.1}$$

where the shallower layer has $M_{\ell-1}$ neurons and the $z_i$ are the shallower signals. As the ANN is fully connected that corresponds directly to the number of source inputs for the current layer, $\ell$. The $w_{j,i}$ have two subscripts. The subscript is read as the weight on the edge from neuron $i$ to neuron $j$. The numbers on the edges in the example ANN graphs are weights, not signals. Each layer also has an implicit *bias* input that is always 1 ($z_b \equiv 1$). The neurons can use the bias to translate their dot products with their bias' weight, $w_{j,b}$. Thus, a layer $\ell$ with $M_\ell$ neurons has $M_{\ell-1} + 1$ inputs, the previous layer's neurons and the bias. This means that every neuron, $n_j$, needs $M_{\ell-1} + 1$ weights. As the layer $\ell$ has $M_\ell$ neurons, the layer $\ell$ requires $M_\ell \cdot (M_{\ell-1} + 1)$ weights.

Returning to the earlier sine example, we can now interpret Figure 2.4 completely. The bias is the gray node in each layer. Observing the weights on every edge, as expected, the input layer with 3 neurons has a total of 6 weights: 3 for the single input and 3 for the bias, which is 1.0 by definition.

### 2.2.1 Activation Functions

There is one final step to computing a neuron's signal. Following the computation of the per neuron dot products, each neuron applies an *activation function* to its dot product. This constitutes the final step in the computation of a neuron's state and forms a neuron's response, that is, its output signal. A neuron's response is written as $\sigma(u_j)$, where $u_j$ is the $j$th neuron's dot product computed above. So the $j$th's neuron's response, $z_j = \sigma(u_j)$, in layer $\ell$ is:

$$z_j = \sigma(u_j) = \sigma\left(\sum_{i}^{M_{\ell-1}} z_i w_{j,i} + w_{j,b}\right). \tag{2.2}$$

Not any function can act as an activation function. The activation function plays an important role when computing the final state. Dot products can produce arbitrary values. An activation function can tame the dot products. If a specific range is required then an activation function can be selected accordingly. Two common requirements are to either map the scaler product between $[-1, 1]$, or make it strictly positive. Activation functions also add non-linearity to the neuron's response making it possible to handle more challenging problems. Three important activation functions are, tanh (hyperbolic tangent), sigmoid and ReLU. Their curves are depicted in Figure 2.5. While superficially similar, they differ in important ways. Both tanh and sigmoid tend to squish their domain into a narrow range. The former is centered about zero and produces a result between $[-1, 1]$. The sigmoid's range is $[0, 1]$. The sigmoid is historically important lending its symbol, $\sigma$, to the notation for activation functions. As we shall see in Chapter 3, all three have important niches. For the moment we examine the sigmoid function.

The sigmoid was the first activation function (162) and its use was inspired by biological processes. The idea was that a neuron was either "on" or "off." This was abstracted as 0 or 1. While the desired behavior suggests a Heaviside function the sigmoid was attractive for a number of reasons, and certainly has a number of advantages. The sigmoid is continuous, differentiable everywhere and non-linear. As we shall see in Chapter 3, the sigmoid is also very convenient when a derivative is required. The sigmoid function is defined as:

$$z = \sigma(u) = \frac{1}{1 + e^{-u}}. \tag{2.3}$$

Its range is roughly $[0, 1]$ but its interesting dynamics are in the domain $[-3, 3]$. As $u$ grows very negative or very positive the sigmoid becomes saturated and the asymptotic behavior manifests itself; it mimics the Heaviside function and is either

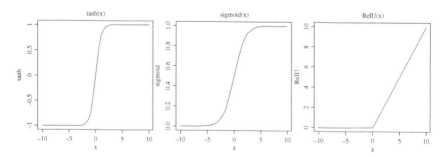

**Figure 2.5** Three popular activation functions. The two on the left are superficially similar, but note the tanh's range is centered on 0.0 and the sigmoid's range is centered on 0.5.

"on" or "off." Ideally weights, the determiners of $u$, avoid saturating the activation functions because adjusting the output becomes more difficult. A neuron that is fixed in the $-10$ish domain will always be $-1$, and may as well be dropped from the network.

More recently introduced, an important family of activation functions for deep learning tasks is the rectified linear unit, ReLU. The ReLU is defined as

$$\text{ReLU}(u) = u^+ = \max(0, u). \tag{2.4}$$

It tends to be deployed in deeper ANNs (ANNs with many hidden layers) for the reasons for which will be exaplined in Section 3.5.4. It adds an element of nonlinearity while its derivative has attractive qualities, which is important when training deep ANNs (42). Saturated weights are less of a problem, but the nonlinearity is far less pronounced. When introduced to the ANN community, it was used to set a record, at the time, for depth in an ANN in AlexNet (89) that also resulted in setting an accuracy record.

We shall refer to the activation function generically as $\sigma(u)$, where $u$ is the scaler product of weights and inputs, but unless specified $\sigma$ is not a particular activation function.

## 2.3 The Feed-Forward ANN Expressed with Matrices

We have seen that the propagation of signals through an ANN proceeds from layer to layer, starting from the input. Each layer is comprised of neurons that need to compute the dot product of its weights with the signal from the previous layer. The computation can be expressed concisely with matrices.

We can express the propagation, or arrival, of a signal at a layer with a matrix multiplication. A matrix of weights, $W_\ell$, can be constructed by populating each row with the weights of an individual neuron; the $j$th row of $W_\ell$ containing the weights for the $j$th neuron. The $i$th column of $W_\ell$ corresponds to the weights on the edges from the $i$th neuron in the previous layer. Thus the matrix element $W_\ell[j, i]$ is the weight for the edge from neuron $i$ in $\ell - 1$ to $j$ in $\ell$. Each row in the $W_\ell$ matrix encapsulates the weights vector of a neuron in that layer, and every layer has its own matrix. Note that if the ANN is not fully connected the missing connections could be represented with zeros in the appropriate matrix entries. The matrix for the hidden layer of the sine in Figure 2.4 is

$$W_{hidden} = \begin{pmatrix} -1.09484 & 0.74208 & 1.48851 \\ -2.76817 & -1.37805 & 1.3605 \end{pmatrix}.$$

We can now express the first step of computing the states of neurons, the per neuron scaler products of arguments and weights, with a matrix multiplication. The dot products of all the neurons in a layer can now be written as

$$u_\ell = W_\ell z_{\ell-1} + b_\ell, \tag{2.5}$$

where $u$ is a vector and $b_\ell$ the vector of bias weights. In computational linear algebra, this is known as a general $Ax + y$, or GAXPY operation (49), and there are many software libraries that implement it efficiently.

Once the per neuron scaler products have been computed the activation function can be applied and a layer's output, $z_\ell$, computed. This results in

$$z_\ell = \sigma(u_\ell) = \sigma(W_\ell z_{\ell-1} + b_\ell). \tag{2.6}$$

Here the activation function has applied on a per element basis of its argument vector, $u_\ell$, producing a new vector of the same dimension, the final result for the layer, $z_\ell$.

We can now express the total computation of an ANN concisely. We define $\mathcal{L}$ as the ordered list of the layers of our ANN, that is, $\{ \ell_1, \ldots, \ell_{depth} \}$. The computation of the response for a feed-forward ANN can be expressed with the following algorithm:

---

**Algorithm 2.1** Feed-Forward and Fully-Connected ANN Computation

---

1: **procedure** ANN($x$)
2: $\quad z_{\ell-1} \leftarrow x$
3: $\quad$ **for** $\ell \in \mathcal{L}$ **do**
4: $\quad\quad u_\ell \leftarrow W_\ell \cdot z_{\ell-1} + b_\ell$
5: $\quad\quad z_\ell \leftarrow \sigma(u_\ell)$
6: $\quad$ **end for**
7: $\quad \hat{y} \leftarrow z_\ell$
8: $\quad$ **return** $\hat{y}$
9: **end procedure**

---

The procedure can be invoked as $\hat{y} = \text{ANN}(x)$. Returning to the running sine example, the argument, $x$, is a scalar, the angle in radians. There are 3 layers, so there will be 3 iterations through the loop. The routine would produce the ANN's approximation of sine($x$) in the final iteration and assign it to $\hat{y}$ prior to returning it to the caller.

## 2.3.1 Neural Matrices: A Convenient Notation

For clarity of exposition, we introduce a notation based on standard linear algebra. We define a new object, the neural matrix. It is the same as a normal matrix but includes an extra column. The first column consists of the bias weights for a layer. For a layer $\ell-1$ with $m$ neurons and a layer $\ell$ with $n$ neurons the weight matrix looks like:

$$W_\ell = \begin{pmatrix} w_{1,b} & w_{1,1} & w_{1,2} & \cdots & w_{1,m} \\ w_{2,b} & w_{2,1} & w_{2,2} & \cdots & w_{2,m} \\ \vdots & & & & \\ w_{n,b} & w_{n,1} & a_{w,2} & \cdots & w_{n,m} \end{pmatrix}. \tag{2.7}$$

To make this work there is an implied 1.0 in the first position of the input vector,

$$z_{\ell-1} = \begin{pmatrix} 1.0 \\ z_1 \\ \vdots \\ z_m \end{pmatrix}, \tag{2.8}$$

where the shallower response vector has been prefixed with 1 and the remaining entries pushed down. The dot product and bias translation can now be written more concisely as

$$u_\ell = W_\ell z_{\ell-1}. \tag{2.9}$$

Revisiting the example in Figure 2.4 the resulting neural matrix is

$$W_{hidden} = \begin{pmatrix} -0.53813 & -1.09484 & 0.74208 & 1.48851 \\ -0.65412 & -2.76817 & -1.37805 & 1.3605 \end{pmatrix}. \tag{2.10}$$

It is just notional sugar for expressing $Wz + b$. This is proposed for notational convenience only; it has no mathematical implications. In the remainder of the text, $Wz$ can be construed as $Wz + b$.

## 2.4 Classification

Classification is an important application of ANNs. Many problems can be framed as classifiers even if at first appearances it does not appear to be the case. Classifiers have applications in making disease predictions, image recognition, giving legal advice, and many more. Classification is one of the most important applications of ANNs. In this section, the rudiments of ANN classifiers are motivated and presented. An ANN trained as a classifier is also known as a classifying neural network (CNN). More commonly, CNN means convolutional neural network (see Chapter 6). The context usually determines which one is meant.

Thus far, the ANNs have been computing continuous functions. The ANN has produced a smooth curve. Simple scaler functions were learnt so the curves were easily plotted (see Figure 2.3). These were simple examples of regressing on sine data. Classification is a different problem. Given a vector for input a, classifying ANN must predict which class from a finite and mutually exclusive set of classes the example belongs. The output is not a number. It is the category to which the example belongs. This is an extremely powerful construction. An example is a diabetes classifier. Given a patient's data, the ANN will make a diagnosis, one of either {Healthy, Diabetes}. Image recognition is also a classifier. For example, a classifier might accept a JPEG image and classify it as one of either a dog or a cat, or even enumerate all of the objects that the image contains.

Note that any object, such as a JPEG, can be flattened into a vector. For example, in the case of a two-dimensional black and white image, laying each row out sequentially in memory produces a vector. Indeed, copying is usually not even required; that is, how images are frequently represented physically in computer memory. The transformation can remain abstract, and the area of memory containing the item is simply reinterpreted.

There can be a choice of how to frame a problem, as a regressor or a classifier. For example, an ANN regressor might predict a stock price. By comparing the current stock price with the predicted stock price, an analyst can make a recommendation of either {Buy, Sell, Hold}. Alternatively, the ANN could simply be trained to make the recommendation in the first place by building a classifier instead of a regressor. In this case, the ANN's output would be the recommendation, not a number (the predicted stock price). Examples of both approaches can be found here (123).

ANN classifiers compute predictions very similarly to regressors. They differ in one important respect: the output. The input layer and the hidden layers are the same, but the final output is treated differently. Classifiers need to perform an extra step to produce their final prediction. The sine regressor is a mapping, $\text{ANN} : \mathbb{R} \to \mathbb{R}$; its input and output are continuous. The range of a classifier is categorical. Classifiers look like, $\text{ANN} : \mathbb{R}^d \to \mathbb{K}$, where $\mathbb{K}$ is the set of categories. An example of $\mathbb{K}$ is $\mathbb{K} = \{\text{dog, cat}\}$. This set must be represented mathematically so that the classifier can compute with it. The first step in constructing a classifier is to identify a strategy for dealing with the set $\mathbb{K}$ mathematically. The remainder of this section examines how categorical variables are handled. The special case of binary classification is dealt with first. A binary classifier has only two categories to choose between.

### 2.4.1 Binary Classification

A binary classifier is the simplest form of classification. There are only two possible outcomes, and it forms an important special case. A diabetes classifier is an example of a binary classifier, there are only two classes in the set of outputs. The set $\mathbb{K}$ comprises of the two valid choices {Healthy, Diabetes}. A natural

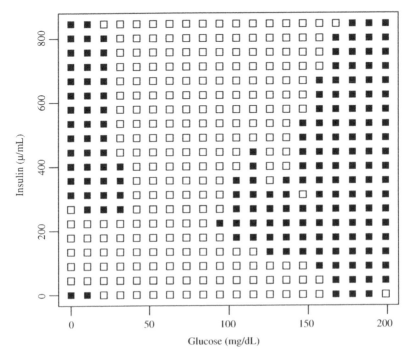

**Figure 2.6** A binary diabetes classifier. The predictors are continuous, but the output is categorical. The grid depicts the decision boundary for a single patient but plotted for glucose and insulin levels. A Black square is a prediction for diabetes and gray is healthy.

course to pursue would be to adapt a regressor to classification by imposing an interpretation on the output. As there are only two classes, then the convention might be that the class `Diabetes` is 0 and the class `Healthy` is 1. This is a regressor masquerading as a classifier, that is, its output is continuous and not categorical. The trouble is that an ANN is unlikely to produce such tidy results every time. Results such as 0.99 and 0.5 are exceedingly likely. With a further refinement this could be made practicable by adopting the convention of rounding the result to one of either 0 or 1. This does work.

Figure 2.6 shows the decision boundary of a binary classifier for diabetes classifier trained with an open source dataset.[1] The patients in the dataset have 8 diagnostic predictors (so $x$ is an 8-tuple) and the correct label, healthy, or diabetic. The 8 predictors are continuous, but the result is categorical. This classifier has the form, $\text{ANN} : \mathbb{R}^8 \to \mathbb{K}$. The ANN was trained with the topology $\{20, 20, 1\}$. Principle component analysis (PCA) revealed that the most important predictors in the dataset were found to be glucose and insulin levels. The patient shown in Figure 2.6 was

---

1 Released by the National Institute of Diabetes and Digestive and Kidney Diseases.

selected randomly from the training set. Six of the patient's predictors were kept constant, while the glucose and insulin values were iterated over to produce the plot. This results in a graphical projection of the decision boundary with respect to insulin and glucose. It is clearly more complex than a simple line. In the full 8-dimensional space, the structure is *very* complicated. The power of deep learning lies in its ability to find decision boundaries in highly complex feature spaces. Note that graphing a classifier is very different from a regressor. This is a binary outcome so color can capture the results.

## 2.4.2 One-Hot Encoding

Many classifiers have more than two possible categories. Clearly, a binary classifier is not sufficient for those applications and a means of supporting more than two outcomes is required. A classifier needs to select a particular class from a finite set of classes in its range; it is discrete. Binary classification suggests itself as a natural starting point. The idea can be extended by assigning an integer to each class, starting at zero and increasing by one for each unique class. This would result in $\mathbb{K} = \{$ dog $= 0$, cat $= 1$, giraffe $= 2$, gorilla $= 3\}$. The method could be construed as function, $f : \mathbb{R}^d \rightarrow \mathbb{N}_0$, the range being the natural numbers, and implemented with a single output neuron. In practice, this does not work well. With further refinement, it forms the basis of a useful approach.

A efficient approach is to elaborate the idea of per class labels to produce a computationally feasible range. The categories have integers assigned as described above, but instead of a single output neuron each class has a dedicated output neuron. Let $K = |\mathbb{K}|$, the number of classes. Then the output layer of the ANN has $K$ neurons. The integer identifiers for the classes are interpreted as their indices in the output layer. Thus, in the Diabetes/Healthy example, the final layer consists of Diabetes, neuron 0, and Healthy is neuron 1. The convention yields a model with domain and range: ANN : $\mathbb{R}^8 \rightarrow \mathbb{R}^2$, and in general ANN : $\mathbb{R}^d \rightarrow \mathbb{R}^K$. While the output is a vector of continuous values, the information is delineated in a per class neuron. Each neuron can be treated in isolation.

The proposed topological practice suggests a means of expressing a datum's class: a vector. Consider the problem of classifying a genus of flower, the iris: $\mathbb{K} = \{$setosa$=0$, versicolor$=1$, virginica$=2\}$. Then $K = 3$. The iris "versicolor" would be represented as a vector, [ 0, 1, 0 ]. The class of a datum is represented as having a 1 at the class' index and zeros in every other position. Representing classes in this fashion is known as one-hot encoding. An example ANN classifier for an iris is presented in Figure 2.7. One-hot encoding assumes membership of one class is mutually exclusive with membership in another class, that is, an example can only be a member of a single class. This is known as the single label classification problem.

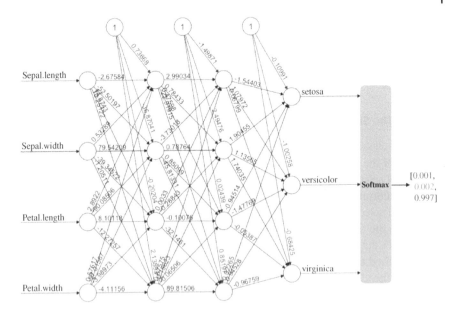

**Figure 2.7** A trained classier for the Iris dataset. There are 4 predictors and 3 classes. Each class has an output. The outputs are used by the softmax function to make a prediction. In this example, `virginica` is the predicted class.

Problems where an example can be a member of more than one class simultaneously are called multilabel problems, and one-hot encoding is not appropriate. The multilabel problem is framed differently. See Section 4.3 for details.

Categorical features are one-hot encoded vectors. A vector representing a category is populated entirely with zeros except for the position corresponding to the class of $x$, which will contain a 1. This can remain abstract. The one-hot encoded vector can, in turn, be encoded simply with the index of the 1 in the vector, for example, [0, 0, 1] is summarized as 2 – the index of the 1. A one-hot encoded vector is discrete, so it is a mass function, not a density function, which is continuous, so the representation is accurate. For applications with many categories, this can save a great deal of memory and copying.

The iris classifier was built with a famous dataset[2] introduced by Ronald Fisher in 1936 (117), a father of modern statistics and inventor of likelihood (116). Known as the iris dataset, it is frequently used with introductions to machine learning. It has 4 continuous predictors and 3 classes; so the classifier looks like, ANN : $\mathbb{R}^4 \rightarrow \mathbb{R}^3$. Note the difference between this example and the `sine` ANN. There are 3 classes so we have 3 output neurons, not the 1 continuous output neuron of

---

2 It is also sometimes referred to as Anderson's Iris Data Set as Edgar Anderson collected the data.

the regression ANN, or the binary classifier. While the number of predictors happens to correspond with the number of input neurons this is by no means required (see the sine example above). As it is a dense ANN, we can write the topology as $\tau = \{\ 4, 4, 3\ \}$. The ANN has a depth of 3, and there is one hidden layer comprises 4 neurons.

### 2.4.3 The Softmax Layer

An ANN classifier has $K$ output neurons; therefore, the ANN will produce a value in each of the $K$ output neurons. There still remains the question of which class the ANN selected; the output will often not be purely one-hot encoded. The $K$ output neurons can produce any value. Ideally, we would have an interpretable means of selecting which output neuron to believe. One means of deciding is to construe the output of the ANN as a probability distribution, then interpreting the ANN's output is as simple as accepting the class with the highest probability. This method is also compatible with the representation of the ground truth, the one-hot encoded vectors. To that end, a *softmax* layer is appended to the output of a classifier ANN (44).

A softmax layer accepts the vector of the output responses from the ANN and processes them to produce a set of "probabilities." The raw output of the ANN is knows as *logits*. softmax processes logit to produce a probability distribution over the possible classes. The probability of the class is computed as

$$\hat{p}_j = \text{softmax}(z) = \frac{e^{z_j}}{\sum_k^K e^{z_k}}, \tag{2.11}$$

where $z$ is the output vector of the ANN, the logits. It computes the probability for the class, $j$. The denominator is the sum over all the responses and thus normalizes each entry of the output vector. To make the final prediction the ANN needs all the probabilities. The vector of all the probabilities, is $\hat{p}$, so $\hat{p} = \text{softmax}(z)$.

The softmax function has a number of desirable properties. The result looks like a probability distribution. Its output vector sums to 1, and all the entries have the property, $0 \leq \hat{p}_j \leq 1.0$ for $j$th entry of $\hat{p}$. Making a final prediction is now straight forward. The ANN selects the class with the highest probability. The index of the entry with the highest probability in $\hat{p}$ is the ANN's predicted class.

The softmax function imposes order on the potential chaos of the ANN's output neurons. Softmax is occasionally referred to as an activation function because it replaces the usual activations in the output layer of the ANN, but it is more like a distinct layer. No one output probability can be computed without all of the output signals, so it is dense. This property seems more like a fully-connected layer than an activation function.

There are two potential numerical pitfalls to avoid when using softmax. The first is a division by zero, and the second is overflow. The sum can become enormous if the logits are large and positive. This is particularly likely at the beginning of training an ANN. It is a good idea to subtract the largest logit from every element in the logits vector ($z$). Translating the logits by the maximum $z_j$ achieves two things. The first is that at least one of the $z_j$ will be zero, which means one term in the denominator's sum will be 1.0, obviating a division by zero. The second is that the remaining terms will be negative and so the sum cannot overflow. Underflow and catastrophic cancelation are not a problem. The class with the maximum value will produce a 1.0 by construction. The 1 dominates the sum so that class, $j$, is the most probable (and the softmax will look like a one-hot encoded vector).

Armed with softmax an algorithm for an ANN classifier can be described Algorithm 2.2.

---

**Algorithm 2.2** ANN Classifier

---
1: **procedure** CLASSIFY($x$)
2:     logits ← ANN($x$)
3:     $\hat{p}$ ← softmax(logits)
4:     $\underset{index}{argmax}\ \hat{p}_{index}$          ▷ index of highest probability is the predicted class
5:     **return** index
6: **end procedure**

---

We conclude with a brief numerical example. Let $x = (5.6, 2.8, 4.9, 2)$, an example from the iris dataset. Then the classifier computes as follows:

1. $z = ANN(x) = (-2.1, 5.2, -1)$
2. $\hat{p} = softmax((-2.1, -1, 5.2)) = (0.0006737164, 0.002023956, 0.9973023)$
3. $max(\hat{p}) = 0.9973023$
4. the index is 2
5. the predicted class is $\mathbb{K}[2]$ : virginica

All the steps can be carried out inside a model. The application would be oblivious to the individual steps. The model should simply accept the predictors and return the predicted class to the application.

## 2.5  Summary

ANNs can be viewed as graphs. The graphs can be defined as a list of widths of its layers. Layers consist of perceptrons that compute state by evaluating the dot product of its weights with the input signal and finish with an activation function. The activation functions introduce nonlinearity. The entire computation can be expressed with a series of iterative matrix multiplications. Two types of ANNs have been introduced, regressors, and classifiers. Regressors and classifiers differ in that classifiers are categorical. Classifiers use softmax to map the ANN's logits to a synthetic probability distribution over the categories.

## 2.6 Projects

1. Implement Algorithm 2.1 in your favorite computer language. Use the weights in the `sine` and `cosine` examples to test it.
2. Measure the time taken to perform a matrix vector multiplication. Plot a graph for the time taken as a function of the $N$, the number rows in a square matrix. What is the relationship?
3. The binary classifier example in Section 2.4.1 was implemented with a regressor and the `sigmoid` activation. The outcomes equally shared the space $[0, 1]$. What would have to change to accommodate the other two activation functions presented in the chapter?

# 3

# Training Neural Networks

In Chapter 2 it was shown how ANNs compute values and perform the tasks of regression and classification. In this chapter, we will learn how ANNs are created. ANNs depend on good values for weights to produce accurate results. Creating an ANN is the process of constructing a graph and then finding the appropriate weights. The latter task is accomplished by training the ANN, the topic of this chapter.

There are two stages in the life-cycle of an ANN. The stages are training and inference. Inference formed the subject of Chapter 2, it is the application of the ANN – the trained model; it has appropriate weights and is ready to be used to make predictions on data that is has never seen before. Inference is the second stage of the life-cycle. The first stage is training. A model cannot be used until is has been trained. The raw clay of the function, a graph with bad weights, must be molded to fit the constraints of the problem's defining dataset. There are multiple steps in the course of training and accepting a model, and they will be introduced to produce a working training framework.

ANNs are defined by their weights. The values of the weights determine the behavior of an ANN. The weights are found during the process of training the ANN. Training an ANN requires a dataset. The dataset is used to train the ANN so it is called the training set. The ANN "learns" from the training set. Training an ANN consists of fitting weights to the ANN such that the ANN emits the desired values with respect to the training set. During training, the weights of the ANN are reconciled with the training data. The correctness of the ANN is measured against the training set. In this sense, the model (ANN) is "fitted" to the data. This is an example of supervised learning (105) because the dataset must also include the answer, also known as the ground truth or labels, so that the ANN's result can be verified and its accuracy quantified. The error is used to correct the ANN. Once the error is sufficiently low, the training is said to have converged. Convergence will be clarified below.

*Demystifying Deep Learning: An Introduction to the Mathematics of Neural Networks,*
First Edition. Douglas J. Santry.
© 2024 The Institute of Electrical and Electronics Engineers, Inc. Published 2024 by John Wiley & Sons, Inc.

## 3.1 Preparing the Training Set: Data Preprocessing

ANNs learn from experience; they get better over time. The experience comes from exposure to the training set. Training requires good data to constrain the ANN. The training set is presented repeatedly to the ANN until is has learnt its lesson sufficiently well. Clearly, the quality of the data is critical: garbage in, garbage out. Taking a little care at the beginning of the process will go a long way to improving results and reducing training time (the number of training cycles required for convergence).

Prior to training the data typically needs to be preprocessed. There are many sources of data, and it can take many forms. The data could be jpeg images, natural language text, or the results of instrument readings. Whatever the source and form of the data, it must put into a useable state for training. Preprocessing the data leads to better behaved dynamics in the model and faster convergence. ANNs are sensitive to the values in a training set. To increase our chances of successful training, we require numerical stability and control over inputs. Preprocessing is means of achieving all of those goals. There are a number of points that need to be considered.

Recall that ANNs compute their values with multiple matrix multiplications and activation functions. Matrix multiplications are linear transformations that scale and rotate their arguments, and it is important that the transformations behave well. It is undesirable to use weights that cause the arguments to explode or disappear. Activation functions are interesting between $-1$ and $1$. The final state of a neuron is the activation function applied to a neuron's dot product of weights and inputs, $u$. A neuron whose weights uniformly produce strongly asymptotic behavior in the activation function (e.g. $-1$ or $1$ for the `tanh`) are not contributing to the inference. The weights of such a neuron are known as saturated. Saturated neurons are not helpful. To keep the activation functions interesting, $u$ should be within the unsaturated domain of the activation functions.

It is also important to ensure that predictors have the correct relative influence on the dot products at the input layer. Consider a dataset with two predictors with means that are orders of magnitude apart. For example, half-lives of radioactive material measured in 100s years and masses measured in $10^{-5}$ kg. There is a difference of 7 orders of magnitude between the features. Even if the mass is the more important feature, it will be dominated by the enormous values of the half-lives. Moreover, if the half-lives are converted from years to seconds a completely different model will be obtained (and probably even less useful). What we really want to capture is the distribution of a feature. Of interest are the relationships between the individual features. The choice of units should not matter, nor should the relative scale of the features. The chances of saturating the activations functions is very high indeed if large numbers are used in the input training set.

Ideally the data will make it easy for the scaler products to produce values within the interesting domains of the activations functions. To make that more likely, two basic steps of preprocessing are adopted: they are translation and scaling. Both steps are performed on a per feature basis. These steps are only performed on numerical features. Translation should ensure that the input data starts centered on the center of interesting activation dynamics, and scaling ensures that the input data does not stray outside the interesting activation domain.

Typically, features are centered at 0.0. The first step is to translate the mean of the distribution of the features to zero. This is done by computing the per feature mean and then subtracting it element-wise from the feature. Each feature is treated separately. Iterating over the features, the mean is computed and then subtracted element-wise. The effect of this translation is that the distribution of every feature is now centered about zero, that is, has a mean of 0.0.

The second step is to "normalize" the data. Normalization of the data is effected by scaling it with an appropriate per-feature scaler value. There are a number of ways of selecting an appropriate scaler. One way it is to compute the max ($|x_i|$) of a feature and then dividing every element of said feature with the maximum. This produces values in the feature that are $-1 \leq x_i \leq 1$.

Z-scoring is another way to normalize a numerical feature. The standard deviation of the feature is computed and then every element is divided by it. This results in each element of a feature being the count of the number of standard deviations that it is away from the mean, which is zero by construction. Z-scoring is usually preferable to scaling by the maximum.

Normalization is the process of scaling the data to make it more amenable to the linear transformation that multiplication by the weights matrix effects. Scaling with either the maximum or standard deviation preserves the relationships between the data. Moreover, it would appear at first glance that the compact domain produced by scaling with the maximum is superior. This begs the question, why is Z-scoring recommended? The answer lies in the application of the ANN. Training produces a model that has learnt the data, but applications are usually interested in performing inference with data that the model has never seen before. Training with the narrow domain $[-1, 1]$ can produce a model that is not good at dealing with unseen data. The problem is the special nature of multiplication in that domain. Numbers in that subset grow smaller with multiplication, which is the opposite with values outside the subset, which grow larger. During training the weights will specialize for the former case. Unseen data, even after pre-processing, may fall outside the subset $[-1, 1]$. The values will grow larger with multiplication, that is, behave completely differently than training data. This effect can produce poor predictions. Z-scoring produces a compact normalized training set while handling unseen data better. This is because the model was trained with data outside $[-1, 1]$, and the weights will not have specialized to the exclusion of values outside that subset; the model will be more robust. Handling unseen data is usually the most important consideration.

Recalling the discussion of activation functions in Section 2.2.1, three particularly important activation functions were proposed. There are many more possibilities, but those selected are important as an introduction to the trade-offs attendant to selecting an activation function. The range of `tanh` and `sigmoid` are very similar. It may not be clear why both are used. Some rules of thumb can now be suggested. The `sigmoid` function has a range of [0, 1]. Observe that half of the `sigmoid`'s interesting domain is not in its range. ANNs are stacks of layers, the output of one layer acting as the input for the next. The `sigmoid` produces output that the deeper layer will have to translate to make full use of its `sigmoid`'s domain. This makes it harder to train. The `tanh` should be preferred as it has a range of [−1, 1]; it is centered. The `tanh` was introduced as an activation function once the dynamics of training ANNs was better understood. `sigmoid` is used when the interpretation of the output is a probability. This is not uncommon so the `sigmoid` still occupies an important niche. Finally, observe that preprocessing ensures that the training set is in the interesting area of the activation functions' domains. Starting the ANN's computation with sympathetic input speeds up training and produces better results.

Data preprocessing needs to be incorporated seamlessly into a model's workflow. There are two choices of when to do it when training. One choice is to perform all preprocessing a priori in a batch. As described above, the means are calculated, the data translated and normalization performed on a copy of the dataset; it never needs to be done again in the course of training. Another option is to compute the per feature means and scaling factors then incorporate them as an ante-layer in the ANN directly. When arguments arrive at the ante-layer, they are processed prior to passing them on to the first dense layer of the ANN. The arrangement is depicted in Figure 3.1. Both methods are correct and the choice is a trade-off, but the latter is often chosen. There are a number of reasons for this recommendation.

First, once the model is trained and ready to be deployed, then data used for inference will also need to be preprocessed. To ensure correctness, the parameters used for preprocessing of the training set will have to be retained for use with the application, even if batch preprocessing was employed. Incorporating the preprocessing as a layer in the ANN obviates a whole class of bugs where ANNs are invoked with unprocessed arguments. The second reason is a question of resources. It is a terrible idea to modify training data, it should always be kept as a record. Preprocessing the training data batch style requires creating a copy, and this can be prohibitive. The one seeming advantage of batch preprocessing prior to training is that it is only done once. The ante-layer ANN may seem wasteful, doing the same thing to the same data over and over again each training epoch, but compared with the computation of computing the ANN's value, and the weight updates, it is really just noise. Relative to the expense of training, preprocessing

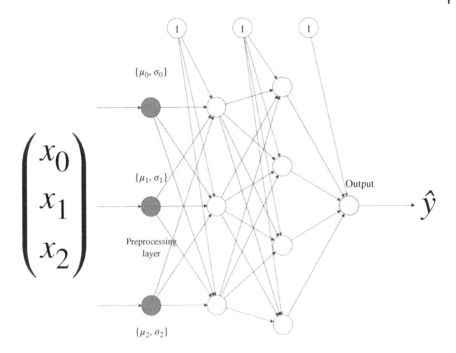

$$\begin{pmatrix} x_0 \\ x_1 \\ x_2 \end{pmatrix}$$

**Figure 3.1** An ANN with a preprocessing layer. The preprocessing nodes are in the first layer. The translation and scaling are performed on a per feature basis. The data are passed directly to the ANN from the training set unmodified. Training a preprocessing layer consists of learning the per-feature means and standard deviations.

examples multiple times by incorporating an ante-ANN preprocessing layer is not as onerous as it might seem. The advantages far out-weigh the drawbacks. The ante-layer is "trained" by computing the per feature means and standard deviations and storing them in the layer.

## 3.2 Weight Initialization

Before the weights of an ANN can be trained, they will need to be initialized. Intuitively it might seem that initializing the weights to zero is indicated. It is a common starting value in many algorithms and data structures, but it does not work when training ANNs. What is important is ensuring that all weights in a layer start with *different* values. Zero is not necessarily precluded, but only one weight in a layer should be initialized with zero. The initial values need to be different to ensure that they evolve in different directions during training. Consider a layer in an ANN. All the neurons receive the same input. If every neuron had the same weights they would all give the same answer, which is pointless. The point of having multiple neurons is to increase the capacity of a layer to learn; the weights need to be different to so that all of the neurons can contribute.

The neurons not only need to be different, but ideally they should be in a certain range. The ranges of activation functions are most interesting in certain subsets of their domains. The internal scaler product of a neuron, $u$, should be, $-1 \leq u \leq 1$. This suggests that the weights should be initialized thus: $w \sim U[-1, 1]$, where U is the uniform distribution. While this might be appropriate it turns that we can do better. The magnitude of the scaler product will also depend on the number of source neurons – the more there are, the greater the magnitude of $u$. Glorot and Bengio (48) suggest that it is important to ensure that the variance of the weights is high. High variance ensures that the weights are widely dispersed and contributing, not overlapping. The following is their proposed method for initializing weights:

$$ w \sim U \left[ -\frac{\sqrt{6}}{\sqrt{M_{in} + M_{out}}}, \frac{\sqrt{6}}{\sqrt{M_{in} + M_{out}}} \right], \tag{3.1} $$

where the $M$s denotes the numbers of the neurons in the surrounding layers. Equation (3.1) is known is known as Glorot initialization. The formulation accounts for the number of weights in the surrounding layers by shrinking the centered subset appropriately.

It is also very common to sample the initial values for weights from a Gaussian distribution. Many deep ANNs employ this technique. The method's use in Deep Learning seems to have emanated from its use in AlexNET (89), a very successful system that broke accuracy records at the time. The successful use of Gaussian initialization has not been explained, but it is widespread (62). AlexNET also introduced ReLU as an activation function for Deep Learning, which has a very different dynamic domain. The latter point may explain the success of the method. More advanced methods of initialization exist, such as orthogonalization (71), but Glorot is the most commonly implemented.

And a final implementation note. ANNs do not have unique solutions. The solution depends entirely on the weight initializations, which are random. The weights do not converge to some unique combination. If determinism is required, for example, when debugging, control of the order of initialization and the seeding of the pseudo-random number generator is required. When developing libraries, it is a good idea to print out the seed for the random number generator before running any code. If a problem is observed in the run, then it can be reproduced. Rare bugs are very difficult to fix if there is no means of reproducing them reliably.

## 3.3  Training Outline

ANNs are trained with example data; the training set. Unlike the historical method of solving for functions, ANNs are empirically constrained functions. We do not define the desired function with a law of nature such as an energy or a conservation of mass constraint, we specify the function directly with data by example. The *data* defines the function, that is, the desired behavior of the ANN. The real function is unknown. The ANN is an approximation to the unknown function, that is, $ANN \equiv \hat{f} \simeq f$.

The model is defined by its training set, the data that empirically constrains how the ANN should behave. The training set might consist of a set of photographs and labels if it is a classifier, or a set of vectors and continuous outputs if it is a regressor. In both cases, there is a set tuples that consists of the inputs, that is, predictors, $x_i$. The data also includes the correct output, $y_i$, the desired response. This is also known as the ground truth. Datasets that include the correct answers are known as labeled data. It is the requirement for the inclusion of the answers in the dataset that makes this an example of supervised learning. Without the answers we do not know if the training is proceeding well or needs to be adjusted.

Given the training set, the role of training is to reconcile the weights of the model with the data, that is, to *fit* the weights to the model; thus, a synonym for training is fitting. Fitting a model consists of presenting the training data to the ANN repeatedly until the desired behavior is observed. The examples comprising the training set define the correct behavior. Elements from the training set are presented to the ANN until it "learns" the data. The process of fitting a model consists of a sequence of distinct and discrete training epochs where the training data are presented to the ANN, errors are computed and the weights are updated (and, hopefully, improved). But what does *learn* mean? How do we know when training is completed?

Fitting the model is driven by globally optimizing an objective function over the training set. By global we mean over the entire training set. ANN objective functions are generally minimized. Let $\hat{y} = ANN(x)$, the ANN's response, and $x$ an example from the training set. Then the general form of the problem is

$$GOF^t = \frac{1}{N} \sum_{i}^{N} Loss(\hat{y}_i^t, y_i), \tag{3.2}$$

at epoch $t$, and where there are N elements in the training set. The global objective function (GOF) is a sum of the per training example loss functions. Training an ANN is the act of finding the weights that minimize the objective function. The local per example loss function quantifies the accuracy of the ANN and must be differentiable. The ANN's result in the local loss function, $\hat{y}_i^t$, is superscripted to denote that the output changes every epoch (as it learns and improves). The ground truth never changes.

Computing the current value of the GOF constitutes the basis of a training epoch. To compute the global loss, we need to run through the training set and compute the per training example losses. At the end of the epoch, the weights are updated to new values based on the results of computing the objective function. The updated weights should improve the global loss function.

Training terminates when the objective function converges. What this means varies between loss functions. The objective functions used in this book have a minimum of zero. It is, however, common practice to terminate earlier than that. A sufficiently small threshold for the objective function can be specified below which the model is accepted. The threshold is determined by the tolerances of the application. This question is examined more closely below as loss functions are introduced.

The convergence of the objective function is the gauge of training progress. At the end of training, the ANN should have weights that minimize the GOF. The outline of the process is presented in Algorithm 3.1.

---

**Algorithm 3.1** Training an ANN with a Global Objective Function

---

1: **procedure** $\text{TRAIN}(\epsilon_{threshold})$
2:     $\text{GOF} \leftarrow +\infty$
3:     **while** $\text{GOF} > \epsilon_{threshold}$ **do**
4:         $\text{GOF} \leftarrow 0.0$
5:         **for** $x, y \in$ *Training Set* **do**
6:             $\text{GOF} \leftarrow \text{GOF} + \texttt{ComputeLoss}(x, y)$
7:         **end for**
8:         $\text{GOF} \leftarrow \text{GOF} \div \text{N}$
9:         $\texttt{UpdateWeights}()$
10:     **end while**
11: **end procedure**

---

Each iteration of the while loop constitutes a training epoch. All the elements of the training set are evaluated, and the current value of the objective function is computed. Once the individual losses have been calculated, the weights are updated. When the objective function is sufficiently small the algorithm terminates. At this point, training is said to have converged. This form of training is called batch training because every epoch uses the entire dataset; it is processed as a batch.

In summary, training consists of a number of discrete steps, called epochs, where the ANN is used to compute a per training datum loss. A GOF summarizes the individual losses to produce a global loss value. Training continues until the objective function falls below the required tolerance. The weights are updated at the end of each epoch, and the solution is improved.

## 3.4   Least Squares: A Trivial Example

Before we present the training of ANNs, it is instructive to briefly examine a trivial example of training a model with a dataset. The exercise will motivate the actual technique. Consider a model with a single layer and the identity activation function, then $ANN(x) = Wx$ (this is a neural matrix so the bias is the first column). Let us examine the properties of a linear ANN.

Training a neural network is the task of finding the weights for the matrix, $W$, that reconciles the ANN output with the training set examples. Consider the problem of training the ANN to learn the trigonometric sine function. The first step is to obtain a training set. The training set consists of a set of tuples with the input arguments and the expected answer. The following training set would be appropriate: $\{(x_1, y_1 = \sin(x_1)), \ldots, (x_N, y_N = \sin(x_N))\}$, a list of angles in radians and their sine.

One solution that suggests itself is to minimize the error with the classic least squares: $\min |Xw - y|_2$. The standard least squares solution is to employ the matrix $QR^1$ decomposition, $X = QR$. This yields the solution, $Rw = Q^Ty$. The solution for an example sine training set is depicted in Figure 3.2. It is clear from visual inspection that it is not a good fit. The solution produced a line that did indeed minimize the error with respect to the cost metric, but sine is nonlinear. The errors are still far too high for the model to be useful. We can see the role of the bias term in this trivial example. If the $y$-intercept had to be zero the fit would be even worse. But even with the bias translation, it is clear that a single layer of linear neurons is simply incapable of learning sine. This begs the question, can the solution be improved by making the network deeper?

A deeper model can be created by employing $h$ layers, $W_1, W_2, \ldots, W_h$. The trouble is that the $h$ matrices convolve to a single matrix: $W_1 \cdot W_2 \cdot W_h = W_c = $ a single matrix; a linear transformation. No matter how many layers are added, they are mathematically isomorphic to a single layer weighted with the convolved matrix, $W_c$ (though computing the convolved matrix with IEEE arithmetic may produce

---

1  See Appendix A for a review of $QR$.

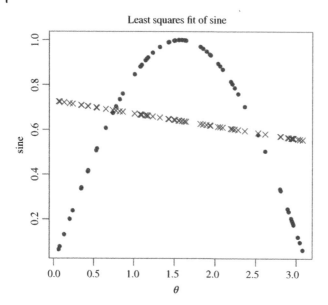

**Figure 3.2** The fit of a least squares solution to a random sample of points and their `sine`. The training set is plotted as points. The results of the computed model are plotted as crosses. The slope is negative because there are more points in the training set on the right side of the curve.

a different result). This can be used to model lines, planes, and hyperplanes, but most interesting problems are extremely nonlinear. It is precisely this nonlinearity that Minksy and Papert used to argue that ANNs were a research dead end (131). Early learning rules were mostly variants of least squares. An improvement can be made by treating the dataset piecewise and dividing the dataset into ranges, but this presents its own problems and remains unsatisfactory.

To learn nonlinear relations requires the introduction of nonlinearity. ANNs get their nonlinearity from activation functions. That is the role of the activation function: they bend the decision boundary around subsets that are not linearly separable. An example is depicted in Figure 3.3. The problem on the right is linearly separable, and least squares is capable of learning it. The problem on the left has a more complex decision boundary. It is not linearly separable. The problem on the left requires more elaborate mechanisms for a satisfactory model. The nonlinear activation functions make possible learning nonlinear decision boundaries.

While the nonlinear models are very successful at dealing with nonlinear problems, they lack interpretability. Least squares results in a solution that can be easily interpreted as a relationship. A trained ANN is a black box. It may make predictions very well, but they usually do not admit of interpretation making it difficult to draw broad conclusions.

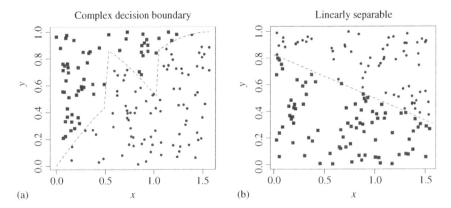

**Figure 3.3** The decision boundaries for two classification problems. The example depicted in subfigure (b) features two classes that are neatly separated by a straight line; it is linearly separable. The classification problem presented in subfigure (b) is far more complicated. Its two classes cannot be differentiated with the superposition of linear boundaries.

## 3.5 Backpropagation of Error for Regression

To handle nonlinear decision boundaries, ANNs must be nonlinear. To that end, a nonlinear learning process was developed in 1986 (34), called backpropagation of error. It remains the basis of training ANNs down to this day. In this section we present how modern ANNs are trained.

It has been shown in Chapter 2 how a feed-forward ANN computes values by accepting an input and then propagating the signal, layer by layer, through the network. The answer pops out of the last layer. When training an ANN, the local loss function computes the per-example error with the ANN's result. The error is used to improve the network. Starting with the error computed with the result and the ground truth, a correction is calculated. The correction is pushed in the reverse direction backward through the graph. As will be seen, the error signal is the *gradient* on the loss function surface. This section describes the resulting method.

Continuing with the `sine` example, a topology for its graph is required. The topology of the graph in Figure 3.4 is {3, 2, 1}. This is the graph that will be used in the derivation. The model will use the `sigmoid` activation function. The nonlinearity introduced will improve the solution when compared to the least-squares model. This topology will not produce an accurate model of `sine`, more neurons are needed, but its simplicity will make the presentation of the concepts clear in what follows below. This model's topology is sufficiently simple that layers can be clearly labeled. The layers are named, {input, hidden, output}. As there is a hidden layer, this is a Deep Learning model (but trivial).

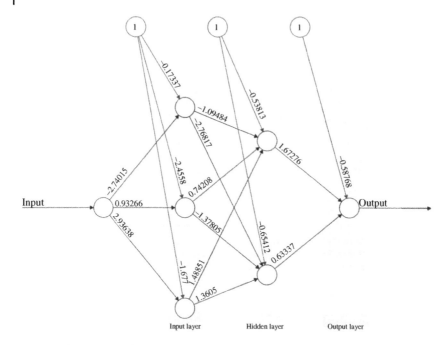

**Figure 3.4** A trained ANN model that has learnt the sine function. The layers are labeled.

At the start of the first epoch of training, the first example is presented to the untrained model. From the input layer, the signal propagates through the network, and as the weights are initialized randomly, we can expect nonsense in the output neuron. To progress further, there are two immediate requirements. We need a means of measuring the accuracy of the ANN's answer, or how "wrong" it is, and the means must be quantitative and differentiable. There must also be a mechanism for using this information to update the weights and thus improve the solution. We address ourselves to meeting these requirements in the rest of the section. The starting point is the GOF:

$$GOF^t = \frac{1}{N} \sum_i^N Loss(\hat{y}_i^t, y_i). \tag{3.3}$$

The work of a training epoch is computing the individual *loss* terms. When training an example is selected from the training set, $(x_i, y_i = \sin(x_i))$, and compute $\hat{y}_i = ANN(x_i)$. Now, almost certainly, we will have $\hat{y}_i \neq y_i$. A loss function will determine the quality, or lack thereof, of $\hat{y}$. For regression, the standard measure is the squared error loss function:

$$Loss = \frac{1}{2}(y - \hat{y})^2, \tag{3.4}$$

where $y$ is the ground truth and $\hat{y}$ is the response of the ANN. The squared error loss function punishes large differences and forgives smaller differences. As the difference is squared the result is always positive, which makes it useful in a sum.

Returning to the objective function, it can now be defined more precisely for regression. To measure the quality of the fit for the entire training set, we employ the mean squared error (MSE). The MSE is the objective function for regression. The global loss function is the mean of all the errors of all the examples from the training set:

$$GOF^t = MSE^t = \frac{1}{N} \sum_{i}^{N} \frac{1}{2}(y_i - \hat{y}_i^t)^2. \tag{3.5}$$

As the MSE $\to$ 0 the accuracy of the model is improving, that is, converging. In practice it is rarely exactly zero. A nonzero threshold is specified below which the fit can be tolerated. When the loss of the ANN falls below the threshold the training process is halted and the model is ready for use. The threshold is left to the application to select.

Having computed a response with an example from the training set the loss, the metric for (in)accuracy, is calculated. The loss needs to be used to improve the accuracy of the ANN so that the ANN can learn from its experience (exposure to an example from the training set). Recall that the object of fitting a model to a training set is to look for the appropriate weights for the ANN. It is now clear what that means: we want values for the weights that reduce the MSE. An update for the weights is required at epoch, $t$, such that,

$$w^t = w^{t-1} + \Delta w^t, \tag{3.6}$$

is an improvement. The object of the training epoch is to compute the weight updates, $\Delta w$. Ideally, the update to a weight would decrease the MSE. An update to the weights is required that decreases the loss. To that end, the weight updates need to be related to how the MSE is changing. In other words, we want to relate how the loss is changing with respect to how the weights are changing. The following equation captures the relationship:

$$\Delta w \propto -\frac{\partial L}{\partial w}, \tag{3.7}$$

where $L$ is the loss function, in this case, squared error. It is negative because this is a minimization problem. The desired direction of travel is toward minima and away from maxima, that is, it needs to descend. If the slope is positive, that is, increasing, we want to go in the opposite direction. If the slope is negative, decreasing, then we simply keep going.

The canonical means of achieving this is a method known as backpropagation of error. The backpropagation procedure computes the derivative of the loss and uses the chain rule from the Calculus to propagate the error gradient backward through the ANN's graph; this is known as the backpropagation phase or the backward pass of training. We use a recurrence equation and dynamic programming to update every weight in the ANN starting from the loss function.

To start, the backpropagation algorithm computes the loss with an example from the training set. This is the forward pass as the responses go forward through the ANN's graph in the usual computation. With the ANN's result, $\hat{y}$, the loss is computed and then the gradient is forced backward through the ANN's graph. This is the backward phase.

The first step is to compute, $\hat{y}_j = \text{ANN}(x_j)$, with the $j$th example from the training set. With $\hat{y}$ available the loss is computed. The inceptive step of backpropagation is the derivative of the loss. Differentiating the loss with respect to the output of the ANN we obtain:

$$\frac{\partial L}{\partial \hat{y}} = \frac{\partial}{\partial \hat{y}}\left(\frac{1}{2}(y - \hat{y})^2\right) = -(y - \hat{y}). \tag{3.8}$$

This is the how the loss is changing with respect to the output neuron, $\hat{y} \equiv z_{output}$. We now have $\frac{\partial L}{\partial \hat{y}}$, but we need to compute the $\frac{\partial L}{\partial w_i}$ for each weight in the ANN's graph. The backpropagation algorithm is a means of doing just that. To start we will compute the update for the weights of the terminal layer, the output layer.

## 3.5.1 The Terminal Layer (Output)

To begin, recall that the output neuron computes its state as follows: $\hat{y} = \sigma(u = W_{output}z_{hidden})$, $\sigma$, the activation function, is the sigmoid function in our example. The chain rule is used to propagate the derivative to every weight in the output layer of the ANN as follows. For each weight $i$ in the output layer:

$$\frac{\partial L}{\partial w_i} = \frac{\partial L}{\partial \hat{y}} \cdot \frac{\partial \hat{y}}{\partial u} \cdot \frac{\partial u}{\partial w_i}. \tag{3.9}$$

The chain rule from the Calculus has been used to decompose the monolithic problem of computing $\frac{\partial L}{\partial w_i}$ rendering it more tractable. There are three intermediate computations required to get the final result for the weight update, and they are easy to compute. Equation (3.9) represents a path of derivatives that the gradient, $\frac{\partial L}{\partial \hat{y}}$, must travel along through the graph to where it is needed. In the sine example, the output neuron has 3 weights. The BPG equation (3.9) will be used 3 times, once for each of the weights, $i = \{0, 1, 2\}$.

Using Eq. (3.9), we can compute the gradient for each of our weights in the output layer. Observe that there are 3 derivatives on the right-hand-side (RHS). It follows that the individual derivatives on the RHS need to be computed, and once obtained, the final derivative is calculated for the weight update. We proceed by computing each derivative individually and then composing them to produce

**Table 3.1** Important Activation Functions

| Activation Function | Definition | Derivative |
|---|---|---|
| Sigmoid function | $\sigma(u) = \frac{1}{1+e^{-u}}$ | $\sigma(1 - \sigma)$ |
| Hyperbolic tangent (tanh) | $\sigma(u) = \tanh(u)$ | $1 - \sigma^2$ |
| Rectified linear unit (ReLU) | $\sigma(u) = \max(0, u)$ | $\begin{cases} 0 & u \leq 0 \\ 1 & u > 0 \end{cases}$ |

the desired term in the weight update equation. We have computed $\frac{\partial L}{\partial \hat{y}}$, so that leaves $\frac{\partial \hat{y}}{\partial u}$ and $\frac{\partial u}{\partial w_i}$.

Proceeding from left to right we start with, $\frac{\partial \hat{y}}{\partial u}$. Recall that $\hat{y} \equiv z_{output} = \sigma(u)$, it is short-hand for the terminal activation function; the final output of the neuron, so $\frac{\partial \hat{y}}{\partial u} = \frac{\partial \sigma}{\partial u}$. As such it depends on the choice of activation function. Our ANN employs a `sigmoid` activation function so we need to compute its derivative. Recall the definition of the `sigmoid` function (Table 3.1):

$$\sigma(u) = \frac{1}{1 + e^{-u}}. \tag{3.10}$$

Let $v = 1 + e^{-u}$, then we can re-write the `sigmoid` as, $\sigma = \frac{1}{v}$, thus:

$$\frac{\partial \hat{y}}{\partial u} = \frac{\partial}{\partial u} \left( \frac{1}{v} \right)$$

$$= -\frac{1}{v^2} \cdot \frac{dv}{du}$$

$$= -\frac{1}{v^2} \cdot -e^{-u}$$

$$= \frac{e^{-u}}{v^2}$$

$$= \frac{(1 - 1) + e^{-u}}{v^2}$$

$$= \frac{v - 1}{v^2}$$

$$= \frac{v}{v^2} - \frac{1}{v^2}$$

$$= \frac{1}{v} \left( \frac{v}{v} - \frac{1}{v} \right)$$

$$= \sigma(1 - \sigma). \tag{3.11}$$

Recalling that $\hat{y}$ is a synonym for $\sigma(u)$ we obtain:

$$\frac{\partial \hat{y}}{\partial u} = \sigma(1 - \sigma) = \hat{y}(1 - \hat{y}). \tag{3.12}$$

This is a very convenient form, we already have $\hat{y}$, and this was one of the reasons why the `sigmoid` was originally so attractive. The last derivative is obtained by differentiating the scaler product with respect to the weight in question:

$$\frac{\partial u}{\partial w_i} = \frac{\partial}{\partial w_i}\left(\sum_j w_j z_j\right) = z_i. \tag{3.13}$$

We now have the three derivatives required for the evaluation of (BPG):

$$\frac{\partial L}{\partial \hat{y}} = -(y - \hat{y}), \tag{3.14}$$

$$\frac{\partial \hat{y}}{\partial u} = \hat{y}(1 - \hat{y}), \tag{3.15}$$

and

$$\frac{\partial u}{\partial w_i} = z_i. \tag{3.16}$$

Composing the individual derivatives to produce the final form results in:

$$\frac{\partial L}{\partial w_i} = \frac{\partial L}{\partial \hat{y}} \cdot \frac{\partial \hat{y}}{\partial u} \cdot \frac{\partial u}{\partial w_i} = -(y - \hat{y}) \cdot \hat{y}(1 - \hat{y}) \cdot z_i \tag{3.17}$$

While there are 3 weights to update in the output layer, observe that only the last derivative, $\frac{\partial u}{\partial w_i}$, is different across all three updates, indeed, it is the only quantity that varies. The first two derivatives (shaded) are common across all 3 updates. This quantity is special and referred to as $\delta$. In general, when the activation is unknown, the delta is written as

$$\delta = \frac{\partial L}{\partial \hat{y}} \cdot \frac{\partial \hat{y}}{\partial u} = \frac{\partial L}{\partial u}. \tag{3.18}$$

In our example, the activation has been specified, it is the `sigmoid` activation function. The the shaded factors in Eq. (3.17) comprise the delta,

$$\delta = -(y - \hat{y}) \cdot \hat{y}(1 - \hat{y}). \tag{3.19}$$

This is not abstract or symbolic, we have both values to hand, $y$ is from the training set and $\hat{y}$ was computed by the ANN in the forward pass. The delta is trivially computed. This leads to the actual weight updates.

We are now in a position to compute the updates for the weights in the output layer for use in the following epoch:

$$w_i^{t+1} = w_i^t - \Delta w_i^{t+1} = w_i^t - \eta \cdot \frac{\partial L}{\partial w_i} = w_i^t - \eta \cdot \delta \cdot z_i, \tag{3.20}$$

where we have introduced $\eta$, a *learning rate*, to scale the update. The learning rate is there to regulate the size of the update. The three updates for the weights for the output neuron are

$$w_b^{t+1} = w_b^t - \Delta w_b = w_b^t - \eta \cdot \frac{\partial L}{\partial w_b} = w_b^t - \eta \delta, \tag{3.21}$$

recall the bias is always 1.0.

$$w_0^{t+1} = w_0^t - \Delta w_0 = w_0^t - \eta \cdot \frac{\partial L}{\partial w_0} = w_0^t - \eta \delta \cdot z_{hidden,0}, \tag{3.22}$$

and finally

$$w_1^{t+1} = w_1^t - \Delta w_1 = w_1^t - \eta \cdot \frac{\partial L}{\partial w_1} = w_1^t - \eta \delta \cdot z_{hidden,1}, \tag{3.23}$$

where the output vector from the hidden layer has been treated like an array. The $z_{hidden}$ vector forms the input for the output neuron in the feed-forward phase of the ANN.

### 3.5.2 Backpropagation: The Shallower Layers

Having computed the updates for the weights for the output neuron it remains to continue the backpropagation of the gradient to the remaining weights shallower in the ANN graph (we continue to use the convention that the output neuron is the deepest layer, that is, with respect to the feed-forward phase).

The inceptive step of the recurrence has been computed with $\delta$ in the output layer. Continuing with the `sine` example, let us compute the weight updates for the hidden layer. There are 2 neurons in the hidden layer, each with 4 weights. All of the weights need to be updated so there are 8 separate weight updates to compute. This is done by continuing to apply backpropagation.

To compute the weight update in the next layer, we need to propagate the gradient through the output layer to the hidden layer. Recall that we computed $\delta$ in the output layer. Expanding $\delta$ in the output layer yields:

$$\delta_{output} = \frac{\partial L}{\partial \hat{y}} \cdot \frac{\partial \hat{y}}{\partial u_{output}} = \frac{\partial L}{\partial u_{output}}.$$

This is the basis of the recurrence. We will use the deeper $\delta_{output}$ to compute the shallower $\delta_{hidden}$. Every neuron in the network has a $\delta$. We have seen how to compute a weight update with a delta, thus with delta computed we know how to compute a neuron's weight updates. It is possible to proceed as in the output layer to compute the updates for the individual weights in the hidden layer. We need,

$$\delta_{hidden} = \frac{\partial L}{\partial u_{hidden}},$$

and we can compute this quantity with the $\delta$ from the output layer:

$$\delta_{hidden} = \frac{\partial L}{\partial u_{hidden}}$$

$$= \frac{\partial L}{\partial u_{output}} \cdot \frac{\partial u_{output}}{\partial \sigma_{hidden}} \cdot \frac{\partial \sigma_{hidden}}{\partial u_{hidden}}$$

$$= \delta_{output} \cdot \frac{\partial u_{output}}{\partial \sigma_{hidden}} \cdot \frac{\partial \sigma_{hidden}}{\partial u_{hidden}}, \tag{3.24}$$

where there are two quantities that have not yet been computed. They are $\frac{\partial u_{output}}{\partial \sigma_{hidden}}$ and $\frac{\partial \sigma_{hidden}}{\partial u_{hidden}}$.

Note that the bias for the output layer does not play any part in the backpropagation. The bias weight receives updates like all other weights in a layer but does not contribute to further propagation of the gradient; it does not receive signals from shallower layers in the graph, it is an input (a BPG terminus). Also bear in mind that $z_{hidden} = \sigma(u_{hidden})$, the sigma notation is used to emphasize that it is a differentiable activation function.

Computing the $\delta_{hidden}$ derivative propagates the gradient between layers. Once the delta is obtained, the weight updates are computed as they were in the output layer. Every time the gradient is propagated back across layers, the deltas will be computed. There are two neurons in the hidden layer so there will be two deltas. Recall that $u_{\ell+1} = \sum_i z_{\ell,i} \cdot w_i$ (the scaler product in the output layer). We need to compute the following twice, for $i \in \{0,1\}$:

$$\frac{\partial u_{output}}{\partial \sigma_{hidden,i}} = \frac{\partial}{\partial z_{hidden,i}} \left( \overset{neurons\ in\ hidden}{\underset{j}{\sum}} z_j \cdot w_{output,j} \right) = w_{output,i}. \tag{3.25}$$

The derivative is the weight on the edge from the shallower neuron to the deeper one. At this point, a pattern is emerging with respect to the layers. The final form of Eq. (3.24) for computing the $\delta$ for a neuron can be generalized:

$$\delta_\ell = \delta_{\ell+1} \cdot \frac{\partial u_{\ell+1}}{\partial \sigma_\ell} \cdot \frac{\partial \sigma_\ell}{\partial u_\ell}, \tag{3.26}$$

and the general form for computing the per neuron $\delta_{\ell,i}$ for a layer, $\ell$, and bearing in mind that it is the shallower layer, is

$$\frac{\partial u_{\ell+1}}{\partial \sigma_{\ell,i}} = \frac{\partial}{\partial z_{\ell,i}} \left( \overset{neurons\ in\ \ell}{\underset{j}{\sum}} z_j w_j \right) = w_i, \tag{3.27}$$

where $w_i$ is the weight on the edge between the two neurons. We already know how to compute the last derivative for the `sigmoid` activation function:

$$\frac{\partial \sigma_{hidden}}{\partial u_{hidden}} = \sigma(1 - \sigma) = z(1 - z), \tag{3.28}$$

where $z$ is the neuron's output. During training the responses for all of the neurons must be retained for the backpropagation phase. During ordinary use the responses can be discarded as soon as the deeper layer has consumed them, but they required when training. It is this requirement for retention that is the connection to dynamic programming.

There are two neurons in the hidden layer. Each neuron has a $\delta$ so we need to compute two of them. We can now compute the two $\delta$s that we need in the hidden layer. The resulting $\delta$s are

$$\delta_{hidden,0} = \delta_{output} \cdot w_0 \cdot \sigma_{hidden,0} \cdot (1 - \sigma_{hidden,0}), \tag{3.29}$$

and

$$\delta_{hidden,1} = \delta_{output} \cdot w_1 \cdot \sigma_{hidden,1} \cdot (1 - \sigma_{hidden,1}). \tag{3.30}$$

With the two $\delta_{hidden,i}$ computed the weight updates for the hidden layer can be computed as they were in the output layer.

The passage of the gradient through the output layer to the hidden layer by way of computing the $\delta$s is general. Backpropagation pushes the gradient backward through the network's layers through the graph from delta to delta, updating the weights in each layer as they are reached, and halting at dead ends (a bias or an input layer). The gradient passes through a layer to a neuron, $i$, using the deeper layer's $\delta$ with:

$$\delta_{\ell,i} = \delta_{\ell+1} \cdot w_i \cdot \frac{\partial \sigma_{\ell,i}}{\partial u_{\ell,i}}, \tag{3.31}$$

where no assumptions have been made about $\sigma$.

Proceeding with the sine example, the gradient has now reached the input layer. Notice that in this layer each input neuron is connected to the two deeper hidden neurons. It is clear that the earlier expression for the gradient crossing layers is too simple. Where neurons are connected to multiple deeper neurons, they need to absorb the gradient from all of their connected deeper neurons. A neuron needs the *total derivative*. The total derivative is just the sum of all the gradients passing backward through the neuron. Hence, the following is performed for each neuron in layer, $\ell$,

$$\delta_{\ell,i} = \frac{\partial \sigma_{\ell,i}}{\partial u_{\ell,i}} \cdot \sum_{j}^{\ell+1} \delta_{\ell+1,j} \cdot w_{j,i}, \tag{3.32}$$

where $w_{j,i}$ is the weight on the edge connecting the two neurons (row $j$ and column $i$ in the deeper layer's $W$ matrix). In the sine example, there are 3 neurons in the input layer, and we know the form of $\frac{d\sigma}{du}$ because the activation function is known (sigmoid), so we have,

$$\delta_{input,0} = z_0(1 - z_0) \cdot (w_{0,0} \cdot \delta_{hidden,0} + w_{1,0} \cdot \delta_{hidden,1}), \tag{3.33}$$

$$\delta_{input,1} = z_1(1 - z_1) \cdot (w_{0,1} \cdot \delta_{hidden,0} + w_{1,1} \cdot \delta_{hidden,1}), \tag{3.34}$$

and lastly

$$\delta_{input,2} = z_2(1 - z_2) \cdot (w_{0,2} \cdot \delta_{hidden,0} + w_{1,2} \cdot \delta_{hidden,1}). \tag{3.35}$$

The above 3 equations can be written more concisely[2] as

$$\delta_{\ell,i} = z_i(1 - z_i) \cdot \sum_{j}^{\ell+1} \delta_{\ell+1,j} \cdot w_{j,i}. \tag{3.36}$$

Once the input neurons compute their deltas the updates for their weights can be computed by multiplying them with $\frac{\partial u_i}{\partial w}$ as demonstrated with the output layer. These are the elements of the input tuple for the ANN. In the case of the input for the `sine` ANN, it is the argument to the ANN, the $x$ from the training set.

In summary, we can now see how propagating the gradient backward through the graph is used to update all of the weights in an ANN. Backpropagation consists of computing the weight updates for the output layer, in the course of which we also compute the output neuron's $\delta$. The $\delta$'s then percolate backward through the ANN until the input layer is encountered, and the last weight updates are performed. Once all of the weights in the ANN have been updated we run through the training set again and measure the improvement. This continues until the MSE is below the halting threshold. Because the weights are changing in the direction that reduces the MSE, the objective function should be reduced over the repeated training epochs. The `sine` example is trivial, and as presented backpropagation may seem cumbersome, but it can be expressed more elegantly.

As with ANN computation in the forward pass, backpropagation can be expressed more succinctly with matrices. Let $\delta_{\ell+1}$ be the vector of $\delta$s for layer $\ell + 1$. Then,

$$\phi_\ell = W^T_{\ell+1} \cdot \delta_{\ell+1}, \tag{3.37}$$

is the vector of total derivatives for layer $\ell$. Note that the upper-case $T$ superscript denotes the matrix transpose, not $t$, the epoch. The matrix multiplication sums the products of the weights and the deltas on a per shallower neuron basis. To compute the $\delta_{\ell,i}$ one more step is required:

$$\delta_\ell = \left(\frac{\partial \sigma_i}{\partial u_i}\right) \otimes \phi_\ell, \tag{3.38}$$

where $\otimes$ is the element-wise[3] vector multiplication operator. $\delta_\ell$ is the vector of deltas for the layer. The vector on the left-hand side of the multiplication is the per neuron $\delta$ so $i$ ranges over all the neurons in the layer, $\ell$.

The per weight gradient for the entire layer can now be written as the outer product:

$$\Delta W_\ell = \delta_\ell \cdot z^T_{\ell-1}, \tag{3.39}$$

---

2 It must be emphasized, this expression is for the `sine` example. The shaded factor is the specific derivative of the sigmoid activation function.
3 The Hadamard product.

where $z$ is the vector of the outputs of the shallower layer and thus forms the input for the current layer. Recall that a vector times the transpose of a vector produces a square matrix,[4] not a scaler. At the input layer of the ANN $z_{\ell-1}$ is the argument to the ANN from the training set. Finally, the weight update is

$$W_{\ell}^{t+1} = W_{\ell}^{t} - \eta \cdot \Delta W_{\ell}^{t+1}, \tag{3.40}$$

where $W$ is the matrix of weight for the layer, $\ell$. All the ingredients for an algorithm are now in place.

### 3.5.3 The Complete Backpropagation Algorithm

Having derived the recurrence equation, we now present a coherent and complete algorithm for backpropagation of the gradient of the loss function through the graph of a feed-forward ANN. We define $\mathscr{L}$ as the ordered list of the layers of our ANN. The complete backpropagation procedure is described in Algorithm 3.2.

---

**Algorithm 3.2** Training an ANN

---

1: **procedure** TRAIN($epsilon_{threshold}$)
2:     GOF $\leftarrow +\infty$
3:     **while** GOF $> \epsilon_{threshold}$ **do**
4:         GOF $\leftarrow 0.0$
5:         **for** $x, y \in$ *Training Set* **do**
6:             GOF $\leftarrow$ GOF + ComputeLoss $(x, y)$
7:         **end for**
8:         GOF $\leftarrow$ GOF $\div$ N
9:         UpdateWeights ()
10:     **end while**
11:     **return** GOF
12: **end procedure**

---

The routines, ComputeLoss and UpdateWeights in Algorithm 3.2 constitute the kernel of a training epoch. They are presented in Algorithm 3.3. The recurrence is initiated with the computation of the training loss for a training datum. The resulting gradient is then pushed backward through the model's graph. During a training epoch, ComputeLoss is called for each element in the training set. Once all of the examples in the training set have been processed UpdateWeights is invoked. Thus, the $\Delta W$s accumulate over an epoch and are applied once as the last step. Consequently, it is the net gradient of the epoch that is used for the weight update.

---

4 The outer product, see Appendix A for details.

---

**Algorithm 3.3** Routines Implementing Backpropagation of Error

---

1: **procedure** COMPUTELOSS($x, y$)
2:    $\hat{y} \leftarrow \text{ANN}(x)$              ▷ Forward pass
3:    $loss \leftarrow \frac{1}{2}(y - \hat{y})^2$
4:    $\phi_\ell \leftarrow \nabla loss$
5:    **for** $\ell \in \mathscr{L}$ in reverse **do**         ▷ Backward pass
6:        $\delta_\ell \leftarrow \left(\frac{\partial \sigma_i}{\partial u_i}\right) \otimes \phi_\ell$
7:        $\Delta W_\ell \leftarrow \Delta W_\ell + \delta_\ell \cdot z_{\ell-1}^T$     ▷ Accumulate net gradient
8:        $\phi_{\ell-1} \leftarrow W_\ell^T \cdot \delta_\ell$          ▷ Gradient for next layer
9:    **end for**
10:   **return** $loss$
11: **end procedure**
12: **procedure** UPDATEWEIGHTS
13:   **for** $\ell \in \mathscr{L}$ **do**
14:      $W_\ell \leftarrow W_\ell - \eta \cdot \Delta W_\ell$
15:      $\Delta W_\ell \leftarrow \varnothing$           ▷ zero out the gradient matrix
16:   **end for**
17: **end procedure**

---

The net gradient is used for a number of reasons. Updating the weights can be expensive – there may millions of them. Moreover, updating them in the middle of the epoch will affect all further iterations in the epoch. This can lead to suboptimal and superfluous, even counterproductive, updates if care is not taken. Amortizing the cost of a weight update over multiple loss calculations nets out contradictory directions of travel. Netting out the gradients ensures that the update reflects the information from the entire dataset.

In closing, we observe that Loss (ANN, $x$, $w$) is high-dimensional function. With backpropagation we are exploring the loss function in an effort to minimize it by descending its gradient. During training the parameters of the ANN, the weights, $w_i$, are variable and the training set is constant, that is, they reverse roles. Once the model is trained the weights are constant, they are parameters, and it is the arguments to the ANN that are variable.

### 3.5.4 A Word on the Rectified Linear Unit (ReLU)

The role of the activation function in an ANN is to introduce nonlinearity. If care is not taken in selecting the activation function carefully training can be degraded, and in the worst case, pointless. For shallow networks sigmoid and tanh offer strong nonlinear properties and convenient derivatives. In deeper networks, ReLU is almost exclusively the activation function of choice. The reason is demonstrated here.

The rationale is as follows. Recall that `sigmoid` is a mapping, $[0, 1]$. The derivative will be zero when the neuron is saturated (one of the extrema). For unsaturated neurons, the interesting range of the function, `sigmoid` maps to $(0, 1)$. Its derivative is $\psi = \sigma(1 - \sigma)$, thus its derivative will be even smaller. Consequently, as the error is propagated backward through the network the gradient grows successively fainter through each layer – and in deeper networks simply disappears (the vanishing gradient problem). The desire to implement deep ANNs led to a re-examination of activation functions. Let us examine the derivative for the `sigmoid` activation. Its maximum is

$$\frac{d\psi}{d\sigma} = 1 - 2 \cdot \sigma \implies \sigma = \frac{1}{2}. \tag{3.41}$$

Thus, the maximum for the derivative is $0.25$. `sigmoid` and its derivative are plotted in Figure 3.5. As the error propagates backward through the network, at best, it is scaled by a quarter in each layer:

$$\delta_{\ell,i} = \delta_{\ell+1} \cdot w_i \cdot \frac{\partial \sigma_{\ell,i}}{\partial u_{\ell,i}} \leq \delta_{\ell+1} \cdot w_i \cdot 0.25, \tag{3.42}$$

It can be viewed as attenuating the error at a rate of $0.25^{depth-\ell}$. The example `sine` used so far is, strictly speaking, a Deep Learning model, but in spirit it is not what comes to mind when people think of Deep Learning. The state-of-the-art Deep Learning models today have more than 20 layers. Training such deep networks simply could not be done if `sigmoid` was used throughout.

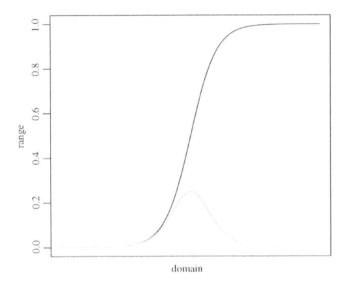

**Figure 3.5** The sigmoid activation function plotted in black. Its derivative is superimposed in gray. The derivative acts to attenuate the error signal between layers.

The ReLU activation has a very different range, $[0, \infty)$. Its derivative is either 0 or 1, a Heaviside function; consequently, the error signal can penetrate further back up the stack of layers. Gradients flow backward unimpeded, or are stopped dead. This is a critical property for training Deep Learning models. The more layers in a model the more an ANN can learn. It does, however, introduce another problem: the "dead neuron." Should a neuron's scaler product consistently produce negative values it can never learn its way out of the hole; the derivative will be zero forever. Care must be taken to ensure the trap is avoided (99). One means is to use a slower learning rate. The slower learning rate gives neurons the chance to avoid death. Note that while the learning rate might be lower it is still a win as ReLU makes it possible to train deeper networks than previously possible. For shallower networks, such as the sine example, the non-linearity of sigmoid is a win.

## 3.6 Stochastic Sine

A vital tool for training ANNs is a pseudo-random number generator. Random numbers are vital for initializing weights and computing expectations. Training ANNs does not have a single, unique, solution. The same data used with the same hyperparameters will result in a different trained model every time. This is the result of the random nature of weight initialization. This can lead to trouble when debugging, so we re-iterate, record the seed for the random number generator to realize some determinism when debugging should it be required.

To emphasize the random nature of training the graph in Figure 3.6 depicts the loss curve for four different training runs of the sine ANN. Each loss curve is different, that is normal. In broad terms they all behave the same way, but the individual weights will be different. The diminishing returns of continuing to train following the initial large reductions in error are evident. Following 10 epochs all the runs exhibit a heavy tail of incremental improvements. The dark black model had the highest loss and the dotted one the smallest. This was just "luck" and the nature of random algorithms; the only difference between the runs was the seed used to initialize the random number generator.

The progress of one solution is evident in Figure 3.7. The figure graphically portrays the evolution a single model over multiple training epochs. An ANN with the topology of $\{3, 2, 1\}$ was trained to learn sine. The model was trained over 125 epochs, and its output was graphed every 25 epochs. The family of curves depicts the history of the model as it learning sine. When initialized the ANN is random, but after 25 epochs, the straight line is obtained; this is the oldest curve in the graph. Over time the curves move toward the solid black sine curve. The darker the hue, the more epochs of training it has received. The model slowly moves closer

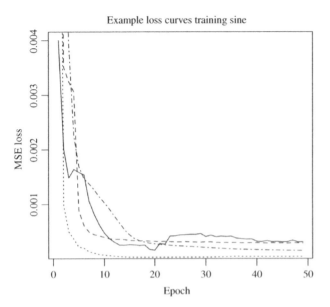

**Figure 3.6** MSE loss for four training runs of a sine ANN. They all show the same distinctive precipitous decline followed by a very heavy tail. The topology was {3, 2, 1}.

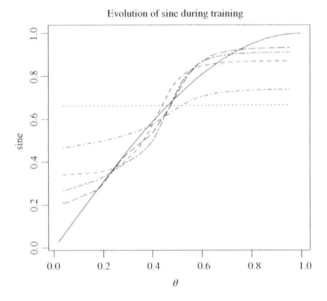

**Figure 3.7** The output of an ANN learning the sine function. The black curve is the ground truth. The remaining curves demonstrate the evolution of the model as it learns. The straight line is the initial random weights. The over time the output of the model approaches the ground truth as the weights improve. Plots are taken every 25 epochs.

to `sine` as the MSE comes down. The differences between the curves of subsequent epochs become less pronounced over time, this is reflected in the heavy tails in the loss graph.

## 3.7  Verification of a Software Implementation

The previous sections have demonstrated how to train ANNs, but we have not discussed the implementation. Implementing the backpropagation algorithm in software libraries can be challenging as there are so many "moving parts." Once the code is written, and a test program runs without crashing, is the implementation correct? Perhaps the test program even converges, the backpropagation implementation may still have one of the more pernicious errors that delays convergence and retards accuracy.

Implementing software libraries correctly and robustly is critical. Developers build their applications on top of libraries. The use of a library is supposed to save the developer work with code reuse. Debugging applications are challenging enough without worrying about components outside of their control. When bugs are encountered, investigation begins by ruling out unlikely sources of the problem. This assumption narrows the field of search. For example, programmers usually rule out compiler bugs, interpreter bugs, and libc errors initially because they are trusted. When implementing a neural network software library, its correctness must be verified to ensure that it can be trusted. The application being built on top of it is difficult enough to get right without basic routines failing. Working with large amounts of data is fraught with perils and tracking down problems is notoriously difficult. In this section, we discuss a useful approach to validate a software implementation of backpropagation to ensure correctness.

ANN models are assembled by combining layers implemented in a software library. So far we have only encountered three types of layers in this text and a single way to connect them (dense). The introduced layers are the preprocessing layer, dense layer, and softmax. It is important to verify that not only do the individual layers work, a process called unit testing, but that when combined in a model they continue to work properly, known as integration testing. Following successful integration testing, confidence in the implementation *may* be warranted.

A powerful technique to verify the correctness of the implementation of a numerical algorithm is cross validation. When implementing numerical algorithms, it is important to verify an implementation with known results of a computation for comparison. The alternate results may be produced by hand or simply computed with a different means on a machine. If the results agree, then that suggests that confidence in an implementation is warranted. In the case of a preprocessing layer, this is fairly straight forward. The statistics computed by a preprocessing layer are easily verified with other software packages such as R or MatLab. The other types of layers in an ANN library are more challenging. We want to verify the correctness of the implementation of backpropagation in the layers. This is not a job for an application developer training a model. Verification needs to be performed by the people writing the software libraries that application developers use. It is also useful when doing research. Verifying an implementation of a new layer is vital to ensure that the experimental results can be trusted.

Verification of an implementation can be performed by computing the expected gradient with differencing equations. Consider the gradient at some weight, $w_i$, in the neural network. Then the backpropagation implementation will compute $\frac{\partial L}{\partial w}$. We wish to confirm that the quantity, $\frac{\partial L}{\partial w}$, is correct. We can verify the result by computing it directly with the definition of a derivative. Both results should agree and confirm the correctness of the backpropagation implementation. The classical definition of a derivative is

$$\frac{dL}{dw} = \lim_{h \to 0} \frac{L(w+h) - L(w)}{h}.$$ (3.43)

Notice that we have used $L$, the loss, and not the ANN, as we need the derivative of the loss with respect to the weight, not the ANN per se. That is how $\frac{\partial L}{\partial w}$ is computed. The derivative is computed by selecting a datum from the training set and computing `ComputeLoss ((x, y))`. The loss is recorded, $w + h$ is then used in a second invocation. The new loss is computed and the approximate derivative calculated. If we obtain "acceptable,"

$$\frac{dL}{dw} \approx \epsilon \frac{\partial L}{\partial w},$$ (3.44)

results for every weight in the layer, then we can have confidence that our backward propagation code works correctly.

In a real computer, implementation such a naïve numerical differentiation is unreliable. This can quickly lead to trouble and require large, and potentially meaningless, choices of $\epsilon$. It must always be borne in mind that the real number line does not exist in a computer. An arithmetically correct algorithm is not necessarily correct when implemented in a computer. The above definition of a derivative must be approximated with the discrete representation in a computer. Employing a truncated Taylor series expansion we can get an idea of the arithmetical and analytical error that we can expect,

$$L(w+h) = L(w) + L'(w) \cdot h + O(h^2),$$ (3.45)

rearranging leads to,

$$\frac{L(w+h) - L(w)}{h} = L'(w) + O(h).$$ (3.46)

We can see that this naïve approach leads to error that is linear in $h$. The error is very high for an application such as verifying the correctness of gradient propagation through an ANN implementation. By using a centered form of approximating the derivative, we can compute the gradient a second way that is far more accurate,

$$\frac{dL}{dw} = \lim_{h \to 0} \frac{L(w+h) - L(w-h)}{2h}. \tag{3.47}$$

It is centered because the computation looks in both directions around $w$ giving us a better idea of local behavior. The improvement can be quantified by expanding the Taylor series by a further term and doing it in both directions,

$$L(w+h) = L(w) + L'(w) \cdot h + \frac{L''(w) \cdot h^2}{2!} + O(h^3), \tag{3.48}$$

and,

$$L(w-h) = L(w) - L'(w) \cdot h + \frac{L''(w) \cdot h^2}{2!} - O(h^3), \tag{3.49}$$

subtracting the two equations and the second-order terms cancel. Solving for the derivative we are interested in produces an expression with second-order error:

$$\implies \frac{L(w+h) - L(w-h)}{2h} = L'(w) + O(h^2) \approx \frac{dL}{dw}, \tag{3.50}$$

and we can see that the error is now quadratic in $h$. The first-order errors cancelled themselves out, taking with them many numerical problems as well. In practice, in a computer implementation, $h$ must be chosen very carefully.

There are now two means of computing the gradient anywhere in a neural network. They will rarely agree exactly so we still need a means of comparing the results. The following is used,

$$\frac{|bprop| - |diff|}{|bprop| + |diff|}, \tag{3.51}$$

where $bprop$ is the value from backpropagation and $diff$ is the result of the centered differencing equation. The closer to zero the better. The comparison can be done at any point in an ANN's graph.

Some important practical details to consider, it is best to only take a couple of training steps before performing the verification. Too late and the gradient will be too faint (the ANN is growing accurate so the error is small). Too early and the results can be erratic. It is also recommended to use double-precision floating point variables for verification. The deeper in the network, the smaller $h$ can be (deeper is closer to the loss function, and the stronger the signal will be). A good starting point for $h$ is $10^{-7}$. The entire process is shown in Algorithm 3.4. It verifies the $\delta$s of a dense layer.

---

**Algorithm 3.4** Verify Gradient

---

1: **procedure** VERIFYLAYER(layer $\ell$, tolerance $\epsilon$, differential $h$, datum $x$)

2:   $G = \texttt{ComputeBPROP}(x)$                             ▷ Compute and store the $\delta$s

3:   **for** *neurons*$(i) \in \ell$ **do**

4:     save $\leftarrow u[i]$

5:     $u[i] \leftarrow u[i] + h$

6:     $z[i] \leftarrow \sigma(u[i])$

7:     $\texttt{Compute}(\ell + 1, z)$                         ▷ only need to compute deeper layers

8:     diff $\leftarrow \texttt{Loss}()$

9:     $u[i] \leftarrow$ save - $h$                            ▷ Now difference in the other direction

10:     $z[i] \leftarrow \sigma(u[i])$

11:     $\texttt{Compute}(\ell + 1, z)$

12:     diff $\leftarrow$ diff - $\texttt{Loss}()$

13:     diff $\leftarrow \frac{diff}{2 \cdot h}$

14:     ratio $\leftarrow \frac{|diff| - |G[i]|}{|diff| + |G[i]|}$

15:     $\texttt{assert}(\text{ratio} \leq \epsilon)$

16:     $u[i] \leftarrow$ save

17:     $z[i] \leftarrow \sigma(\text{save})$

18:     $\texttt{Compute}(\ell + 1, z)$                         ▷ ante-state fully restored

19:   **end for**

20: **end procedure**

---

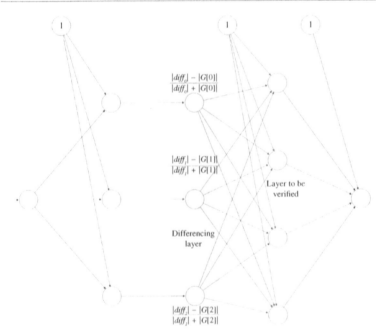

**Figure 3.8** An ANN with a differencing verification layer. The differencing layer is verifying the backpropagation of error of the immediately deeper layer.

**Table 3.2** Verification Results

| BPROP | Differencing | Ratio |
|---|---|---|
| 0.001181 | 0.001181 | 0.000000 |
| 0.000791 | 0.000791 | 0.000000 |
| −0.002559 | −0.002559 | 0.000000 |
| 0.000381 | 0.000381 | 0.000000 |
| −0.000849 | −0.000849 | 0.000000 |
| −0.017801 | −0.017801 | 0.000000 |
| 0.006248 | 0.006248 | 0.000000 |
| −0.002292 | −0.002292 | 0.000000 |
| −0.018861 | −0.018861 | 0.000000 |

Comparison of values computed with backpropagation of error and differencing. The ratio of zero indicates good agreement between both methods suggesting correctness of the BPROP implementation.

When new types of layers are implemented and added to a library, they can be verified with the above algorithm. A model can be created with the new type of layer and with a generic dense layer above it (shallower). If backpropagation is flowing correctly through the new type of layer, then the instrumentation in the dense layer will confirm it (Figure 3.8).

It is important to bear in mind that differencing assumes a continuous function; dense layers are continuous. Many types of ANN layers, such as the max pooling and convolutions found in Chapter 6, have important discontinuities that need to be accounted for when the above method is used. Differencing can still be used but the discontinuities must be accounted for.

The Table 3.2 presents examples of output of the verification Algorithm 3.4 for an ANN implementing sine with two hidden layers of 5 and 4, respectively. It is clear that the library that was used to build the model is correct. A value of $h = 0.0000001$ was used.

## 3.8 Summary

This chapter introduced the rudiments of training ANNs. It was seen that pre-processing the data is critical to success. The basis of learning is employing a quantitative "loss" function to measure progress. The loss function must be differentiable. Backpropagation of error from the loss function is used to update the

ANN's weights. It is the backward phase of training that constitutes "experience" from which a model learns. Verification of implementations is critical to gaining confidence in results and detecting silent problems.

## 3.9 Projects

1. Recall the material on numerical stability in Section 1.4 and apply it to computing the derivative for the `sigmoid` function. The following equality is mathematically correct, $\sigma(1 - \sigma) = \sigma - \sigma^2$. But are they floating point equivalent? Which form of the equation is better suited to a computer? Validate your belief with an argument and computer experiments.
2. Explain why preprocessing was not required for the example in project 1 in Chapter 2.
3. The algorithms in Algorithm 3.3 have been implemented in a Python notebook that can be found here, https://github.com/nom-de-guerre/DDL_book/tree/main/Chap03. Use them to implement Algorithm 3.2. Test it by training the `sine` example.

# 4

# Training Classifiers

This chapter presents how to train classifier artificial neural network (ANNs). The loss functions required are motivated and derived. The inherent and fundamental supporting concepts are also demonstrated. Chapter 3 detailed how to train a regressor ANN. Backpropagation of the loss gradient was used to compute updates for every learnable parameter in an ANN's graph. The loss is a quantitative metric for the incorrectness of an ANN's output. Classifiers differ substantively from regressors in only one particular: the loss function. The loss function is very important as it not only measures progress, but its derivative is the inceptive step of the backpropagation of error. mean squared error (MSE) is not appropriate for classification so we begin by motivating an appropriate loss function for classification.

## 4.1  Backpropagation for Classifiers

Having demonstrated how to train ANN regressors, we now proceed to the more important class of ANNs, classifiers. We can use backpropagation to train classifiers, but the inceptive step is different. The difference lies in the choice of loss function. In this section, we motivate and present an appropriate loss function for classifiers. The loss function is then differentiated to initiate the back-propagation recurrence for classifiers. We begin by motivating our loss function.

Recall that an ANN classifier has the softmax function at the output layer. Softmax accepts the logits from the output layer of the ANN and produces a synthetic "probability" distribution in the form of a vector. The probability distribution is over the possible classes. It is discrete and expresses a degree of belief; the maximum probability is selected as the final prediction for the class of the argument. As with regressors, a classifier needs to learn from a training set of examples. The training set for a classifier takes the form $(x_1, p_1 = $ [one-hot encoded vector]$_1$), $\ldots$ , $(x_N, p_N = $ [one-hot encoded vector]$_N$) , where $x$ is a vector of predictors, and the ground truth is a probability distribution.

*Demystifying Deep Learning: An Introduction to the Mathematics of Neural Networks,*
First Edition. Douglas J. Santry.
© 2024 The Institute of Electrical and Electronics Engineers, Inc. Published 2024 by John Wiley & Sons, Inc.

Let $\mathbb{K}$ be the set of classes, that is, the range of the classifier, and $K = |\mathbb{K}|$ be the number of classes. Softmax produces a vector of probabilities, and the training examples use one-hot encoded vectors, which can also be interpreted as a discrete probability distribution. The two distributions, $p_i$ and $\hat{p}_i$, need to be quantitatively compared to compute a loss. The MSE does not make sense when comparing distributions in the form of probability mass functions; they are not continuous. To train a classifier, we need a loss function that is more appropriate, a measure of similarity between probability distributions.

### 4.1.1 Likelihood

Before the loss function is presented, a brief digression is indicated to introduce the idea that the loss function is based on the notion of *likelihood*. Likelihood is often used colloquially as a synonym for probability, but it is subtly different. It is easiest to grasp the difference with a simple example. Suppose someone claims to have a fair coin, an equal probability for either a head or a tail, and plays a game with you. Over the course of 15 tosses 12 heads and 3 tails are observed. Is the coin fair?

Coin flips are distributed binomially, $P(X = S|\theta) = \binom{N}{S} \theta^S (1 - \theta)^{N-S}$, where $S$ is the number of tails and we have conditioned on the parameter, $\theta$, the probability of a tail. The binomial distribution could be used to compute the probability of $X = 3$ tails, as it is claimed that the coin is fair and it is assumed that $\theta = 0.5$. This results in a probability of the observed outcome of 0.0138855, or 1.4%: but it is the claim that the coin is fair that needs to be addressed. We are really interested in the value of $\theta$ that explains the observations. The task is to fit observed data to a distribution, not make a prediction (we have the data). The object is to find the most likely value of $\theta$ that explains the observed data. The tool for such problems is called a *maximum likelihood estimator* (MLE).

Probability is used to predict data, and likelihood is used to explain data. All of $X, S$, and $N$ are known. $\theta$ is the variable, so we use a likelihood function to find $\theta$. For discrete probabilities, the likelihood function is the probability function with the outcome fixed and the parameters varied. For more details and a thorough introduction see (110).

The likelihood function for the binomial distribution is conditioned on the observed data:

$$\mathcal{L}(\theta|X = 3) = \binom{15}{3} \theta^3 (1 - \theta)^{12}. \tag{4.1}$$

The object is to find $\theta$ that maximizes the likelihood function. Its graph is presented in Figure 4.1. $\theta = 0.5$ seems very unlikely. The maximum likelihood lies in the gray region of the curve. A more plausible value for $\theta$ lies between 0.15 and 0.3, hence

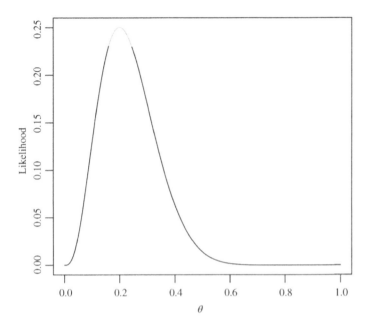

**Figure 4.1** Likelihood for the fairness of a coin following 15 tosses and observing 3 tails. The portion of the curve that is gray is where the likelihood is highest indicating that $\theta$ is like found there, between $[0.1, 0.3]$. This suggests that the coin is likely unfair.

we conclude that the coin is not fair. The notion of likelihood is very powerful, and it can be used to train categorical ANNs.

### 4.1.2  Categorical Loss Functions

A meaningful loss function for a categorical ANN must account for the discrete distribution over the categories. We want to measure the degree of difference between a computed distribution and the ground truth distribution, not continuous values. To that end, we employ an MLE for a local loss function. Treating the softmax layer as the final layer in the model, then the output of the ANN is a vector of probabilities distributed over the classes,

$$\hat{p} = \text{ANN}(x \mid w) = (\hat{p}_1, ..., \hat{p}_K), \tag{4.2}$$

here the ANN is conditioned on the weights. What is the likelihood of the probabilities computed by softmax with the weights? The output of softmax is a vector of random variables, and we are interested in their joint distribution. If we view the elements of the vector produced by softmax as probabilistically independent, then by the chain rule for probability we want to choose weights, $w$, that maximizes:

$$f(\hat{p}|w) = f(\hat{p}_1, ..., \hat{p}_K|w) = f(\hat{p}_1|w) \cdot \ ... \ \cdot f(\hat{p}_K|w), \tag{4.3}$$

where we have conditioned on our parameters, the weights. Given the output of softmax, $\hat{p} = \{\hat{p}_1, ..., \hat{p}_K\}$, we want to maximize the likelihood that $\hat{p}$ represents the ground truth, $p$. The likelihood function, $\mathscr{L}$, for independent conditionals is

$$\mathscr{L}(\hat{p}; w) = \text{argmax}_w \prod_{i}^{K} \hat{p}_i^{p_i}. \tag{4.4}$$

In other words, the loss function for classification is the response of the ANN exponentiated to the ground truth (the expected number of times they should appear), the one-hot encoded vector from the training set. This function is maximized when all the $\hat{p}_i = p_i$. When training categorical ANNs all the $p_i$ will be zero except for one item, the target class.

The problem with this loss function is that it is a product, and underflow is a serious problem. There is also the ironic problem of correct progress, one zero factor, which is desired given one-hot encoding, and there is no information at all. It is more convenient to work with a sum. To that end the natural logarithm is taken, written `log`, of the MLE. The choice of base $e$ is not mathematically required, but it will be prove to be a very convenient choice when differentiating `softmax` below. Taking the negative logarithm of $\mathscr{L}$ yields a more convenient function (the exponents are probabilities). We give it below for an ANN with $K$ possible classes:

$$Loss(p, \hat{p}) = -\sum_{k}^{K} p_k \log(\hat{p}_k), \tag{4.5}$$

where we are iterating over a one-hot encoded vector. This function compares the ground truth with the computed vector. Only one $p_k$ is nonzero (it is 1, the target class), and the rest are zero. Maximizing the original likelihood function is done by minimizing the loss function.

The loss function can also be arrived at with information theory (26). In the context of information theory, the loss is known as $H$, the *cross entropy*. Information theory uses a logarithm with base 2, and this gives units of Shannons, or Shannon bits, after Claude Shannon. Claude Shannon is the father of modern information theory. He published a seminal paper, "A Mathematical Theory of Communication," published in Bell Labs' internal journal, *Bell System Technical Journal*. Shannon developed information entropy as a means of computing the optimal length of messages for distributions (such as the frequency of letters in a language, e.g. English or Arabic). Cross entropy can be interpreted as the loss of information when using a suboptimal encoding.

With the definition of an appropriate local loss function, the global objective function can be defined. Training a classifier ANN attempts to minimize:

$$GOF^t = -\frac{1}{N} \sum_{k=1}^{N} \sum^{K} p_k \log(\hat{p}_k^t), \tag{4.6}$$

where there are $N$ training examples and $K$ categories. Again, as with the MSE, as the cross entropy $\rightarrow 0.0$ the information loss approaches zero and the model is converging. It is rare for the cross entropy to actually reach zero, and it is standard procedure to specify a loss threshold below which training is halted. The threshold specified depends on the application. In practice, the inner sum does not need to be computed as the $p_k$ will all be zero except for the target class, which is 1, so only one term is nonzero. The simplified version is

$$GOF^t = -\frac{1}{N}\sum_{}^{N} \log(\hat{p}^t_{target}). \tag{4.7}$$

The MLE is used to seed the backpropagation of error to train a classifier. The strategy is the same as for a regressor measured with MSE. The weight updates that reduce the loss function need to be computed, so we need the $\frac{\partial L}{\partial w}$ for every weight in the ANN. The output of a classifier is different from a regressor owing to the softmax function. The softmax accepts the raw output of the ANN, logits, and from that point backpropagation is no different from a regressor. The strategy then is to differentiate from the loss function to the logits then perform backpropagation as usual.

## 4.2 Computing the Derivative of the Loss

The recurrence needs to be initiated and so the derivative of the loss function is required. From the loss function, the gradient will pass through the softmax layer to reach the output layer of the ANN. Cross entropy must be differentiated, then softmax and finally the gradient will reach the output layer of the ANN. Once the gradient reaches the logits, the backward pass proceeds as usual. The object of this section is to show how to compute the $\frac{\partial L}{\partial z_i}$ of the logits.

Recall that an ANN classifier has $K$ output nodes. An ANN then has $K$ logits, the length of the $z_{output}$ tuple. For the remainder of the section, subscripts on $z$ are the index into the tuple. The $z_i$ are the inputs to softmax (for example 3 in the iris model). The object is to compute the $K$ values of $\frac{\partial L}{\partial z_i}$. This means that we need to differentiate,

$$Loss(p, \hat{p}) = -\sum_{k=1}^{K} p_k \log(\text{softmax}(z_k)), \tag{4.8}$$

where we have convolved softmax with cross entropy. Let $\hat{P}(z)$ be the softmax function. Then we begin by recalling the definition of softmax. For the class $i$, its softmax probability is

$$\hat{p}_i = \hat{P}(i) = \frac{e^{z_i}}{\sum_{k}^{K} e^{z_k}} \tag{4.9}$$

and,

$$\hat{p} = (\hat{P}(0), ..., P(K-1))^T, \tag{4.10}$$

the vector of all the softmax probabilities.

To compute the $\frac{\partial L}{\partial z_i}$ we start by differentiating the loss with respect to the output of the neuron for each class $i$.

$$\frac{\partial L}{\partial z_i} = \frac{\partial}{\partial z_i} \left( -\sum_k^K p_k \cdot \log(\hat{p}_k) \right)$$

$$= -\sum_k^K p_k \frac{1}{\hat{p}_k} \frac{\partial \hat{P}(k)}{\partial z_i}$$

$$= -p_i \frac{1}{\hat{p}_i} \frac{\partial \hat{P}(i)}{\partial z_i} - \sum_{k \neq i}^K p_k \frac{1}{\hat{p}_k} \frac{\partial \hat{P}(k)}{\partial z_i}, \tag{4.11}$$

where the problem has been split into two cases. The first term is the case where $i$ is the class with which we are differentiating with respect to; we have broken it out of the sum. The second term is the sum containing the remaining $i \neq k$ terms. Our strategy is to deal with the two cases separately and recombine the results. The first case is

$$-p_i \frac{1}{\hat{p}_i} \frac{\partial \hat{P}(i)}{\partial z_i}. \tag{4.12}$$

Let us compute

$$\frac{\partial \hat{P}(i)}{\partial z_i} = \frac{\partial}{\partial z_i} \left( \frac{e^{z_i}}{\sum_j e^{z_j}} \right). \tag{4.13}$$

We employ the product rule to differentiate. Let $A = e^{z_i}$, and $B = \left( \sum_j^K e^{z_j} \right)^{-1}$. Then $AB = \hat{p}_i$. This leads to,

$$\frac{\partial}{\partial z_i}(AB) = A'B + AB'$$

$$= AB + AB'$$

$$= \hat{p}_i - e^{z_i} \cdot B^2 \cdot e^{z_i}$$

$$= \hat{p}_i - \hat{p}_i^2$$

$$= \hat{p}_i(1 - \hat{p}_i)$$

$$= \frac{\partial \hat{P}(i)}{\partial z_i}.$$

Substituting $\frac{\partial \hat{P}(i)}{\partial z_i}$ back into Eq. (4.12) we obtain,

$$\implies -p_i \frac{1}{\hat{p}_i} \frac{\partial \hat{P}(i)}{\partial z_i} = -p_i \frac{1}{\hat{p}_i} \hat{p}_i(1 - \hat{p}_i) = p_i \hat{p}_i - p_i. \tag{4.14}$$

The second term containing the residual classes is the sum,

$$-\sum_{k \neq i}^{K} p_k \frac{1}{\hat{P}_k} \frac{\partial \hat{P}(k)}{\partial z_i}. \tag{4.15}$$

Employing a similar strategy as above, we use the product rule to differentiate $\frac{\partial \hat{P}(k)}{\partial z_i}$.

Let $A = e^{z_k}$, and $B = \left( \sum_{j}^{K} e^{z_j} \right)^{-1}$. Then,

$$\frac{\partial \hat{P}(k)}{\partial z_i} = A'B + AB'$$

$$= AB'$$

$$= -e^{z_k} \cdot B^2 \cdot e^{z_i}$$

$$= -\hat{P}_k \hat{P}_i. \tag{4.16}$$

Substituting back into Eq. (4.15) we find:

$$-\sum_{k \neq i}^{K} p_k \frac{1}{\hat{P}_k} \frac{\partial \hat{P}(k)}{\partial z_i} = \sum_{k \neq i} p_k \frac{1}{\hat{P}_k} \hat{P}_k \hat{P}_i = \sum_{k \neq i} p_k \hat{P}_i. \tag{4.17}$$

Recombining our results obtained for Eqs. (4.12) and (4.15) we reconstitute the original equation:

$$-p_i \frac{1}{\hat{P}_i} \frac{\partial \hat{P}(i)}{\partial z_i} - \sum_{k \neq i}^{K} p_k \frac{1}{\hat{P}_k} \frac{\partial \hat{P}(k)}{\partial z_i} = p_i \hat{P}_i - p_i + \sum_{k \neq i}^{K} p_k \hat{P}_i$$

$$= -p_i + \sum_{k}^{K} p_k \hat{P}_i$$

$$= -p_i + \hat{P}_i \sum_{k}^{K} p_k$$

$$= \hat{P}_i - p_i. \tag{4.18}$$

The full sum was reassembled and we take advantage of the fact that $\sum_{k}^{K} p_k = 1$ to simplify the final expression. Thus, we arrive at,

$$\frac{\partial L}{\partial z_i} = \hat{P}_i - p_i. \tag{4.19}$$

The expression cross-entropy's derivative looks very similar to the derivative of the squared error used for regression, a simple difference between the computed answer and the ground truth. This is the inceptive step of the recurrence for backpropagation when training classifiers. It does not look very different from the squared loss for regression, but note that it is applied to every class, that is, the $K$ outputs of the ANN, e.g. all three species of iris in the example classifier. Moreover, $p_i$ is zero for every class except the target class, in which case it is 1.

### 4.2.1 Initiate Backpropagation

It should be noted that the activation function for the output neurons of a classifier should be the identity, so $\frac{\partial \sigma}{\partial u} = 1$ in the output layer, which means that $\delta_i = \hat{p}_i - p_i$. With the $K$ $\delta$s computed for the output layer, the standard back-propagation algorithm proceeds as described for regressors. The weight updates are computed as the gradient is propagated back through the ANN's graph. The procedure is depicted in Figure 4.2.

Lastly, training can be a long process with each step improving on the earlier one; we do not want to waste earlier work with carelessness. Training should propagate gradients backward, not numerical problems. It is important to catch IEEE numerical errors early. The IEEE values of NaN and $\pm\infty$ can result in many places. The special values of $\pm\infty$ will result in NaN if used in a calculation. One of the easiest ways to introduce NaN is in the evaluation of the loss function. A NaN in the loss will spread and destroy all of an ANN's net weight gradients accumulated

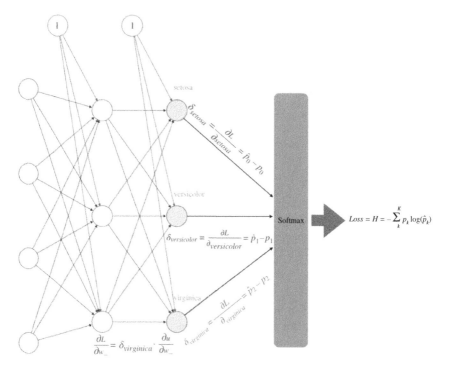

**Figure 4.2** Detail of an iris classifier's terminal layer. The softmax layer runs into the loss function where the back propagation begins. It is differentiated with respect to each class, $k$.

so far in the training epoch, $\Delta W_i = \sum_j^{epoch \, so \, far} \frac{\partial L_j}{\partial w_i}$, and if not caught, the weights themselves during the weight update. If the weights are destroyed, the training has to be restarted. It is important to monitor the values for NaN to detect and contain the problem early. It is too expensive to check after every floating point operation, and usually not necessary. It is best to place the checks strategically in the code. There are two important places that should be considered, and it is strongly advised to implement both. The first is following the computation of a training item's loss. It is advisable to verify that it is valid number as backpropagation flows from this starting point. If the result is invalid, then skip the example for this epoch, or substitute a sensible value. The second safety checkpoint should be in `UpdateWeights`. Verify each of the updates prior to use. If an NaN gets into the weight itself training will have to be restarted, so protect them – they represent all progress thus far. Should an NaN be detected in a weight update skip that particular weight and continue updating the remaining weights. The remaining good updates will hopefully move the solution out of the bad neighborhood on the loss surface. If it is a frequent occurrence, then there is probably a bug in the implementation.

## 4.3 Multilabel Classification

The classifying neural networks presented so far are known as *multiclass* problems. Given a set of categories, $\mathbb{K}$, a datum could only be a member of one of the classes. For example, an iris flower can only be one species. Membership in the categories is mutually exclusive. There are, however, problems where membership of multiple classes is desirable, that is, a datum can be a member of more than one category. The problem is known as *multilabel* classification. To solve this problem, a different technique is required, and we present it here.

Consider the problem of classifying an email by subject matter. Emails frequently touch on many subjects. A forensic examination of a batch of emails might be interested in the following topics, $\mathbb{K} = \{HR, Finance, Budget, Criminal\}$. Forcing an email to be a member of a single category would clearly lose a great deal of information. To that end we permit an email to be a member of multiple classes. The training set for such a classifier could not use one-hot encoding. In this problem, an email can have multiple labels. To account for the difference, the problem is known as multilabel classification.

Multilabel classification refers to the fact that a datum can have more than one label. Multiclass classification is framed very differently. The fundamental difference is the relationship between the outputs. The mutually exclusive class membership of multiclass problems can be represented with one-hot encoding, which can be efficiently represented with a single integer, the index of the "1" in said vector. Softmax produces a distribution over the output vector. Multilabel classification is different as membership in all the classes is *independent*. The question of membership of one class has no bearing on membership in another class. Thus multilabel class membership can be treated separately with respect to each category. Each class can be interpreted, and treated, as a binary classifier.

### 4.3.1 Binary Classification

A multilabel classifier has an output node for each class in $\mathbb{K}$. It differs from a multiclass classifier in that there is no terminal softmax layer. Instead, a normal dense layer is used with the `sigmoid` activation function. The range of the `sigmoid` function is $[0, 1]$, so the `sigmoid`'s output can be interpreted as a probability. Again, let $K = |\mathbb{K}|$, then a multilabel classifier has $K$ terminal nodes and produces $K$ independent probabilities (Figure 4.3).

There remains the question of interpreting what a multilabel ANN is predicting. Softmax produces a probability distribution and so the maximum probability is the prediction of the CNN. Multilabel CNNs produce $K$ probabilities, but which of the $K$ is the ANN suggesting? The prediction is performed by specifying a threshold probability, typically 0.5, above which a probability is construed as being a prediction for the class. The probabilities can be mapped to a vector of class membership using the threshold. This produces a vector with multiple 1's and 0's indicating the CNN's prediction. The final output could also be a boolean vector of logical values, `True` or `False`.

### 4.3.2 Training A Multilabel Classifier ANN

Training a multilabel classifier is relatively straight forward. The first step is to select a loss function. As it is a classification, problem the cross entropy loss function is appropriate. The cross entropy function is

$$H = -\sum_{k}^{K} p_k \cdot \log(\hat{p}_k).$$

(4.20)

The special case of binary classification is simpler. A datum is either in the class or it is not. This is captured in the following formulation for a class, $k$:

$$loss_k = -[p_k \cdot \log(\hat{p}_k) + (1 - p_k) \cdot \log(1 - \hat{p}_k)].$$

(4.21)

This leads to the local loss function,

$$loss = \frac{1}{K} \sum_{k}^{K} loss_k.$$

(4.22)

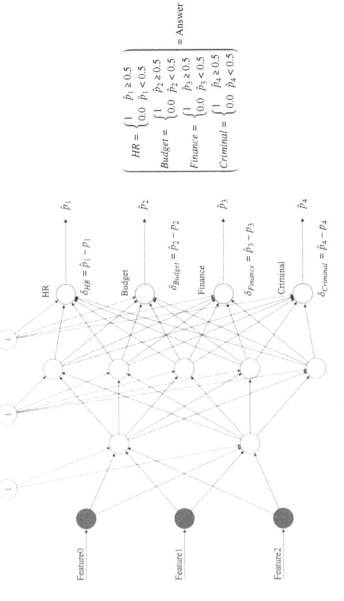

$$HR = \begin{cases} 1 & \hat{p}_1 \geq 0.5 \\ 0.0 & \hat{p}_1 < 0.5 \end{cases}$$

$$Budget = \begin{cases} 1 & \hat{p}_2 \geq 0.5 \\ 0.0 & \hat{p}_2 < 0.5 \end{cases}$$

$$Finance = \begin{cases} 1 & \hat{p}_3 \geq 0.5 \\ 0.0 & \hat{p}_3 < 0.5 \end{cases} = Answer$$

$$Criminal = \begin{cases} 1 & \hat{p}_4 \geq 0.5 \\ 0.0 & \hat{p}_4 < 0.5 \end{cases}$$

HR

$\delta_{HR} = \hat{p}_1 - p_1$

$\hat{p}_1$

Budget

$\delta_{Budget} = \hat{p}_2 - p_2$

$\hat{p}_2$

Finance

$\delta_{Finance} = \hat{p}_3 - p_3$

$\hat{p}_3$

Criminal

$\delta_{Criminal} = \hat{p}_4 - p_4$

$\hat{p}_4$

Feature0

Feature1

Feature2

**Figure 4.3** An example of a multilabel classifier. The outputs corresponding to the 4 classes are independent. The final output is a vector with 4 entries mapped to category membership based on a probability threshold. The per class $\delta$s are indicated.

The global objective function to minimize is

$$GOF = \frac{1}{N} \sum^{N} \frac{1}{K} \sum_{k}^{K} loss_k, \tag{4.23}$$

where there are $N$ examples in the training set.

A multilabel CNN can be trained with backpropagation. To initiate the inceptive step, the loss function must be differentiated. It is much simpler to derive as there is no `softmax` function, just `sigmoid`. As the classes are all treated independently, the work is greatly simplified. The special case of binary cross entropy is the beginning of the backwards pass:

$$\frac{\partial L}{\partial \hat{p}_k} = \frac{\partial}{\partial \hat{p}_k} \left( -(p_k \cdot \log(\hat{p}_k) + (1 - p_k) \cdot \log(1 - \hat{p}_k)) \right), \tag{4.24}$$

this leads to,

$$\frac{\partial L}{\partial \hat{p}_k} = \frac{-p_k}{\hat{p}_k} + \frac{-(1 - p_k)}{1 - \hat{p}_k} \cdot -1$$

$$= \frac{-p_k \cdot (1 - \hat{p}_k) + \hat{p}_k \cdot (1 - p_k)}{\hat{p}_k \cdot (1 - \hat{p}_k)}$$

$$= \frac{\hat{p}_k - p_k}{\hat{p}_k \cdot (1 - \hat{p}_k)}. \tag{4.25}$$

This was a relatively simple derivative to compute, but numerically it is fraught with danger. Luckily, it does not need to be evaluated[1] . The computed probability is $\hat{p}_k = \sigma(u_k)$. As the activation function is known, it is the `sigmoid` function, and recalling that the derivative of the `sigmoid` function function is $\hat{p}_k \cdot (1 - \hat{p}_k)$, the expression can be simplified. It is best to work with the per class $\delta$. It can be easily computed,

$$\delta_k = \frac{\partial L}{\partial \hat{p}_k} \cdot \frac{\partial \hat{p}_k}{\partial u} = \frac{\hat{p}_k - p_k}{\hat{p}_k \cdot (1 - \hat{p}_k)} \cdot \hat{p}_k \cdot (1 - \hat{p}_k) = \hat{p}_k - p_k. \tag{4.26}$$

With $\delta_k$ computed the backpropagation of error takes places as usual. The terminal layer computes the deltas using this numerically stable method, updates its weights, and propagates the error back through the network.

## 4.4 Summary

Backpropagation of error is used for training classifiers, but a different loss function is employed. Multiclass classification is prediction of membership in a

---

1 Never forget that computing is different from doing mathematics. This is a classic example of anticipating the computational pitfalls and obviating them.

mutually exclusive set of categories. One-hot encoded vectors are used to represent the set. The loss function is cross entropy across the distribution produced by softmax. Multilabel classification provides for membership of a datum in multiple categories. Each category is treated independently. Instead of softmax, the `sigmoid` activation is used. The loss is special case of cross entropy, per category binary cross entropy.

## 4.5  Projects

1. The webpage, https://github.com/nom-de-guerre/DDL  book/tree/main/ Chap04, contains a Python notebook implementing an Iris classifier. It is missing the `softmax` layer. Write a routine that accepts the logits from the classifier and produces the network's prediction and its probability.
2. Topology plays an important role in the performance of a model. Using the Iris classifier plot, the loss of the network is ($M_{input}$, $M_{hidden}$, loss).
3. Project the predictors and inference to ($x, y, z$, color) space, where color is the species predicted. This means that 1 predictor out of the 4 will have to be dropped. Does the choice of projector make a difference to the decision boundary?

# 5

# Weight Update Strategies

In Chapters 3 and 4 it was seen that the training of artificial neural networks is the act of fitting weights to models with respect to a training set. While the updates to weights was related to how the loss function is changing, how to precisely quantify the update was not discussed. In this chapter, we examine the process of updating weights more closely and present some strategies for selecting the updates efficiently. The treatment consists of two prongs. The training step itself is examined followed by a closer look at the individual weight updates themselves.

An important consideration for training is the batch size used for a training epoch. The training process, as described, is a sequence of discrete steps called epochs. During each epoch, `ComputeLoss` is called for every element in the training set. `ComputeLoss` performs backpropagation, and the per weight net gradients are accumulated. The weights are only updated after the net gradients are computed. The net gradient reflects all of the information in the training set. A training step that makes use of the entire training set is called a batch step. Batch steps are not always desirable. There are alternative methods, one of which is *stochastic gradient descent*. It forms the topic of Section 5.1.

## 5.1   Stochastic Gradient Descent

There are occasions when training sets are so large that batch training is undesirable or even infeasible. Stochastic gradient descent (SGD) is an alternative means of training artificial neural networks (ANNs) (93). SGD is the basis of almost, if not all, deep learning (DL) training. SGD is not a method confined to use with training ANNs, nor did it originate with ANNs or even with machine learning. It is a general technique used in optimization problems framed as fitting the parameters of a function with respect to data. Its modern origins lie in the 1950s and was known as the Robbins–Monroe method, but arguably reached maturity in the

*Demystifying Deep Learning: An Introduction to the Mathematics of Neural Networks,*
First Edition. Douglas J. Santry.
© 2024 The Institute of Electrical and Electronics Engineers, Inc. Published 2024 by John Wiley & Sons, Inc.

1960s as statisticians began to examine the use of the latest technological marvels, digital computers in the form of mainframes, to deal with experimental data and regression. By then the technique had evolved into stochastic estimation, introduced by Kiefer and Wolfowitz (83). The interested reader is encouraged to read the latter as it is both concise and approachable.

SGD attempts to *approximate* the net gradient by sampling a subset of the gradients, that is, by only using a subset of the training set between weight updates. In "pure" SGD, the weights are updated after each evaluation of ComputeLoss, see Algorithm 5.1. In practice training, ANNs with pure SGD is rarely used. All of the arguments for batch processing adduced above suggest that updating the weights following a single sample is a bad idea. An alternative refinement to SGD is used, called "minibatch," and described in Algorithm 5.2. Instead of updating the weights after every call to ComputeLoss, a random subset of data is sampled from the training set, called a minibatch, and the minibatch is used for the training epoch.

---

**Algorithm 5.1** Pure Stochastic Gradient Descent

1: **procedure** SGD PURE
2:     GOF $\leftarrow +\infty$
3:     **while** GOF $> \epsilon_{threshold}$ **do**
4:         randomly select $x, y \in$ *Training Set*
5:         GOF $\leftarrow$ ComputeLoss$(x, y)$
6:         UpdateWeights ()
7:     **end while**
8: **end procedure**

---

The insight behind mini-batch SGD is that if the describes the problem domain (the ground truth), then a randomly selected subset of the will approximate the gradient well. By repeatedly sampling the training set randomly, then, on average, the correct gradient is computed and the ANN will converge to a good solution. Moreover, many training examples are redundant or superfluous. If data points are sufficiently close together in the input space, then there is no need to use all of them at once. Because the full training set is not used with every epoch, less work is done. Epochs are shorter and solutions are found sooner. The size of the minibatch, by which we mean the percentage of the training set used in a minibatch, varies greatly between applications and datasets.

Figure 5.1 presents the results of training 4 models to recognize the MNIST dataset of hand-written digits. MNIST consists of 60,000 28 × 28 black and white images of hand-written digits and 10,000 further examples for testing. It is a plot of epoch number versus loss demonstrating the progress of training over time. All

---

**Algorithm 5.2** Mini-Batch Stochastic Gradient Descent

---

1: **procedure** SGD
2:    working ← True
3:    streak ← 0
4:    **while** working **do**
5:       GOF ← 0.0
6:       randomly select $X_t \subset$ *Training Set*
7:       **for** $x, y \in X_t$ **do**
8:          GOF ← GOF + ComputeLoss $(x, y)$
9:       **end for**
10:      UpdateWeights ()
11:      GOF ← GOF $\div N_{miniBatch}$
12:      **if** GOF $\leq \epsilon_{threshold}$ **then**
13:         streak ← streak + 1
14:         **if** streak $== n$ **then**
15:            working ← False
16:         **end if**
17:      **else**
18:         streak ← 0
19:      **end if**
20:   **end while**
21: **end procedure**

---

four curves are relatively well clustered signifying that all four models are converging at roughly the same rate; but they are not doing the same amount of work! The run using a minibatch size of 10% is doing roughly 1/10th of the work of a full batch, but it is converging at a similar rate. This claim is borne out by Table 5.1. As the size of the mini-batch decreases, the time taken to train exhibits corresponding decreases as well. The accuracy of the final model (all values represent 100 epochs) does not seem to suffer. It must be emphasized that 10% is not being proposed as a universal mini-batch size. The size will vary widely between problem domains and datasets. But it does demonstrate the advantages of mini-batch training with SGD.

Ideally, the subsets are sampled from the full training set by randomly permuting the order of the training set. During batch training, the training set is iterated over in the same order every time; the order does not matter when the entire training set is used. The best implementation of SGD is to randomly permute the order of the training set. Every time the model has finished iterating over the complete training set, the order is permuted again (so no minibatch is the same). Let $n$ be the number of mini-batches required to consume the entire dataset once (the inverse

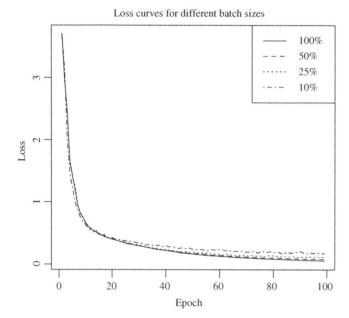

**Figure 5.1** Four training runs using SGD to train a classifier to recognize the MNIST hand-written digits dataset. Each run had a different % of the dataset for a minibatch. All models were trained over 100 epochs.

**Table 5.1** Table of Times and Accuracy for a Sample of %size Minibatchs When Training to Learn MNIST

| % of Training Set | Time (s) | Accuracy (%) |
| --- | --- | --- |
| 100% | 1887.93 | 94.39 |
| 50% | 1059.6 | 96.47 |
| 25% | 618.17 | 96.11 |
| 10% | 286.61 | 94.77 |

of the minibatch). Every $n$ SGD epochs a new permutation of the training data order is computed ensuring entirely different minibatches the next time through. Also, no training example is seen a second time prior to all the other examples being seen at least once. This ensures that all data examples receive equal weight.

Implementing SGD in a permuted serial fashion has some important qualities. With this method, we are still using every element of the training set an equal number of times, that is, each element of the training set is contributing equally to the final model, all the elements of the training set are weighted equally. By changing the order of every $n$ epochs, we are also varying the make up of the minibatches ensuring many combinations of data examples are producing the approximated gradients. Some training libraries implement SGD with sampling with replacement, but this is discouraged as the resulting distribution of samples is very different (and, arguably, incorrect). SGD should not be an implementation of bootstrapping or bagging (36). Sampling without replacement produces better quality updates. SGD minibatch can be implemented efficiently with the "shuffle" algorithm (86).

Detecting convergence when training with SGD can be challenging. Batch training usually exhibits a monotonically decreasing loss function. In contrast, SGD losses can jump around and exhibit jittery behavior. This is owing to the way losses are computed in SGD: they depend on a subset of the data, which is usually much smaller. Sometimes a mini-batch will contain elements that the ANN has learnt yielding a small loss, then the next minibatch might contain all the pathological outliers in the training set producing enormous loss. There are many techniques to cope with the problem. One approach is based on $n$. If the loss is below the threshold for $n$ epochs in a row, then training has probably converged. An even simpler variant is to maintain a sum of the losses. At the point of permuting the training set, the sum is converted to a mean (divided by $n$) and if acceptable training is halted. While simple it does have a drawback. Waiting for the next permutation to test for convergence may postpone acceptance of the solution while doing superfluous work.

Below we contrast and compare the 3 variants of epochs presented thus far:

1. Full batch training was described in Algorithm 3.2. The entire dataset is used in every epoch. The weights are only updated once the comprehensive net gradient representing the entire dataset has been computed. This can be prohibitively slow for large datasets.
2. Pure SGD, described in Algorithm 5.1. The weights are updated after each loss computation. This is expensive and also leads to jerky objective function evaluations; GOF will be very jittery. The pure form of SGD is expensive because updating weights can also take a great deal of time for large ANNs. It is more likely to make "mistakes" as the error gradients are not averaged out before updating the weights resulting in many superfluous weight updates.
3. Minibatch SGD, described in Algorithm 5.2. In each training epoch, a random subset from the training set is selected. The gradient is approximated over multiple examples from the training set, the subset. The idea is that all the approximated gradients will average out over multiple samples. The cost of updating the weights is amortized over more loss calculations than pure SGD. The objective function is far smoother than pure SGD.

SGD is an important means of training ANNs. For the large state-of-the-art problems in DL, it is almost always used. Problem domains where the datasets are smaller, such as medical clinical studies where the number of patients might only be a few hundred, SGD is not as important.

## 5.2   Weight Updates as Iteration and Convex Optimization

The object of training is to find good weights for DL models. Backpropagation of errors permits us to find the errors of weights with respect to the loss function and improve them. It was shown that a weight should be updated proportionally to its derivative, $\frac{\partial L}{\partial w}$. The precise size of the update was, however, glossed over. The update was scaled by a static learning parameter, $\eta$. This is extremely naïve. In reality, what the derivative is really telling us is the direction the function is changing, instantaneously, at that point. The *size* of the update needs to be dynamic to adapt to the changing conditions of the error function.

Using backpropagation of error, we can find the per weight derivatives, but the optimal step size for the weight update is unknown. We want to choose an update to the weight that will reduce the error in the loss metric. Unfortunately, as we shall see, determining the optimal step size is often not tractable. Generally something that is simply "good enough" is used instead. The weight update problem is

$$\Delta w \propto -\eta \cdot \frac{\partial L}{\partial w},\tag{5.1}$$

but what should $\eta$ be?

Consider the two scenarios depicted in Figure 5.2. Starting from point A, the slope is very steep. In this instance, it is desirable to take a small step to ensure that minimum is not missed. The problem when at point B is quite the opposite. The slope is very shallow, and large steps are desirable to get through plains of stasis. Ideally, $\eta$ would be adapted to both situations. $\eta$ should not be static. The scale of the update needs to be adapted dynamically to suit the current conditions.

During training, the weight updates are plotting a course on the surface of the objective function. The training set contains the parameters, they are static, and it is the weights that are variable. The objective function is wandering through weight space seeking a minimum. Let $M_G = \sum_\ell M_\ell$, the number of weights in the entire model. Then it is clear that the objective function, $Loss : \mathbb{R}^{M_G} \to \mathbb{R}$, has an extremely high dimensional domain. The true global minimum is rarely found, and there is no way of verifying it even if by luck it was found; indeed, there is no way of even knowing it. Training continues until an acceptable solution is reached. The search is further complicated as weight updates interfere with each other. At

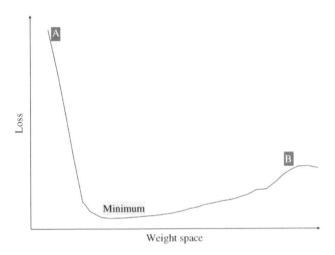

**Figure 5.2** A loss surface for a hypothetical ANN. A static choice for $\eta$ is problematic and would depend on the starting position. The precise shape is not known a priori and so a dynamic choice is required.

epoch, $t$, we might have a good update for some weight, $w_i$, but updating weight $w_j$ may interfere with it; the loss is a function of both of them. Most methods update each weight independently, failing to take account of negative, or positive, side effects on other weights.

Training is an iterative process. An epoch computes the current loss, updates the weights and repeats. The iteration has the form,

$$w_i^{t+1} = w_i^t + \Delta w_i^{t+1}, \tag{5.2}$$

for weight $w_i$. With increasing epoch, the objective function will be reduced and the ANN's weights should converge to a tolerable solution. Iteration is an important means of finding the solutions to equations. The remainder of the chapter is dedicated to presenting a selection of iteration strategies for weight updates. There is no one best approach. Like any complex problem, there are trade-offs to be considered. Often the problem domain must be considered, some update strategies work best with different problems.

### 5.2.1 Newton's Method for Optimization

This section presents Newton's method for optimization. Newton invented an iterative method for convex optimization in the seventeenth century. As we shall see, while it is not practicable for most ANN training scenarios, it does provide insight in to the problem of weight updates that will be useful for more widely implemented algorithms.

Newton was interested in finding the extrema of functions. He used his recently invented Calculus to do so in the setting of convex optimization. Training neural networks is often assumed to be a convex optimization problem (18) so his insights are relevant. Training ANNs is generally concerned with finding minima, as the objective is to minimize the loss function.

Consider a scaler function, $f(w)$. Let us iteratively find a minimum for $f$. Then the object is to find $w$ such that $f'(w) = 0$, a stationary point of $f$. Suppose that, for whatever reason, we cannot solve the equation analytically (exactly). Then we need to use a numerical method to approximate a solution. Training a neural network is the same problem. The training set is constant. The parameters of the ANN, the weights, are what we are solving for. So we want to optimize the objective function by finding appropriate weights.

Newton's method for optimization approximates a solution by starting with an initial guess, then iteratively improving it. To proceed, start with an initial guess for the solution, $w^0$, then compute a new value, $w^1 = w^0 + \Delta w^1$. $\Delta w$ is chosen to improve the guess, that is, $f(w^0 + \Delta w^1)$ should move the solution closer to an extremum.

More generally, at each step, we have $w^{t+1} = w^t + \Delta w^{t+1}$. In the case of ANNs, we want $f$, the objective function, to decrease so movement should be in the direction of decreasing $f$, this suggests that the direction should be $-f'$. So we choose $\Delta w = -\eta \cdot f'(w^t)$. We still need to choose a value for $\eta$, that is, determine how large a step we should take in that direction. Too large a step and we may miss the minimum. Too small a step and we may have to perform many superfluous updates. The step size certainly should not be constant.

Newton invented what is now known as a Newton step to determine the step size. He used the curvature of $f$. Let us approximate $f$ with a second-order Taylor series around our current guess, $w$:

$$f(w + \Delta w) \approx f(w) + f'(w)\Delta w + \frac{f''(w)\Delta w^2}{2!} + \mathcal{O}(\Delta w^3). \qquad (5.3)$$

There remains the choice of $\Delta w$. Newton used his calculus to find $\Delta w$. Differentiating the series with respect to $\Delta w$ and ignoring error terms yield:

$$\frac{df}{d\Delta w} = f'(w) + f''(w)\Delta w. \qquad (5.4)$$

Setting the derivative equal to zero and solving for $\Delta w$ we obtain,

$$\Delta w = -\frac{f'(w)}{f''(w)}, \qquad (5.5)$$

and so as expected our update is proportional to the first derivative, but it is now scaled by the local curvature, the second derivative. The full update is then,

$$w_i^{t+1} = w_i^t - \frac{f'(w_i^t)}{f''(w_i^t)}. \qquad (5.6)$$

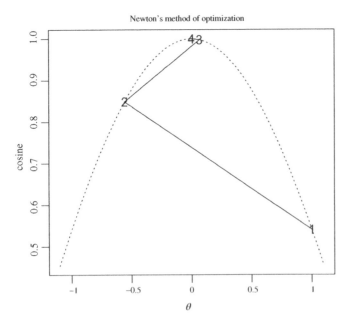

Newton's method of optimization

**Figure 5.3** An example run of Newton's Method for optimization for the cosine function. There are 4 steps until it finds a maximum. Each step is numbered.

This is a very elegant and simple result. An example of Newton's method with a scaler function is depicted in Figure 5.3. The trouble lies in the fact that ANNs are not scaler functions. ANN's can have thousands, and even millions, of parameters to solve for. Applying Newton's method for optimization to ANNs requires the use of matrices.

Extending Newton's method to matrices, we have $g = \nabla Loss(x; w)$, where $g$ is the gradient, $\nabla Loss$, but approximated numerically with backpropagation, and $H = \nabla^2 Loss(x; w)$, where $H$ is the Hessian (not the cross-entropy), the matrix of the second derivatives. Then, $\Delta w = H^{-1}g$, is the vector of updates for the weights. This is an example of a second-order method for training ANNs.

There are two problems with the equation, $\Delta w = H^{-1}g$. The first is constructing the Hessian. Computing the derivatives of the ANN for the Hessian is computationally prohibitive, especially for state-of-the art problems where there can be millions of parameters. The second problem is solving the Hessian. Even supposing that the Hessian could be computed practically, solving such a large matrix is extremely expensive. The Hessian of an ANN is dense, that is, so many elements are nonzero that it cannot be considered sparse. The state of the art for solving matrices of that size, Krylov subspace methods, is targeted at sparse matrices (132). The number of ANN parameters (weights) continues to grow as research progresses and the infeasibility of second-order methods becomes more daunting. Language models have a very large number of parameters. OpenAI's GPT-4 model has 176 billion learnable parameters (108), and NVIDIA's Megatron contains around 500 billion parameters (138). The world is waiting for the first model with 1 trillion learnable parameters. Training such systems is clearly not practical with second-order methods.

Second-order method for training ANNs is an active area of research (4; 101), but the results are rarely used in production systems. Newton's method and the variant, Gauss-Newton, are often the basis of research (156). There are also other formulations such as the Fisher information and natural gradients as contents of the matrices (102). But for the most part, they are impracticable and remain areas of pure research. The most approachable papers have been cited and the interested reader is encouraged peruse them. The salient point is that choosing the size of an update that is optimal is difficult, and the adoption of heuristics is required to improve first-order choices for $\eta$.

In summary, backpropagation is a means of approximating the instantaneous error for a particular parameter, $\frac{\partial L}{\partial w_i}$, but it only determines the *direction* to move. The direction is the only truly safe conclusion to draw. The efficient selection of the step size remains a significant challenge in training ANNs. To fit ANNs first-order heuristic methods of selecting step size are usually used. There are *many* algorithms, but no one single method is best in every scenario. A selection of important examples of weight update strategies is presented below. They address different niches in the ANN problem domain. The choice of which one to use is very much application specific.

Weight update strategies are also known as optimizers. This is because they attempt to minimize the loss function by searching the surface of the loss function with gradients. The context of the chapter is training ANNs, but optimizers have many applications outside of DL and indeed, the development of many of them pre-date DL or machine learning.

## 5.3   RPROP+

The RPROP+ algorithm addresses itself to the problem of choosing a step size for a weight update (73). Like most modern learning rules, it relies on backpropagation to push the gradient through the graph and provide the $\frac{\partial L}{\partial w}$s. RPROP+ computes the step size.

The RPROP+ acronym stands for **Resilient PROP**agation. The original RPROP algorithm was introduced in 1993 (124). The + signifies an amended version of the algorithm that also includes a means of back tracking, a later improvement on the original work. RPROP+ fully embraces the limitation of the first derivative.

The sign of the derivative is the only information that it needs. The intuition of RPROP+ is to continually increase the step size, that is, accelerate, until the sign of the derivative changes, in other words, it accelerates over the surface of weight space until it passes a minimum. The solution will then bounce back and forth over the minimum until it falls in.

The memory requirements are linear in the number of weights. It requires two variables for each weight and thus consumes $2 \cdot M_G$ of memory. For each weight, $w_i$, RPROP+ keeps an update increment, $\eta_i^t$, and its last error, $\frac{\partial L^{t-1}}{\partial w_i}$. The RPROP+ algorithm consists of three cases, and they are implemented in Algorithm 5.3.

---

**Algorithm 5.3** RPROP+ Update Strategy

---

1: **procedure** RPROP
2:      **if** $\frac{\partial L}{\partial w}^t \cdot \frac{\partial L}{\partial w}^{t-1} > 0$ **then**
3:          $\Delta^t \leftarrow \mathbf{min}(\Delta^{t-1} \cdot \eta^+, \Delta_{\max})$
4:          $\Delta w^t \leftarrow -\mathbf{sign}\left(\frac{\partial L^t}{\partial w}\right) \cdot \Delta^t$
5:          $w^t \leftarrow w^{t-1} + \Delta w^t$
6:      **else if** $\frac{\partial L}{\partial w}^t \cdot \frac{\partial L}{\partial w}^{t-1} < 0$ **then**
7:          $\Delta^t \leftarrow \mathbf{max}(\Delta^{t-1} \cdot \eta^-, \Delta_0)$
8:          $w^t \leftarrow w^{t-1} - \Delta w^t$
9:          $\frac{\partial L}{\partial w}^t \leftarrow 0$
10:      **else**
11:          $\Delta w^t \leftarrow -\mathbf{sign}\left(\frac{\partial L^t}{\partial w}\right) \cdot \Delta^t$
12:          $w^t \leftarrow w^{t-1} + \Delta w^t$
13:      **end if**
14: **end procedure**

---

RPROP+ has 5 hyperparameters. The authors suggest the following values for the parameters. They are

1. $\Delta_0 = 10^{-2}$ : the initial weight update size
2. $\Delta_{\min} = 10^{-8}$ : the minimum weight update size
3. $\Delta_{\max} = 50$ : the maximum weight update size
4. $\eta^+ = 1.2$ : rate of acceleration
5. $\eta^- = 0.5$ : rate of deceleration

The authors suggest that RPROP+ is not very sensitive to these choices. The algorithm is very robust with respect to the choice of hyperparameters. The default values suggested in the paper are usually used in implementations.

The RPROP+ algorithm is attractive because it is intuitive and thus easy to understand, and it is also extremely fast for some problems. RPROP+ continually accelerates forward on the surface of the objective function until it passes a stationary point. Then the second and third cases take over as the updates bounce back and forth over the minimum sinking down into it. An example RPROP+ course presented in Figure 5.4.

While RPROP+ is extremely fast, it does have some serious theoretical limitations. RPROP+ is a batch-oriented algorithm. Recall that batch training provides for running through the entire training set computing the total net gradient. The most challenging problems employ SGD, a minibatch scheme. Minibatch methods rely on averaging approximate gradients over multiple training epochs,

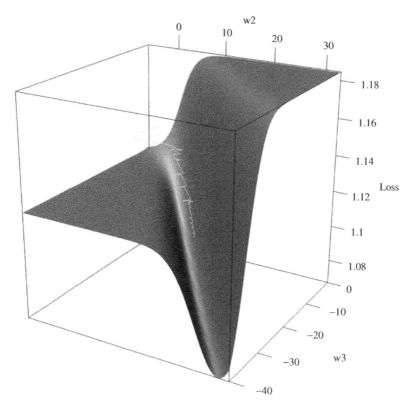

**Figure 5.4** An example path for RPROP+ during the training of a `sine` ANN. It plots the loss as a function in weight space with respect to two of the weights in the same layer. Notice the flat plains and the steep canyons of the loss function. It is crucial to produce updates in response to changing topology.

and the errors can vary widely between epochs. RPROP+ can behave poorly in these circumstances as from line 3 it is clear that following $q$ uninterrupted steps forward, the step size will be $\Delta^{t+q} = \Delta^t \cdot (\eta^+)^q$. Following $r$ moves in the opposite direction slows RPROP+ down by $(\eta^-)^r$, but even when $q = r$ we have $(\eta^+)^q \cdot (\eta^-)^q \neq 1.0$. Put another way, $\Delta^{t+q+r} \neq \Delta^t$. The updates have not cancelled out (with the default parameters it is a net deceleration). This can lead to serious convergence problems with SGD variants. The only way to make the updates average out is to use $\eta^- = 1/\eta^+$, which results in deceleration that is simply too fast.

Despite these limitations, RPROP+ has been reexamined in recent years in a number of contexts (74) and it is widely used in many applications. In practice, it can dramatically out perform the de rigueur weight update schemes when used in conjunction with SGD, but the theoretical problems should be borne in mind. If inexplicable convergence problems are observed, it is a good idea to switch to one of the schemes presented below.

## 5.4 Momentum Methods

Prior to the development of RPROP+, an important family of update strategies was developed based on the the idea of momentum. Momentum was first described in 1964 in a Soviet journal by B. Polyak in the context of first-order iterative solutions (114). Like many standard machine learning algorithms, its roots are not purely machine learning. Momentum was adopted much later as a machine learning technique.

The object of momentum is to smooth the gradient, often with a convex equation, to produce more consistent updates. The convex expression for a momentum strategy is

$$\bar{g}^t = \rho \cdot \bar{g}^{t-1} + (1 - \rho) \cdot g^t, \tag{5.7}$$

where $g^t = \frac{\partial L^t}{\partial w}$ and $\rho$ is a decay factor. $\bar{g}$ is the value used in the weight update. The point of momentum is to introduce the memory of past observations to inform the current update. It is this crude "memory" that approximates the curvature by accounting for how quickly $\frac{\partial L^t}{\partial w}$ is changing. The accumulated history can detect flat plains and steep precipices. The most popular optimizer for updating weights, ADAM, is a member of the momentum family, and we will trace its development by first presenting some of its important precursors to understand how it works.

### 5.4.1 AdaGrad and RMSProp

In 2011, Duchi et al. described a form of momentum adapted to training ANNs that was very simple, but had some very desirable properties (35). They called it AdaGrad, which stands for **Ada**ptive **Grad**ient. The fundamental problem for an update strategy is to adaptively choose a step size dynamically that accounts for the local curvature. RPROP+ throws caution to the wind and adopts the mantra: always accelerate. A more refined approach is to employ a heuristic to capture the local curvature. When the curvature is high, the gradient is steep, and small steps are indicated, otherwise large steps are required. The gradient is computed as usual, but AdaGrad scales the weight update as shown in Algorithm 5.4.

---

**Algorithm 5.4** AdaGrad Weight Update Strategy

1: **procedure** ADAGRAD

2: $\quad \Delta^t \leftarrow \frac{\partial L^t}{\partial w}$

3: $\quad \Delta_{sq}^t \leftarrow \Delta_{sq}^{t-1} + \Delta^t \cdot \Delta^t$

4: $\quad \Delta_w \leftarrow \eta \cdot \frac{\Delta^t}{\sqrt{\Delta_{sq}^t} + \epsilon}$

5: $\quad w^t \leftarrow w^{t-1} - \Delta_w$

6: **end procedure**

---

Every weight requires a variable, the running sum of the square of the gradients. The final update, $\Delta_w$, is the scaled gradient. When the gradient is large dividing by its square attenuates the step size. Small gradients are amplified by the square. $\eta$ is a hyper-parameter, a learning rate, and $\epsilon$ is a small number to avoid division by zero. AdaGrad does well early in training, but $\Delta_{sq}$ grows monotonically and can quickly lead to low rates of convergence. If good weights are not trained prior to the inevitable immobility, then training has to be restarted; ideally, the $\Delta_{sq}$ can just be reset. The momentum variable, $\Delta_{sq}$, needs a decaying factor. This problem was addressed by RMSProp.

RMSProp appeared soon after AdaGrad in 2012 (150). It recognized the need for a decay factor to ensure progress throughout training. This was effected by introducing another hyper-parameter, $\rho$, that decays the history over time. $\rho$ should be a positive value less than unity. The choice of $\rho$ and $\eta$ will depend on the model being trained, and usually some experimentation is required to identify good values. RMSProp is presented in Algorithm 5.5. The algorithm is the same as AdaGrad except for the introduction of a hyperparameter. The additions are in shaded.

---

**Algorithm 5.5** RMSProp Weight Update Strategy

---

1: **procedure** RMSPROP

2:    $\Delta^t \leftarrow \frac{\partial L^t}{\partial w}$

3:    $\Delta_{sq}^t \leftarrow (1 - \rho)\Delta_{sq}^{t-1} + \rho(\Delta^t \cdot \Delta^t)$

4:    $\Delta_w \leftarrow \eta \cdot \frac{\Delta^t}{\sqrt{\Delta_{sq}}+\epsilon}$

5:    $w^t \leftarrow w^{t-1} - \Delta_w$

6: **end procedure**

---

RMSProp was a good improvement, but it still left a great deal to be desired. Choosing the hyperparameters can be difficult, the perennial problem in machine learning, but RMSProp can be used with minibatches and so it is appropriate for use with SGD.

### 5.4.2 ADAM

In 2015, a further refinement was developed called ADAM (84). It is an extremely popular optimizer and possibly the most widely used. ADAM works well with SGD variants, that is, minibatch schemes, as it scales well to large problems. This makes ADAM eminently suitable for use with large training sets. The name, ADAM, is derived from **ADA**ptive **M**oment estimation. It is based on the idea of using momentum to choose the step size. ADAM evolved from RMSProp.

ADAM requires two variables per weight. They are its estimations of the first moment of the gradient (mean) and the estimation of the squared uncentered second moment (variance). The estimations are used to scale the step size based on the recent history of the gradient. The ADAM update rule is presented in Algorithm 5.6.

---

**Algorithm 5.6** ADAM Weight Update Strategy

---

1: **procedure** ADAM

2:    $g^t \leftarrow \frac{\partial L^t}{\partial w^t}$

3:    $m^t \leftarrow \beta_1 \cdot m^{t-1} + (1 - \beta_1) \cdot g^t$

4:    $v^t \leftarrow \beta_2 \cdot v^{t-1} + (1 - \beta_2) \cdot (g^t)^2$

5:    $\hat{m} \leftarrow \frac{m^t}{1-\beta_1^t}$

6:    $\hat{v} \leftarrow \frac{v^t}{1-\beta_2^t}$

7:    $w^t \leftarrow w^{t-1} - \alpha \cdot \frac{\hat{m}}{\sqrt{\hat{v}}+\epsilon}$

8: **end procedure**

---

The authors recommend values of $\alpha = 0.001$, $\beta_1 = 0.9$, $\beta_2 = 0.999$, and $\epsilon = 10^{-8}$. The latter is included simply to ensure that there is never a division by zero. The similarities to RMSProp are evident. The numerator in ADAM's correction is now first-order momentum, and both $v$ and $m$ are bias corrected.

It is instructive to compare ADAM to RPROP+ updates. The ADAM update to the weight, in weight space, is $\Delta w^t = -\alpha \cdot \frac{\hat{m}}{\sqrt{\hat{v}}+\epsilon}$. The authors show that they expect the common case for the update to respect the bound $|\Delta w^t| \leq \alpha$. Contrast this with RPROP+ where the upper bound for an update is $\Delta_{max}$, and a value of 50 is recommended, which is 50,000 times larger than the recommended value of $\alpha = 0.001$. RPROP+ is far more aggressive. Making ADAM efficient generally involves fiddling with the $\alpha$ hyperparameter.

We compare the distribution of values for the full $|\Delta w|$ for both ADAM and RPROP+ for the LeNet5 C5 layer to really observe the dynamics of both heuristics in a realistic setting. The results are depicted in Figure 5.5. The graph makes clear that the bulk of RPROP+'s updates are orders of magnitude greater than

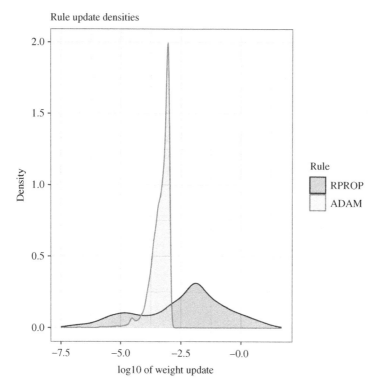

**Figure 5.5** Computed densities of observed weight updates. Training was initiated with the same initial values for weights. The $x$-axis is logarithmic.

**Table 5.2** Comparison of Strategies

| Strategy | Loss | Accuracy (%) |
| --- | --- | --- |
| RPROP+ | 0.3161 | 93.94 |
| ADAM | 0.6866 | 84.4 |

ADAM's (the $x$-axis is logarithmic). There is a barrier that ADAM hits that it seems to want to cross. The wall curve is the effect of $\alpha$ on the update size. Modern implementations of ADAM tend to be more aggressive, and many models using Keras's implementation of the ADAM optimizer use a value of $\alpha = 0.01$.

Of course large weight updates are not useful unless they contribute to earlier convergence. To measure the effect of the larger updates, the losses and accuracy are presented in Table 5.2. The table was produced with 5 runs for each training method. Both models were trained for 100 epochs with SGD, and for each of the 5 runs, the models started with the same initial weights. The RPROP+ algorithm clearly out performed ADAM in this instance. While this is an example where RPROP+ out-performed ADAM despite theoretical limitations, it must be emphasized that LeNet5 is an extremely shallow and simple neural network by today's standards of the state of the art[1].

While slower than RPROP+, ADAM is steady. When training a network with Relu activation functions, ADAM is always selected over RPROP+. To avoid the "dead neuron" effect inherent with Relu, slower training is essential to avoid neuron death; recall that it is not recoverable. RPROP+ can easily shoot into a bad area, it is designed to, but it needs to recover and as Relu is not forgiving (once a neuron is dead its derivative is always zero and can never recover). RPROP+ can kill many neurons with Relu and progress typically comes to a halt well before convergence. Relu (and its variants) are almost always used in the deepest DL models, and ADAM is the optimizer of choice.

# 5.5 Levenberg–Marquard Optimization for Neural Networks

Both ADAM and RPROP+ are examples of first-order methods, that is, they only rely on the first-order derivatives produced with backpropagation. Both strategies employ heuristics to compute the step size. We saw with Newton's method

---

1 LeNet-5 is strictly ordered and comprised of 5 layers. This is small compared to the 20+ layers with skipping in modern visual classifiers.

for optimization that there is important information relevant to selecting a step size in the second derivatives, the curvature, but concluded that the Hessian is too expensive to compute, much less solve. None the less, like a moth drawn to a flame, there remains considerable interest in the research community in pursuing second-order methods. To examine the question more concretely, a relatively simple algorithm is presented in this section. The discussion is really a vehicle for demonstrating why second-order methods are not currently practical while simultaneously demonstrating why people continue to consider them. The method is called Levenberg–Marquard (LM) optimization.

LM optimization uses approximate second order information to compute an update. There are a number of choices of quasi "practical" second-order methods to choose from when deciding which second-order method to discuss, e.g. Broyden-Fletcher-Goldfarb-Shannon (BFGS) (3) and its variant, L-BFGS (97) (the L stands for limited memory), but LM methods are simple while demonstrating the pain/reward trade-off. We follow Hagan's formulation of the problem (58).

An ANN is a function that accepts an argument, a vector $x$, and is parameterized by its weights, $w$. Training the ANN is the process of determining the weights, so the parameters are the variables and the training set is constant. Thus, the roles of arguments and parameters are temporarily reversed during training. To reflect the temporary rôles, we will write $\mathbf{f}(\mathbf{w})$, where $\mathbf{f}$ is the ANN, *not* a loss function. $\mathbf{f}$ is a vector function that accepts the entire training set as an argument and produces a vector, $\hat{\mathbf{y}}$, with all of the computed outputs,

$$\hat{\mathbf{y}} = \begin{pmatrix} ANN(x_1) \\ \vdots \\ ANN(x_N) \end{pmatrix}, \tag{5.8}$$

so we have $\mathbf{f}(\mathbf{w}|\mathbf{x}) = \hat{\mathbf{y}}$, where $\mathbf{x}$ is the parameter, the training set. Let there be $N$ elements in the training set and $M$ weights to fit in the ANN. The domain and range of $\mathbf{f}$ are then effectively $\mathbf{f} : \mathbb{R}^M \to \mathbb{R}^N$ during the training of the ANN with LM.

The object of training is to improve the performance of $\mathbf{f}$ by iteratively finding better weights. We can approximate an update to $\mathbf{f}$ with a first-order Taylors Series: $\mathbf{f}(\mathbf{w} + \Delta\mathbf{w}) \approx \mathbf{f}(\mathbf{w}) + \mathbf{J}\Delta\mathbf{w}$, where $\mathbf{J}$ is the Jacobean matrix. The Jacobian matrix comes from the gradient of a function. The ANN Jacobean has the form:

$$\mathbf{J} = \nabla^T \mathbf{f} = \begin{pmatrix} \nabla^T ANN(x_1) \\ \vdots \\ \nabla^T ANN(x_N) \end{pmatrix}, \tag{5.9}$$

where the $N$ rows are the results of performing backpropagation on the ANN with the $N$ elements from the training set. Note that the ANN is differentiated not a loss function. Let $f_i = ANN(x_i)$, then the Jacobian matrix is generated over a training epoch creating a row of $M$ entries of $\frac{\partial f_i}{\partial w_j}$ for each of the $N$ training examples.

For a training set containing $N$ examples, and an ANN with $M$ weights, we obtain the following Jacobian matrix:

$$\mathbf{J}_{N,M} = \begin{pmatrix} \dfrac{\partial f_1}{\partial w_{1,1}} & \dfrac{\partial f_1}{\partial w_{1,2}} & \cdots & \dfrac{\partial f_1}{\partial w_{1,M}} \\[2mm] \dfrac{\partial f_2}{\partial w_{2,1}} & \dfrac{\partial f_2}{\partial w_{2,2}} & \cdots & \dfrac{\partial f_2}{\partial w_{2,M}} \\[2mm] \vdots & & & \\[2mm] \dfrac{\partial f_N}{\partial w_{N,1}} & \dfrac{\partial f_N}{\partial w_{N,2}} & \cdots & \dfrac{\partial f_N}{\partial w_{N,M}} \end{pmatrix}. \tag{5.10}$$

Each row is the per weight error for an example from the training set. Thus, entry $\frac{\partial f_i}{\partial w_{i,j}}$ is the error for weight $j$ at example $i$ from the training set.

Computing the Jacobean also requires a modification to the usual training epoch. Instead of computing the net gradient by summing the per weight derivatives over the examples, the Jacobean records each derivative individually. The net gradient for $w_j$ is the sum of the $j^{th}$ column in the Jacobean. Both ADAM and RPROP+ only store the net gradient.

The object for the weight update is to reduce the error with the training set. The error reduction can be expressed as $|\mathbf{f}(\mathbf{w} + \Delta \mathbf{w}) - \mathbf{y}|_{min}$, where $\mathbf{y}$ is the vector of the ground truth from the training set, and we are using Euclidean distance. The method is to solve for the vector $\Delta w$ by minimizing the residuals. Substituting for the Taylor series approximation, the following is obtained,

$$|\mathbf{f}(\mathbf{w}) + \mathbf{J}\Delta\mathbf{w} - \mathbf{y}|_{min} = |\mathbf{J}\Delta\mathbf{w} - (\mathbf{y} - \mathbf{f}(\mathbf{w}))|_{min}$$
$$= |\mathbf{J}\Delta\mathbf{w} - (\mathbf{y} - \hat{\mathbf{y}})|_{min}$$
$$= |\mathbf{J}\Delta\mathbf{w} - \mathbf{r}|_{min}, \tag{5.11}$$

where $\mathbf{r}$ is a vector of the residuals (the error). This formulation of the problem can be solved with least squares. The object is to solve for the vector, $\Delta\mathbf{w}$. Observe that $\mathbf{r}$ also happens to be the vector of per training example derivatives of the MSE loss function, $\frac{\partial L}{z_{output,i}}$. The global MSE loss can be computed as $\frac{1}{2N}\mathbf{r}^T\mathbf{r}$. So the matrix formulation naturally led to the usual regressor framing of the problem.

Constructing the normal equations for least squares leads to,

$$\mathbf{J}^T(\mathbf{J}\Delta\mathbf{w} - \mathbf{r}) = 0 \implies \mathbf{J}^T\mathbf{J}\Delta\mathbf{w} = \mathbf{J}^T\mathbf{r}. \tag{5.12}$$

The canonical approach when dealing with least squares problems is to employ the QR decomposition. Decomposing the Jacobean and substituting yields the familiar LS solution:

$$\mathbf{QR} = \mathbf{J} \implies \mathbf{Q}^T\mathbf{QR}\Delta\mathbf{w} = \mathbf{Q}^T\mathbf{r} \implies \mathbf{R}\Delta\mathbf{w} = \mathbf{Q}^T\mathbf{r}. \tag{5.13}$$

As **R** is upper-triangular, the answers are obtained by backward substitution. An enormous advantage of this method is that the matrix $\mathbf{J}^T\mathbf{J}$ does not even need to be formed explicitly, it simply disappears; there are also numerical advantages as well–matrix–matrix multiplication can be numerically unstable. The problem is that the matrix of gradients, **J**, is usually very ill conditioned. To tame it the LM technique can be used. Unfortunately, LM requires $\mathbf{J}^T\mathbf{J}$'s explicit formation. The approach is to shift the spectrum of the Jacobean, which makes it easier to solve. This is a trust region technique; the local surface area is being approximated linearly. The LM method of shifting the spectrum is performed by

$$\mathbf{J}^T\mathbf{J} + \lambda\mathbf{I} = \mathbf{K}, \tag{5.14}$$

and the new system,

$$\mathbf{K}\Delta\mathbf{w} = \mathbf{J}^T\mathbf{r}, \tag{5.15}$$

is solved. The Jacobean's spectrum has been shifted by the scaler $\lambda$. $\lambda$ is adjusted dynamically in response to current stability of the Jacobean during training. One solace is that a matrix multiplied by its transpose is symmetric so it is only half the work to produce. A second nice quality of the matrix **K** is that it is positively definite and so specialized methods for the solving the matrix can be used.

The LM method works by dialing the $\lambda$ factor as needed. The more badly behaved the Jacobean, the larger $\lambda$ grows, and it degrades to gradient descent; this is inferior to the heuristic methods described thus far as the updates are strictly proportional to $\frac{\partial L}{\partial w}$, with nothing clever to regulate the step size ($\eta = 1$). This can be seen as

$$(\mathbf{J}^T\mathbf{J} + \lambda\mathbf{I})\Delta\mathbf{w} = \mathbf{J}^T\mathbf{r} \implies \Delta\mathbf{w} = (\mathbf{J}^T\mathbf{J} + \lambda\mathbf{I})^{-1} \cdot \mathbf{J}^T\mathbf{r}. \tag{5.16}$$

Approximating the inverse of $\mathbf{K}^2$ the asymptotic behavior becomes clear, as does the effectiveness of the method,

$$\Delta\mathbf{w} = (\mathbf{I} - \frac{\mathbf{J}^T\mathbf{J}}{\lambda} + ...) \cdot \mathbf{J}^T\mathbf{r}, \tag{5.17}$$

and so as $\lambda \to +\infty$ the update approaches $\Delta\mathbf{w} \to \mathbf{J}^T\mathbf{r}$, which is gradient ascent (hence the update is subtracted in Algorithm 5.7). When $\lambda$ is small, then the matrix, $\mathbf{J}^T\mathbf{J}$, uses its approximate curvature information to yield a good update. The entries of look like,

$$J_{i,j} = \sum_k \frac{\partial f_i}{\partial w_{i,k}} \cdot \frac{\partial f_j}{\partial w_{k,i}}. \tag{5.18}$$

This is a first-order approximation to the Hessian matrix, and the basis of the Gauss–Newton method of optimization (31).

---

2 A Taylor series expansion was used, $(B + A)^{-1} \approx A^{-1} - A^{-1} B A^{-1} + A^{-1} B A^{-1} B A^{-1} - ...$, where $A = \lambda I$.

---

**Algorithm 5.7** Levenberg-Marquardt Optimization

---

1: **procedure** LM STEP
2:   **for** $x \in$ *Training* **do**
3:     $\mathbf{f}[i] \leftarrow ANN(x_i)$
4:     $\mathbf{J}[i,] \leftarrow$ BPG ()                    ▷ Computer derivatives for row
5:   **end for**
6:   loss $\leftarrow \infty$
7:   **while** loss > CurrentLoss **do**
8:     $\mathbf{K} \leftarrow \mathbf{J}^T\mathbf{J} + \lambda\mathbf{I}$
9:     $\mathbf{r} \leftarrow \mathbf{f} - \mathbf{y}$
10:     $\Delta w \leftarrow$ SolveLinear$(\mathbf{K}, \mathbf{r})$     ▷ Cholesky decomposition can be used
11:     $W \leftarrow W - \Delta w$
12:     **for** $x \in$ *Training* **do**
13:       $\mathbf{f}[i] \leftarrow ANN(x_i)$
14:     **end for**
15:     $\mathbf{r} \leftarrow \mathbf{f} - \mathbf{y}$
16:     loss $\leftarrow \frac{1}{2N}\mathbf{r}^T\mathbf{r}$                    ▷ Compute new loss
17:     **if** loss $\geq$ CurrentLoss **then**
18:
19:       $W \leftarrow W + \Delta w$                    ▷ Backout bad update
20:       $\lambda \leftarrow \lambda \cdot 10$                    ▷ Backoff the trust region
21:     **else**
22:       $\lambda \leftarrow \lambda/10$                    ▷ Dial up the trust region
23:     **end if**
24:   **end while**
25:   **return** loss
26: **end procedure**

---

The LM method is very expensive, but it does have some advantages. It is a global solution. The first-order methods presented thus far compute updates for each weight in isolation. Consequently, the updates can, and do, interfere and confound each other. Solving the matrix is globally optimal and the weights do not interfere with each other; they have been accounted for by solving the matrix of simultaneous equations.

There is a cost. First-order methods are $\mathcal{O}(M)$ for both memory and work. Firstorder methods iterate through the weights, compute the update, and apply it. The memory required to train with LM is $\mathcal{O}(M \cdot N)$, the size of the Jacobean. This quickly gets very large for most ANN problems. In addition to storing, the Jacobean the LM matrix has to be formed. This is $\mathcal{O}(M^2)$ space on top of the Jacobean's memory. Forming the LM matrix is $\mathcal{O}(M^3)$ in time. It is clear that

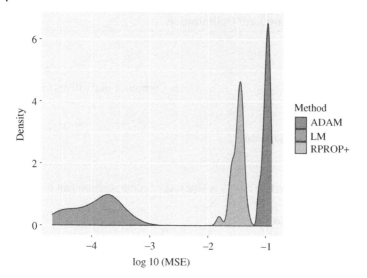

**Figure 5.6**  Densities of log scale losses of models following training. LM losses are centered 2–3 orders of magnitude to the left of the first-order methods.

LM resource demands quickly grow onerous. Both memory and time grow very quickly, so there are very few problems for which LM is appropriate.

Figure 5.6 presents the results of training ANNs to learn sine. The densities of the final losses for 30 attempts to train an ANN per strategy are depicted. ADAM and RPROP+ ANNs were trained for 100 epochs. Comparing LM with ADAM and RPROP+ is potentially problematic. Running LM for 100 epochs would produce spectacular results, but take far more time. The firstorder methods were used to calibrate the comparison. The mean CPU time consumed by the resulting combined 60 runs of the first-order methods was used to run LM. Thus, LM training took the same CPU time, but managed far fewer epochs. The logs of the losses are presented. LM is orders of magnitude better than the first-order methods. The experiment is not meant to be misleading. It must be emphasized that sine is a trivial function to learn. LM it totally impractical for the LeNet-5 experiment in Table 5.2. Medium sized Deep Learning models have millions of weights. The space and time requirements of LM render it totally impractical for such problems. But the dream of such rapid convergence is so promising that researchers continue to examine second order methods.

## 5.6  Summary

Backpropagation reliably finds the direction of the correct update, but not the appropriate size of the step to be taken. The optimal step size is too expensive to compute so heuristics are used to compute it. RPROP+ is an extremely fast heuristic, but can present challenges when used with SGD. ADAM is the de rigueur optimizer used for training Deep Learning models. `ReLU` and its variants are the activation functions of choice.

## 5.7 Projects

The projects below rely on notebooks that can be found here, https://github.com/nom-de-guerre/DDL_book/tree/main/Ch05.

1. The Python notebook sine.ipynb looks for the minimum of `sine`. It contains an implementation of ADAM and RPROP+. Implement Newton's Step. Compare the heuristics' step sizes with Newton's step.
2. The iris classifier iris05.ipynb includes ADAM and RPROP+ optimizers. Plot loss versus epoch for both RPROP+ and ADAM. Experiment with different topologies. Is there an important difference?
3. The website includes a handwritten digit classifier, called MNIST05.ipynb. Plot loss for MNIST for both RPROP+ and ADAM. Do the results differ from the iris experiment?

# 6

# Convolutional Neural Networks

This chapter presents convolutional neural networks (CNNs). For the purposes of this chapter, CNN means convolutional neural network, not classifying neural network. In general, when people use the acronym CNN, it is the former meaning that is intended, a convolutional neural network. CNNs are often classifiers, so a CNN can be classifying neural network. When the latter sense is meant, it is generally written out in full, not as an acronym, to avoid confusion. CNNs have wide application, often in image recognition, but they have many uses including in games, generative artificial neural networks (ANNs) and natural language processing. A CNN is an ANN that includes at least one convolutional layer. They are used extensively in deep learning (DL) performing many vital functions in deep neural networks. This chapter motivates the use of convolutional layers, describes their operation inside an ANN, and demonstrates how to train them.

CNNs were motivated by the observation that cats had neurons dedicated to fields of vision, that is, they could comprehend sub-regions of an image in parallel. A cat's brain divides an image into subimages called receptive fields. The receptive fields have dedicated neurons. Dedicating neurons to receptive fields produces an efficient motion detection mechanism. Fukushima was inspired by the biological use of receptive fields. In 1980, he described how to combine perceptrons with convolutions to produce a "neocognitron" (43). A neocognitron is a multilayer neural network and meets the modern definition of "deep learning." The system used perceptrons to perform image recognition tasks with convolutions. Another point of interest is that two modes of training were described, supervised, and unsupervised. The neocognitron was able to learn and recognize hand-written digits, but it was arguably the work done in 1989 by Yann LeCun et al. (91) that set the pattern for modern CNNs. It was the first paper to describe the use of backpropagation of error to train a CNN. LeCun recognized that introducing

*Demystifying Deep Learning: An Introduction to the Mathematics of Neural Networks,*
First Edition. Douglas J. Santry.
© 2024 The Institute of Electrical and Electronics Engineers, Inc. Published 2024 by John Wiley & Sons, Inc.

convolutions simultaneously addressed many problems that were believed to render ANNs infeasible for practical image recognition.

## 6.1 Motivation

Images are much larger inputs than the example datasets that have been discussed thus far. Such large inputs require special handling to efficiently process them. When performing image recognition, many properties are required. The algorithm should be shift invariant, that is, it should not matter where precisely an object is in an image, it should be detected. Images can be large. It is a challenge to both quickly and reliably recognize items in an image.

Consider a color image with a resolution of $1024 \times 1024 \times 3$. There are 3 colour channels, one for each of red, green, and blue (RGB). RGB images can be thought of as 3 images exclusively in one of each of the 3 color channels. An RGB image is a volume, not an area (2 dimensional grid). Such objects can be encapsulated in a *tensor* (the reader is directed to section 12.4 in (49) for a brief introduction). To invoke an ANN, the example image could naively be construed as a vector with a length of 3,145,728. Passing such a large vector to a fully connected ANN would result in an enormous number of weights. An input layer with 100 neurons would require 314,572,900 weights (the additional 100 weights accounts for the bias). Such a large number of weights present an enormous problem in many respects. The weights consume space (memory), increase training time, and add latency when performing inference with the final model. Large numbers of fully connected neurons with dedicated weights can also generalize poorly as they tend to overfit during training.

Image classification attempts to look for spatial relationships. If a nose is detected, then there are probably one or two eyes nearby. A spoon will look like a spoon no matter where it is located in an image. The Figure 6.1 depicts a sample of hand-written twos. The examples are taken from the modified National Institute of Standards and Technology (MNIST) hand-written digit dataset. The dataset is a combination of two datasets. Both consist of hand-written digits

**Figure 6.1** Five examples of hand-written twos from the MNIST dataset. The images are $28 \times 28 \times 1$ (gray scale). There are no simple rules that define what a two looks like.

and their labels, but from two separate sources (US Post Office employees and highschool students). The full MNIST dataset includes a training set of 600,000 digits and a test set consisting of 10,000 digits for a total of 70,000 examples. All 10 digits, 0–9, are represented approximately equally. It was introduced in a paper describing a very famous DL model, LeNet-5 (92). MNIST digits are convenient to use as examples as they are relatively small, $28 \times 28 \times 1$, where the 1 denotes that it is gray-scale, which makes an MNIST digit a 2 dimensional array, not a volume.

The MNIST dataset contains all 10 digits, but we will restrict ourselves to the twos for the moment. Implementing a model to recognize twos requires learning what a "2" looks like. A curve implies finding a line in predictable direction, and vice-versa. A two has defining features that can be recognized, but perhaps are difficult to specify formally. Moreover, a two is a composite of a number of distinct features in the image. Humans can recognize them immediately (and they complain about the hand writing if they cannot). The same can be said of all digits and the Latin alphabet, which is relatively simple when compared to other alphabets such as the Japanese alphabet. Instead of writing down rules to distinguish the different symbols, it is desirable for an ANN to simply learn how to recognize them. The techniques that are developed can be used to recognize anything.

## 6.2 Convolutions and Features

The object of convolutions is to discern features in an image that differentiate higher order objects in the image. Decomposing an image into features makes, it easier for a system to distinguish between and recognize macro structures. The result is a smaller image that contains more useful information. The resulting image consumes less memory as it is smaller. The memory consumption, however, tends to go up, not down, as there are usually multiple features produced in parallel. This results in multiple smaller maps that collectively consume more space than the original. The information gleaned in the feature maps is worth it and makes the task of recognition easier.

The pivotal concept at the center of convolutions is the *kernel*. A kernel is used by applying it to a submatrix of an input matrix producing a scaler. The scaler is recorded in a new matrix, the *feature map*. The kernel is applied repeatedly to different submatrices in the image. Each application of the kernel produces a scaler that is stored in the feature map. The feature map contains the feature that is the result of applying the kernel; what the kernel is looking for. The result is a new feature map that is smaller than the input. The feature map contains information about the original matrix that should make interpreting its contents easier.

The process starts by applying the kernel to the top-left of the input matrix. The computation is performed, the result stored, and the kernel is moved along to the right and the operation repeated with the new submatrix. Applying the kernel and sliding over to the new submatrix are repeated until the end of the image is reached on the right. At this point, the algorithm returns to the first column on the left, but slides down. The number of slots to move along (the number of columns), or the number of rows to move down, is known as the *stride*. The stride is one of the hyperparameters of convolutional layers. An example of the process is shown in Figure 6.2. For clarity of exposition, input matrices and kernels are assumed square. Neither object is required to be square and in real applications are frequently not. MNIST images are square.

To be useful, the kernel should extract meaningful information from the original image. One means of identifying features is to hardcode some masks and use them as kernels. By applying masks to an image, it is possible to identify vertical lines, horizontal lines, and diagonals. Each mask produces a feature, and applying them to the original image decomposes the image in a different way with respect to the feature. The masks can be interpreted as *filters*. The mask looking for vertical lines is filtering the image with respect to vertical lines. The matrices in Eq. (6.1) are examples of filters. Applying all 4 masks produces 4 separate feature maps. The idea is that patterns associated with digits will emerge. Comparing feature maps, intradigit should find similarities, and comparing feature maps interdigit should identify differences. Assuming a kernel size of $3 \times 3$, the following constitute the

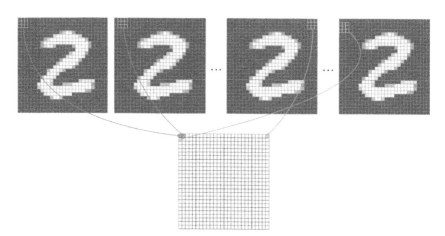

**Figure 6.2** The repeated application of a kernel to produce a feature map. The kernel is applied to every submatrix resulting from traversing the image by the stride. The $28 \times 28$ MNIST image is convolved to a $26 \times 26$ image produced from the $26 \times 26$ convolutions resulting from a stride of 1.

masks required:

$$k_{hor} = \begin{pmatrix} 0 & 0 & 0 \\ 1 & 1 & 1 \\ 0 & 0 & 0 \end{pmatrix},$$

$$k_{ver} = \begin{pmatrix} 0 & 1 & 0 \\ 0 & 1 & 0 \\ 0 & 1 & 0 \end{pmatrix},$$

$$k_{dTop} = \begin{pmatrix} 1 & 0 & 0 \\ 0 & 1 & 0 \\ 0 & 0 & 1 \end{pmatrix},$$

$$k_{dBot} = \begin{pmatrix} 0 & 0 & 1 \\ 0 & 1 & 0 \\ 1 & 0 & 0 \end{pmatrix}. \tag{6.1}$$

The convolution consists of taking a mask, e.g. $k_{hor}$, and element-wise applying a binary operator logically, the *not exclusive or* (NXOR). The kernel is applied to a submatrix from the image of the same dimensions as the kernel ($3 \times 3$). The truth table for NXOR is 1 if both arguments are nonzero or if both arguments are zero, that is, both arguments agree. It is zero if the arguments disagree. Applying the mask yields 9 values as there are 9 binary operations between the mask and the submatrix. To produce the final scaler, the results are summed; a value of 9 is a perfect match, 0 connotes a complete difference. The kernel is summarizing a submatrix with a scaler, that is,

$$\text{kernel} : \mathbb{R}^{3 \times 3} \to \mathbb{R}. \tag{6.2}$$

The resulting kernel is

$$\overset{rows}{\underset{i=1}{\sum}} \overset{columns}{\underset{j=1}{\sum}} k_{i,j} \odot subm_{i,j}. \tag{6.3}$$

The procedure is repeated until all of the submatrices in the image have been processed and the feature matrix is filled.

Figure 6.2 graphically depicts the process for an example MNIST "2". An MNIST image is a $28 \times 28$ grayscale matrix. The mask is $3 \times 3$, with a stride of 1. As the stride is 1, the convolution moves over one column following each computation. Once the last column is reached, computation returns to first column, but moves down a row. A stride of 1 creates a great many overlapping convolutions decreasing the chance of "missing something" in the image; the kernel is looking for spatial relationships. The cost is a bigger feature map. The number of rows in the feature matrix is $Im_{rows} - k_{rows} + 1 = 28 - 3 + 1 = 26$. As all objects are square in this example, the resulting feature matrix is $26 \times 26$. There are 4 masks defined in (6.1) leading to 4 feature maps, each $26 \times 26$. The output is therefore $4 \times 26 \times 26 \times 1$. In general, a feature matrix will have dimension,

$$\frac{Im_{rows} - k_{rows}}{s} + 1, \tag{6.4}$$

where $s$ is the stride. In the case of asymmetric kernels or images, then the column width will have to be computed as well.

Note that not all elements in the original image participate in an equal number of times in the convolutions. As described, the pixel in the top right corner, and the top left, each participated in only a single kernel application. The pixels in the center of the top row will contribute to 3 calculations. If there is something important on the edges of the images, then this may not be desirable. Images can be padded to increase the inclusion rate. In the case of an MNIST digit, a $28 \times 28$ image can have zeros added around the edges depending on the desired level of padding. A $28 \times 28$ image can be padded to produce a $29 \times 29$ or a $30 \times 30$ image, whatever is required. To produce a $29 \times 29$ padded image, a row is added to the top and bottom, and a column is prepended and appended to the left and right of the image. The original image is at the center of the padded image. The paddings increase the number of times the edges participate, and the convolutions and the edges receive the full benefit of the kernels. A classifier training to learn the MNIST dataset does not need padding, and the images are centered. Not all applications are so well behaved though. Domain knowledge is required to make a sensible determination.

The results of applying the masks to an MNIST "2" are displayed in Figure 6.3. The left-most image is the original input image of a "2". The remaining images to the right are the feature maps resulting from applying the masks in order of their definition in Eq. (6.1). The darker colors are higher numbers, so closer matches to the kernel. Visual inspection of the results suggests that they are sensitive to

**Figure 6.3** The result of applying the kernels in (6.1) to detect features. The original hand-written two is on the left. The result of applying the masks are in order from left to right. The stride is 1 which results in $28 \times 28$ images convolving to $26 \times 26$.

a number of factors. The masks are looking for patterns that are a single pixel in width. The example "2" does not restrict itself to single pixel width anywhere. Despite that, some feature definition has emerged. Once computed, the feature maps are ready for use with the bottom of the classifier, a FFFC ANN.

With the features computed, they can be further processed by a fully connected ANN. Construing the 4 features as a single, albeit long, vector the features can be passed into the deeper ANN. The feature vector is $4 \times 26 \times 26 = 2704$ elements long. While this is far larger than the $28 \times 28 = 784$ long vector that would result from starting with the original image, it is far more information rich. The important differences between a "3" and an "8" are easier to discern in the feature matrices than the original image. The structural differences emerge more distinctly.

The CNN described is a big improvement on a naive classifying ANN. A number of questions, do, however, immediately suggest themselves. Do the masks that were defined make sense for digits? Are there better kernels that could be used? Ideally, the masks would be well suited to the problem domain. What if more than 4 feature maps are desired? Conceiving bitmasks for use with convolutions is clearly not ideal, and there are only so many sensible masks that suggest themselves. If possible the features should be automatically created during training, not hardcoded a priori. Learned features increase the number of possible useful features as the onus is placed on the CNN to find them, not the human. Features that are learnt would also be well suited to the problem domain as the features were learnt from the training set, the definition of the problem domain.

## 6.3 Filters

The above agruments suggest that a desideratum for the kernels is that they are *learnt*. If kernels are learnt, then domain-specific kernels will result yielding better feature maps. In addition, the number of features is constrained by the needs of the model, not by how many masks can be dreamt up by a human.

The perceptron makes an excellent kernel. A perceptron employed as a kernel is known as a *filter*. Some of its advantages as a kernel include that the perceptron is well understood, including how to train it. A perceptron accepts multiple inputs and produces a scaler, precisely what is required for a kernel. The weights of a perceptron can be used for the values in a mask. Weights are learnt leading naturally to learned features. A $3 \times 3$ kernel can be implemented with a perceptron with 9 weights, and in general a $k_{rows} \times k_{columns}$ kernel can be implemented with $k_{rows} \cdot k_{columns}$ weights (and a bias). Perceptron weights are usually numbered linearly and construed as a vector. This follows from designing them to accept vector arguments in an ANN. The vector interpretation also makes it convenient to implement perceptrons as a row in a weight matrix for a layer. Kernels are small matrices so a means of converting a perceptron's weights to a matrix is indicated. A matrix interpretation can be effected by construing the sequentially ordered weights as a row-order matrix. The weights are mapped unambiguously to a matrix. The following example illustrates the scheme for a $3 \times 3$ kernel:

$$\{w_0, w_1, w_2, w_3, w_4, w_5, w_6, w_7, w_8\} \rightarrow \begin{pmatrix} w_0 & w_1 & w_2 \\ w_3 & w_4 & w_5 \\ w_6 & w_7 & w_8 \end{pmatrix} \tag{6.5}$$

Arranging the weights in a matrix produces a kernel of the correct dimensions, but the kernel must produce a scaler. Matrix multiplication produces a matrix. A scaler is obtained with an extension of the vector dot product, known as the inner product, used by perceptrons. The dot product for a pair of matrices of the same dimension is known as a Frobenius product. The Frobenius dot product is similar to a Hadamard operation except that the final result is a scaler as the results are summed. The Frobenius dot product for a filter and a submatrix is defined as:

$$F(f, subm) = \sum_i^{rows} \sum_j^{columns} w_{i,j} \cdot subm_{i,j}, \tag{6.6}$$

where $f$ is a filter (perceptron), and *subm* is the submatrix. The Frobenius product is a natural extension of how a perceptron computed its intermediate state, $u$, in an ANN; the dot product of its inputs with its weights. Once the Frobenius product has been computed, the perceptron applies its activation function to produce the final result. The final expression for the scaler produced by a perceptron is $\sigma(F)$; this is the filter kernel. The result is stored in the feature map. Modern DL CNNs typically use the RelU activation function for the reasons outlined in Section 3.5.4. It is interesting to note that Fukushima introduced the RelU activation function when describing his cognitron in 1975 (42), but he did not use it in the neocognitron with convolutions (Figure 6.4).

| $Im_{0,0}$ | $Im_{0,1}$ | $Im_{0,2}$ | | |
|---|---|---|---|---|
| $Im_{1,0}$ | $Im_{1,1}$ | $Im_{1,2}$ | $\sigma(w_{0,0} \cdot Im_{0,0} + w_{0,1} \cdot Im_{0,1} + w_{1,0} \cdot Im_{1,0} + w_{1,1} \cdot Im_{1,1})$ | $\sigma(w_{0,0} \cdot Im_{0,1} + w_{0,1} \cdot Im_{0,2} + w_{1,0} \cdot Im_{1,1} + w_{1,1} \cdot Im_{1,2})$ |
| $Im_{2,0}$ | $Im_{2,1}$ | $Im_{2,2}$ | $\sigma(w_{0,0} \cdot Im_{1,0} + w_{0,1} \cdot Im_{1,1} + w_{1,0} \cdot Im_{2,0} + w_{1,1} \cdot Im_{2,1})$ | $\sigma(w_{0,0} \cdot Im_{1,1} + w_{0,1} \cdot Im_{1,2} + w_{1,0} \cdot Im_{2,1} + w_{1,1} \cdot Im_{2,2})$ |

**Figure 6.4** The figure depicts a $3 \times 3$ image and the feature map that results following the application of a $2 \times 2$ kernel when a stride of 1 is used. The $3 \times 3$ image convolves to a $2 \times 2$ feature map. The shaded elements in the submatrix on the left are used in the highlighted element in the feature map on the right. The kernel is depicted with a general activation function, $\sigma$, but it is usual to use RelU.

To produce the feature map, the filter (perceptron kernel) is applied to each sub-matrix as described above with naive masks. A feature map is produced per filter, and the number of filters corresponds to the number of the desired features. The number of filters required is specified as a hyperparameter of the model.

Typically, multiple filters are applied in parallel in one layer of a CNN. The result is multiple feature maps produced from a layer of filters. Continuing with the MNIST example ($3 \times 3$ kernel, stride 1), the input for the filter layer is $28 \times 28$, and assuming 5 filters the output would be $5 \times 26 \times 26$. Once the feature maps have been computed, they can be passed on to a fully connected ANN. Fully connected ANNs expect vectors, and the output of the filter is the wrong shape. Prior to passing the feature maps to the ANN classifier, they must be *flattened*. Flattening is the process of changing the higher order (complicated) shape to a vector. Following with the MNIST example, the $5 \times 26 \times 26$ tensor is flattened to a 3380 element vector. The vector is the shape expected by an ANN's input layer. It should be noted that a good implementation will not perform any copying of data, but merely reinterpret the memory occupied by the tensor. Flattening is not to be confused with *concatenation*. Concatenation is the operation of fusing, or synthesizing, multiple tensors of the same underlying shape. For example, concatenating a $3 \times 20 \times 20$ tensor with a $4 \times 20 \times 20$ tensor results in a $7 \times 20 \times 20$ tensor. It is a very different operation (and almost certainly will involve copying data).

An important interpretation of filters is that of a regularized perceptron. A feature map has a single perceptron processing an input image of many pixels. In other words, convolutions are a form of regularization as they are kernels providing shared weights between two layers. This is described in the section on regularization (Section 7.4). All of the entries in a feature map share the same weights. In consequence, overfitting is far less likely and filters generalize well. Filters extract features learnt from the problem domain; they are learnt during training. It is clear that filters simultaneously perform two important rôles, they regularize the network and automatically perform quality feature extraction. LeCun et al. recognized the utility of perceptrons as filters. It was this insight that motivated them to train perceptrons as filters with backpropagation of error in a CNN (91). The arguments remain valid today, and these are the reasons for their continued widespread use.

## 6.4 Pooling

In a typical CNN, multiple filters are used in parallel in a layer resulting in a corresponding number of feature maps. At this point, the feature maps can be flattened and passed to an ANN, but the resulting vector is rather large (usually much larger than the original image). The feature maps need to be condensed to make them smaller while retaining as much feature information as possible. A useful means of doing so is pooling (122; 134).

The scheme presented here is a convolution called maxpooling (also commonly referred to simply as pooling). The technique is to interpose a pooling layer between a filter layer and a flattening layer. Pooling performs subsampling and condenses the feature information in the feature maps creating new maps. Maxpooling works by summarizing a submatrix with a scaler: the maximum element the submatrix. An example of maxpooling is

$$\underset{a_{i,j}}{\mathrm{argmax}} \begin{pmatrix} 1 & 2 & 2 \\ 3 & 5 & 1 \\ 7 & 4 & 1 \end{pmatrix} = 7. \tag{6.7}$$

It is common to place a maxpooling layer after the first filter layer in a network. The first layer accepts the input image and is therefore the largest. Maxpooling is expected to select the most important aspects of the filter's feature maps. Just like any convolutional kernel, it is applied to the submatrices of an input matrix producing a new result matrix. Every feature map accepted as input is pooled to produce a corresponding output pooled map. The pooled matrices can then be flattened and passed on to a fully connected ANN.

The width of the kernel and the stride are independent hyperparameters of a pooling layer, but the number of result matrices is dictated by the earlier layer. The hyperparameters of both the filter and the pooling layers are often considered together as there is often a target output size, but the resulting pair of hyperparameters are usually different (e.g. a filtering layer with a stride of 1 and kernel width of 5 followed by a pooling layer with a stride of 2 and a width of 2). The number of maxpooling maps is dictated by its input layer.

## 6.5 Feature Layers

With convolutions defined the pieces can be assembled to produce the whole: a CNN. There are 3 hyperparameters defining a convolutional layer with filters. They are the number of the filters (feature maps), the stride, and the dimensions of the filter. The immediately following maxpooling layer, if present, is only free to use different strides and kernel width. For maxpooling layers, the number of output maps is determined by the number of input maps.

It is common to place a pooling layer following the first filter layer in a CNN. Figure 6.5 presents a CNN to classify MNIST digits. The FCFF ANN portion of the model could be quite small, for this example {50, 50, 10} would work well. The convolutional layers of the CNN can be known as the features portion of the CNN, but in modern DL CNNs the distinction is blurred. There can be many filters, and the number of filters, and the number of filter layers, is dictated by the application. The MNIST dataset is a trivial dataset by modern standards, but more challenging images such as those produced by the camera of a mobile phone would require a deeper network. This would include more filter layers, not just a wider filter layer at the top.

It is useful to examine the output of the individual layers to understand what is happening inside the CNN (168). This can be invaluable when debugging. The Figure 6.6 presents the outputs of the convolutional layers of the CNN in Figure 6.5. It was trained to learn the MNIST dataset. The input image was deconstructed into 5 features followed by 5 pooling layers. Problem domain filters have learnt how to recognize features, and maxpooling has summarized the features and the deeper fully connected ANN has an easier job to do.

When considering and designing CNNs, it is helpful to think in terms of the shapes of the tensors. The CNN can be viewed as a pipeline. Data starts at the top and exits at the bottom. In the case of a classifying ANN, the bottom is a softmax layer producing the prediction. Layer after layer shapes and passes on the image. Figure 6.5 depicts the pipeline $28 \times 28 \rightarrow 5 \times 26 \times 26 \rightarrow 5 \times 13 \times 13 \rightarrow 845$. The 5 final maxpool maps are flattened to produce a vector of $169 \times 5 = 845$ elements. 845 is slightly larger than the original 784 vector, but it is packed full of information.

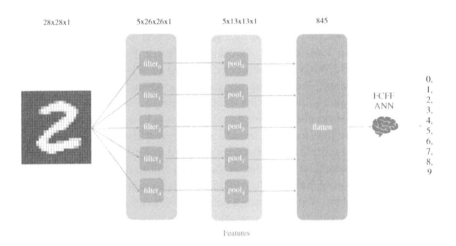

**Figure 6.5** An example of a complete CNN. The CNN is a classifier that accepts examples from the MNIST dataset. The shapes of each layer are inscribed above the layers. There are 5 filters, which each receive a complete copy of the digit, followed by a pooling layer. The strides are 1 and 2, respectively.

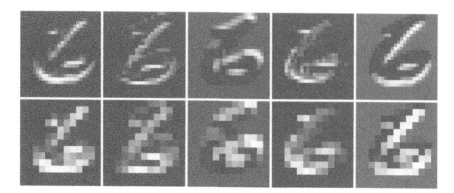

**Figure 6.6** The top row is the result of applying a set of 5 filters to an example "6" from the MNIST dataset. The bottom row presents the result of applying a Maxpool layer to the result. The pipeline is as described in the text.

Convolutions are almost synonymous with DL. The example CNN in Figure 6.5 is trivial by modern standards. A single layer of filters can learn MNIST. The pipeline can be much deeper and include many layers of filters. A more challenging problem would require a deeper CNN. The shallower filters identify useful features and the deeper filters learn compositions of the trivial features. As the CNN gets deeper, the filters learn more complicated artifacts built on the earlier decompositions. The output of filters can be flattened and used as input to a deeper filter layer. A CNN's architecture is dictated by the application, and the shallowest possible should be used. The efficient use of GPUs to train CNNs described in AlexNet (89) set off a race for deeper and wider CNNs. Modern deep networks can have over 22 convolutional layers. Examples include the Googlenet (148) and VGGx (140) networks. Training such large systems requires GPUs and experience. Propagating an accurate gradient so far backward is challenging and prone to disappearing (become zero).

The deepest networks often include a macro structure built with multiple layers to perform a specific job. Googlenet introduced the *inception module*. An inception module combines multiple layers that were designed together to solve a problem. One of the hyperparameters of a filter is the kernel width. An inception module includes a filter layer of multiple filter widths. This is far more challenging than it first appears. The final step of an inception module is to ensure that a consistent shape is passed on (usually with concatenation). The power of the module is that it introduces an element of size invariance in the pipeline. Inceptions module have the capacity to detect an object, e.g. an apple, no matter what size it is when the object is present in an image.

The difficulty and resources required to train DL models have led to the trend of making pretrained models available. An application developer can simply download an appropriate pretrained model and incorporate it in their CNN. The pretrained model can be specialized by appending some appropriate layers and then training. Generally, only the new layers are trained, and the pretrained model is frozen. The result is a specialized model appropriate for the application. The required training to specialize is usually trivial compared to training the full model.

## 6.6 Training a CNN

The training of convolutional layers is based entirely on backpropagation of error. There is nothing in particular that makes convolutional layers challenging to incorporate in a backpropagation scheme. Mathematically, filters and pooling are straight forward. Filters are merely perceptrons, and it has been shown how to train them earlier in Section 3.5. Consequently, both types of layers can be dropped in to a general backpropagation framework. There are, however, some nonmathematical considerations respecting the implementation of the layers. Recall that the CNN can be divided into two distinct pieces, they are the features portion of the network and the fully connected ANN that performs classification. The feature layer is shallower in the network, on top of the classifying ANN. Using the example CNN in Figure 6.5, the task of this section is to expatiate the flow of the gradient through the features section of the network.

The inceptive of step of backpropagation for a CNN is the same as for an ANN; moreover, it is the ANN that is responsible for it: the computation of the loss function. The error is computed normally for a classifier as described in Section 4.2. Backpropagation of the error then takes place up to the interface between the features section of CNN and the fully connected ANN. The weights in the fully connected ANN are updated as usual. The shallowest layer of the fully connected ANN contains deltas, $\delta$, and the gradient must cross into the features portion of the CNN. The first layer encountered is the flattening layer. What is now required is an algorithm to perform the backpropagation through the 3 layers, in order of backpropagation: flatten, pooling, and filter.

### 6.6.1 Flatten and the Gradient

Gradient flow through the flattening layer is trivial reflecting its simple job. To begin recall that the $\delta$s in the fully connected layer are

$$\delta_i = \frac{\partial L}{\partial u_i} \tag{6.8}$$

and these are the basis of propagating the gradient across layers in a fully connected ANN. There are no trainable parameters in the flattening layer. The flattening layer simply reshapes the multiple objects of its input into a single output vector. When transmitting the gradient, it simply does the reverse. The gradient, which is flat when emerges from the ANN, is reshaped to fit the shape the flatten layer expects from its input feature maps. The only task then is to transmit the gradient through the flattening layer. Perceptrons inside of the classifying fully connected ANN propagate the gradient across layers by

$$\phi_\ell = \frac{\partial L}{\partial z_\ell} = W_{\ell+1}^T \cdot \delta_{\ell+1}, \tag{6.9}$$

where $z_\ell$ is the output vector of the flattening layer, $\ell$, and $\phi_\ell$ is the gradient arriving at the flattening layer, $\ell$. The only work to be done by the flattening layer is reshape $\phi_\ell$ to fit the expected input shape. As there are no trainable parameters in the flattening layer, or inflective operations performed on the data, the flattening layer has no effect on the gradient. The gradient is simply transmitted through to be consumed by the immediately shallower layer in the correct shape. Referring back to the example of the CNN depicted in Figure 6.5, $\phi_\ell$ is a vector of 845 elements. It is reshaped to $5 \times 13 \times 13$ and then propagated backward.

### 6.6.2 Pooling and the Gradient

Gradients arriving at the pooling layer are expected to be in the same shape as the output. For every element in the pooling layer's result matrix, there will be an entry in the gradient map. The example pooling layer in the Figure 6.5 has a $5 \times 13 \times 13$ output shape. Consequently, the gradient will also have the same shape when it arrives, $5 \times 13 \times 13$. Once the gradient arrives at a pooling layer, it must be passed through. The gradient that emerges from a pooling layer will have the same shape as its input. Backpropagation will ensure that the $5 \times 13 \times 13$ gradient is passed on to the $5 \times 26 \times 26$ input shape that it received. Every element in the input set to the pooling layer must have a value for the gradient flowing back through it. A pooling layer does not have any learnable parameters so no updates are required inside the pooling layer. The pooling does, however, perform an operation on its input. The effects of the operation must be reflected in the gradient that flows through.

The kernel for maxpooling is $\mathsf{max}(subm)$. The gradient must be passed through the kernel so the derivative of max is required. The max function is not continuous, so it is not differentiable everywhere, but it is differentiable. Let $\alpha = \mathsf{max}(subm)$. Then $\alpha$ is the result of the application of the pooling kernel. Using the definition of a derivative, the gradient can be computed for the max function at that point:

$$\frac{d\mathsf{max}}{d\,subm} = \lim_{h \to 0} \frac{\mathsf{max}(subm + h) - \mathsf{max}(subm)}{h} = \lim_{h \to 0} \frac{\alpha + h - \alpha}{h} = 1. \tag{6.10}$$

Equation (6.10) is the key to passing the gradient through a pooling layer. A similar argument with the limit approaching from the other side yields the same,

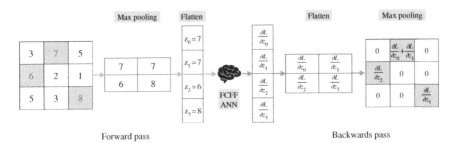

**Figure 6.7** An example of a pooling layer in a forward training pass and the resulting backpropagation of error. The $3 \times 3$ input image is pooled with a $2 \times 2$ kernel and a stride of 1, convolving to a $2 \times 2$ feature map. The ANN computes and propagates the gradient as usual until it reaches the flattening layer. The gradient is reshaped and passed on to the pooling layer. The pooling layer assigns the gradient based on the results of the forward pass (the maxima).

defined, result. Thus we conclude that the derivative for max is defined and equal to either 1 or 0; 1 for the max and zero for all the other arguments. This is intuitive as the arguments that are not the maximum have no effect on the downstream computations. For a pooling layer, $\ell$, $\phi_\ell = \frac{\partial L}{\partial z_\ell}$ is passed back to the maxima and is zero for all other arguments. A pooling layer does not contain any trainable parameters so it merely passes the gradient through, albeit selectively, similarly to the flattening layer. The gradient has the same shape as the input, so the gradient emanating from the pooling layer in Figure 6.5 would be a tensor of shape $5 \times 26 \times 26$.

Mathematically pooling layers do not present any challenges to backpropagation. A pooling layer does, however, require some bookkeeping during training. When computing the maxima for the feature map, a pooling layer needs to record which $a_{i,j}$ produced maxima so that the gradient can be passed back efficiently. In the event of a tie, for example, the background of an image, the gradient should be split equally among all of the inputs in the submatrix. This is not always done and should not be assumed when using third-party libraries (Figure 6.7).

### 6.6.3 Filters and the Gradient

Filters differ from the previous two layers in an important way. Filters have learnable parameters, they are perceptrons, and so they require updating in addition to transmission of the gradient. There is, however, an important difference between perceptrons in dense layers and a filter. The perceptrons encountered so far are in a fully connected layer with dedicated weights. Filters are more complicated as the weights are shared. The weight's loss in a dense layers is computed as

$$\frac{\partial L}{\partial w_i} = \frac{\partial u}{\partial w_i} \cdot \frac{\partial L}{\partial u} = z_i \cdot \delta \qquad (6.11)$$

There is a one to one relationship between a perceptron's weight, $w_i$, and the input $z_i$. The 1:1 relationship permitted the use of Eq. (3.39), a standard matrix product. A filter's weights are not dedicated, and they are shared with several incoming values. There are multiple $z_j$ for the $w_i$ in a filter. There is a further complication in that there is also more than one $\delta$ per weight in a filter. Every entry in the feature map will produce its own $\delta$. The $u$ in Eq. (6.11) is the single vector dot product of the weights and the input, but in a filter it is one of many Frobenius products. Again, one for each entry in the feature map. Indeed, all the terms in red are assumed to have one value in the pure perceptron context, but they have multiple values in the filter setting and must be accounted for in an updated scheme. Equation (6.11) must be modified before it can be used with a filter.

The shared weights of a filter require a change to Eq. (6.11). The plan is to break up the problem into two pieces. To begin the set of $\delta$s are computed, then the final weight update is computed. To arrive at the correct form of loss equation, the feature map must be examined. The filter is producing a map, not just a single value, and an entry in a feature map is computed as

$$z_{i,j} \equiv O_{i,j} = \sigma(F(f, subm_{i,j})). \tag{6.12}$$

The computation is not different from the dense perceptron per se, and it is simply applied repeatedly to many permutations of the inputs producing many distinct results. This is reflected in the indexing. Instead of a single result, there is a map of them. To propagate the gradient backward simply requires doing the same thing, but in reverse. This will produce a map of $\delta$s that can in turn be used to compute the losses. The immediately deeper layer, $\ell + 1$, propagates the gradient in the form of a map. The gradient is a correctly shaped tensor containing the $\frac{\partial L}{\partial O_{i,j}}$s, and these are used to calculate the $\delta$s. The $\delta$s are computed by multiplying them with the derivative of the activation function.

$$\delta_{i,j} = \frac{\partial L}{\partial O_{i,j}} \cdot \frac{\partial O_{i,j}}{\partial F_{i,j}}. \tag{6.13}$$

Figure 6.8 demonstrates the flow. It continues from the pooling example. The general form of activation derivative is shown, but in practice the activation is usually RelU. With the table of $\delta$s computed, the final weight updates can described.

The shared weights of the filter produced a map of results consequently the gradient must flow back through each entry to the weights. The loss for a weight is computed by applying Eq. (6.11) repeatedly, once for each dot product the weight participated in to produce the map. The total derivative for a weight is the sum over all the losses resulting from all of the convolutions that it produced,

$$\frac{\partial L}{\partial w_m} = \sum_{i,j}^{convolutions} x_{p,k} \cdot \delta_{i,j}. \tag{6.14}$$

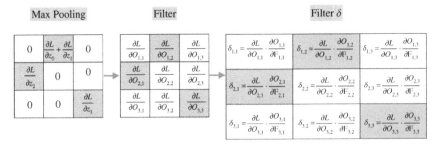

**Figure 6.8** Backpropagation from a pooling layer to a filter. The filter gradient table is simply the Maxpooling gradient renamed (relabeled). The gradient is used to compute the $\delta$s producing a $\delta$ for each instance of weight sharing (convolution). In this example, only 3 of the $\delta$s are nonzero, the blue ones.

**Figure 6.9** Some example weight updates in a filter. A weight accumulates the loss for every element in the feature map that it participated in. This can in turn be computed as a Frobenius product between the table of $\delta$s and the submatrix of the input image that the weight touched. The kernel is $2 \times 2$ and the stride is 2.

Note that $x_{p,k}$ has different indexing, it the argument from the input map that produced the convolution. This equation can be expressed as a Frobenius product between the input image and the map of $\delta$s. The Frobenius product is computed for each weight in the filter. The submatrix of the input image changes to match those elements that the weight touched when computing the feature map. The process is depicted graphically in Figure 6.9.

For the example in Figure 6.5, the backpropagation would be terminated at this point, but it is a trivial example with a single feature layer. State-of-the-art DL CNNs have many filter layers. It follows that the gradient must be transmitted through a filter to shallower layers. The dedicated weight form of interlayer gradient passage is Eq. (6.9). Not only are the weights shared in a filter but the elements of the input are as well. It is clear that the gradient propagation equation must also be emended to deal with convolutions.

The same strategy that was employed for derivatives of filter weights can also be used for the gradient's passage. For a particular point in the input image, the total gradient is accumulated by summing all of the losses emanating from the convolutions in which it participated. The actual computation is similar to the filter weights. Instead of a single computation, the dedicated weight version is applied repeatedly. The result will be a gradient in the same shape as the layer's input.

$$\frac{\partial L}{x_{p,k}} = \overset{convolutions}{\underset{i,j}{\sum}} \delta_{i,j} \cdot w_k. \tag{6.15}$$

The maximum length of a sum for any point in the transmitted gradient is the kernel width squared. The computation itself can also be expressed as a Frobenius product. Equation (6.15) is the Frobenius of the filter with the $\delta$ map corresponding with the convolutions in which the pixel participated. Prior to use the filter's matrix must be reversed. This is because the input map's elements interact with the filter in the reverse order. An input element can participate in at most filter size number of convolutions. If an element contributes to the maximum number, then it is in the order starting from $w_{n-1}$ in reverse order to $w_0$. To reflect the order of usage, the filter matrix must be reversed, not just transposed, as the diagonal needs to change as well.

$$\text{filter} = \begin{pmatrix} w_0 & w_1 & w_2 \\ w_3 & w_4 & w_5 \\ w_6 & w_7 & w_8 \end{pmatrix} \implies \text{filter}_{BPG} \begin{pmatrix} w_8 & w_7 & w_6 \\ w_5 & w_4 & w_3 \\ w_2 & w_1 & w_0 \end{pmatrix} \tag{6.16}$$

To propagate the error to a shallower layer, a map of the same dimensions as the input is built containing the gradient. The complete prodecure is presented in Algorithm 6.1.

A filter layer may have either a 1:1 relationship with its input, or a 1:many. This exposes a potential dichotomy of two cases respecting the input shape. The example in Figure 6.5 is 1:many. The single input image produces many feature maps. A filter can also accept a number of maps producing a 1:1 relationship. Both cases are handled the same way despite the superficial appearance of a complication. The gradient needs to flow through each element of the input shape, that is, the total gradient of any convolutions that involved the element needs to be accumulated, regardless of the shape of the input. In the case of 1:1, then gradient has the shape nFilters × rows × columns. 1:many simply sums the individual gradient maps to produce the correct shape (and gradient).

The implementation of a convolutional layer must include 3 functions. The layer implements a forward pass, the application of a kernel. It must also include support for a backward pass. The backward pass must update learnable parameters as well as propagating the gradient through it. Any layer that implements this functionality can be dropped in to a CNN library. The importance of designing a flexible API is clear. New convolutional layers must implement the API to be used in a software library. The API should make it easy for new convolutions to be implemented without having to make changes in the rest of the library. Verifying the shapes of the data going between the layers is vital to ensure bugs are caught early.

**Algorithm 6.1** Push a Gradient Through a Filter

1: **procedure** AcceptGradient($G_{\ell+1}$)          ▷ Accepts deeper gradient
2:    **for** f in filters and $G$ in $G_{\ell+1}$ **do**          ▷ Performed per feature in layer
3:       **for** $F_{i,j}$ in f.map **do**
4:          $\delta_{i,j} \leftarrow G_{i,j} \cdot \frac{\partial O}{\partial F_{i,j}}$          ▷ Derivative depends on activation fn used
5:       **end for**          ▷ $\delta$ is a map
6:       PropagateToFilter $(\delta, f)$
7:          ▷ Concatenate or sum, depending on input shape
8:       $G_\ell$.append (ComputeGradient $(\delta, f)$)
9:    **end for**
10:    **return** $G_\ell$          ▷ return the gradient
11: **end procedure**
12: **procedure** PropagateToFilter($\delta, f$)
13:    **for** $w_i$ in f.weights **do**
14:       $\Delta w_i$ += $F(\delta, Im, i)$
15:    **end for**
16: **end procedure**
17: **procedure** ComputeGradient($\delta, f$)
18:    $G \leftarrow \varnothing$
19:    $filter_{BPG} \leftarrow$ Reverse($filter$)
20:    **for** $x_{i,j}$ in $Im$ **do**
21:       $Gi, j \leftarrow F(i, j, \delta, filter_{BPG})$          ▷ Must account for padding
22:    **end for**
23:    **return** $G$
24: **end procedure**

## 6.7 Applications

CNNs have many applications. Their origins lie in image recognition, but their power extends far beyond that field. Convolutions are adept at dealing with shift-invariant data that is also quasi-translation invariant. The world abounds with such problems. The following rules of thumb should be considered when designing a model:

1. 1-dimensional convolutions are useful when performing signal processing. Some examples are text and sound. Text can be a natural language processing problem (see Section 9.4.1 ). Sound can be music, speech – there are many more.

2. 2-dimensional convolutions should be considered when dealing with any kind of grid data. As has been demonstrated, images are of particular importance. This includes object detection and recognition tasks.
3. 3-dimensional convolutions should be considered when working with video and volumetric data. Video can be viewed as a string of 2-dimensional images; video can be dealt with convolutional tensors. Volumetric data is a 3-dimensional image; a data point $(x, y, z, w(= RGB))$. The value specified at the point is often an RGB color. Mineral search, such as geological surveys, commissioned searching for oil produce volumetric data. Medical imaging is an application where CNNs have proved immensely successful. CNNs are already better than human radiologists finding cancer (103).
4. In general, CNNs are useful with multidimensional arrays (tensors).

CNNs can also be used to play games. AlphaGo (139) is the most famous example. It uses a 12-layer CNN, trained with reinforcement learning, to identify potential moves. Go is a game with a great deal of potential symmetry, and convolutions are good identifying them. Multiple-layers identify the recursive nature of the patterns.

## 6.8 Summary

CNN almost always stands for convolutional neural network, not classifying neural network. CNNs are ANNs with at least one convolutional layer. Of particular interest is the filter, it regularizes a neural network while extracting learned features. Filters work on grids by identifying components of interest regardless of where they are in an input grid. They can be trained with normal backpropagation making them attractive for incorporation in ANN software libraries. When designing and reasoning about a CNN, it important to think about the flow of data in terms of shapes and what layers are doing with them.

## 6.9 Projects

The aim of these projects is provide insight and experience into how the performance of a CNN responds to changes in its hyperparameters. The projects are based on the Python notebook that can be found here, https:// github.com/nom-de-guerre/DDL_book/tree/main/Ch06. The notebook is called, MNIST06.ipynb. The site includes directions for obtaining the data (MNIST).

1. Plot the percentage correct of the test set as a function of the number of features in the first layer.
2. Plot the percentage correct of the test set as a function of the width of the FFFC initial dense layer.
3. Plot the time versus percentage correct of the test set as a function of kernel width and number of features.

# 7

# Fixing the Fit

So far this book has demonstrated how to train articial neural networks (ANNs). While theoretically the methods presented thus far should be sufficient to train practical models, there are further points to bear in mind when designing practical software to train models. There are techniques that accelerate convergence of training. Trained models also need to be verified to confirm that they are suitable. These considerations imply that there are a few more ancillary concepts that are required to successfully implement a deep learning (DL) library. We cover the most important points in this chapter.

## 7.1  Quality of the Solution

Once training has been completed, we can be confident that our ANN has learnt the training data to the required degree. The model has converged, and the training loss has sunk below the specified tolerance. In general, however, models are trained for applications that have to deal with data that are not in the training set. The trained ANN must infer correctly from unseen data. The value of a DL model is its ability to perform inference. Therefore, it is important to understand how a trained model will *generalize* to unseen data. Following training, we can use the model with the training data and that results in the training error, but that only tells us about data that our model has already seen. We are really interested in the model's error with unseen data. This error is called the generalization error. Estimating the generalization error is the subject of this section. To that end, we will also introduce some important terminologies and concepts.

Finding a reliable estimation of the generalization error is challenging. A statistical argument could be made that as the training data, and the unseen data are produced from the same underlying, but unknown, process, it follows that the unseen data must be similarly distributed so the generalization error and the

*Demystifying Deep Learning: An Introduction to the Mathematics of Neural Networks,*
First Edition. Douglas J. Santry.
© 2024 The Institute of Electrical and Electronics Engineers, Inc. Published 2024 by John Wiley & Sons, Inc.

training error should be the same. The argument is based on the assumption that the training data and the unseen data are all independently and identically distributed samples, so the model should perform just as well with unseen data. This argument is, however, naïve.

## 7.2 Generalization Error

Let us examine the problem of estimating the generalization error with respect to the MSE loss function. The expectation of the generalization error can be defined as, $\mathbb{E}[(\hat{y} - y)^2]$, which is the expectation of the loss function. The components are $\hat{y} \equiv ANN(x)$, $x$ is the observed predictor, and $y$ is the ground truth. Of course the ground truth will probably not be available in production[1]; if it was available, then there would be no need for the model. None the less some conclusions can be drawn from the expectation. The expression can be expanded by recalling the definition of the variance of a random variable, $\sigma^2 = \mathbb{E}[z^2] - \mathbb{E}[z]^2$. If we rearrange the terms, we obtain $\mathbb{E}[z^2] = \mathbb{E}[z]^2 + \sigma^2$. Letting $z_i = \hat{y}_i - y_i$ the result is

$$\mathbb{E}[(\hat{y} - y)^2] = \mathbb{E}[\hat{y} - y]^2 + \sigma^2. \tag{7.1}$$

There are two terms on the right. The first is the square of the *bias*. The second term is the variance. Let us deal with these two terms separately. But first, it is important to realize that during training the model is the result of both the act of training and the effect of the training set. A different training set, or indeed, just a different seed to the random number generator, would yield a different model. The trained model is very much a variable in this context.

### 7.2.1 Bias

The bias of a model is defined as $bias = \mathbb{E}[\hat{y} - y]$. It is a measure of how wrong a model is relative to the underlying ground truth, or the generative process. Ideally, a model would be unbiased, that is, the bias would be 0. Informally, we can interpret it as a measure of how wrong our assumptions are about the underlying process producing the data. The canonical example is the Bernoulli distribution,

$$P(X = q) = \mu^q \cdot (1 - \mu)^{1-q}. \tag{7.2}$$

It is the special case of the Binomial distribution where $n = 1$ and $q$ takes on the values of either 0 or 1. It is used for binary outcomes. Given a set of outcomes,

---

1 Production means that the Deep Learning model has been deployed and in real use by the application.

$\{q_1, q_2, \ldots, q_N\}$, $\mu$ can be estimated as

$$\hat{\mu} = \frac{1}{N} \sum_{i}^{N} q_i, \tag{7.3}$$

which is an unbiased estimator. The bias is $\mathbb{E}[\hat{\mu} - \mu]$, and we can see that as $N \to \infty$ then $\hat{\mu} \to \mu$ and the *bias* $\to 0$. Thus, it is an unbiased estimator of $\mu$. The estimator understands the underlying process generating the observable data. Of course this is a trivial example of parametric estimation. An ANN is far more complicated and models are more complex objects than simple parametric estimators. The bias is rarely zero. There are a number of interpretations of model bias.

In the context of ANNs, a model with a high bias does not explain the training set well. Recall the example of a least squares fitting of the sine curve in Section 3.4. The bias was extremely high, and intuitively it is clear why: sine is not linear, that is, the model was "wrong." In machine learning (ML) this phenomenon is known as *underfitting*. The trained model does not explain the training data well. The size of the training set can be increased, but the quality of the results will not improve. Low bias is a desideratum of a ML model.

Underfitting of ANNs can occur when either the loss threshold is too high or the loss threshold cannot be met. In the latter case, the ANN's capacity to learn the training set was not sufficiently high. Either there are not enough layers or there are not enough neurons (or both). The more neurons there are the more trainable parameters, and the learning capacity of the ANN is increased. The number of neurons can be increased by either increasing the depth of the ANN or widening a layer.

### 7.2.2 Variance

The second term of generalized error is the variance. It is a measure of how the models produced vary with respect to sampling the underlying process. A training set is a sample of an underlying process or phenomenon. The training set is, in effect, a random variable. For a given statistic, e.g. arithmetic mean, it will vary from training set to training set, but the underlying process itself has an unknown mean. So in a very real sense the model is a function of the training set, which is in turn a random variable. The variance is a measure of how the performance of the model varies with respect to sampling the underlying process. Models with high variance tend to lead to *overfitting*; learning the data too well to the exclusion of generalizing. Low variance of a model is a desideratum. Overfitting is the effect of learning the training set to the point of being unable to recognize similar, but unseen, data. Consider the 5 examples of the hand-written digit, 3, in Figure 7.1. If we trained an ANN to learn the right-most example perfectly, then it would fail to recognize the remaining 4 examples. The model will have overfitted and only

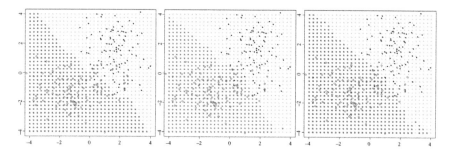

**Figure 7.1**  Sample of hand-written 3s from the MNIST dataset.

recognize the 3 that it learnt to the exclusion of unseen, but genuine 3s. Overfitting can be addressed with a number of mechanisms. For example, the training set can be improved by adding further examples of 3s. More information leads to a more robust model. The training can also be terminated sooner so the ANN's idea of what exactly constitutes a "3" is broader, that is, more *general*. The latter is far more difficult to get right. Ideally, the training process itself could be made more robust.

### 7.2.3   The Bias-Variance Trade-off

Returning to the measure of the generalization error, the expectation $\mathbb{E}[(\hat{y} - y)^2] = \mathbb{E}[\hat{y} - y]^2 + \sigma^2$ can be viewed as, *bias*$^2$ + *variance*. There is a great deal of theory surrounding bias and variance in ML (61). It has been postulated that there exists a fundamental tension when training ANNs, and ML in general, known as the bias variance trade-off. When training a model one has to trade-off the bias against the variance, or vice versa. It is argued that this is a general constraint that applies to all ML models.

Consider the Figure 7.2. For a given training set, we show the decision boundary resulting by varying the hyper-parameter, $k$, for 3 $k$-nearest-neighbors (kNN) models (60). For the same training set, we obtain radically different decision boundaries. For small $k$, the model is extremely sensitive to the slightest change

**Figure 7.2**  kNN models for a static dataset. The data are produced as pairs of normally distributed $(x, y)$, and the classes have different means to produce the geometrical differentiation. From left to right $k = 5$, 10, and 25. Note that the decision boundary becomes far more regular with increasing $k$.

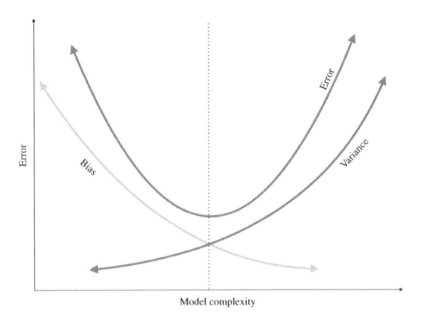

**Figure 7.3** The classical bias-variance trade-off. The minimum of the error occurs as the bias and variance intersect. Underfitting occurs to the left of the dotted line and overfitting to the right.

in the training set, so it has high variance, but we obtain low bias. There are fewer misclassifications of the training set, but any change in the training set will produce a very different model. If we increase $k$ to reduce the variance, we observe that the bias is increasing and the number of misclassifications is also increasing; the decision boundary is becoming straighter and less jagged. Adjusting either of the bias or variance has an inverse effect on the other. Thus, it is suggested that in ML, there is a fundamental tension between overfitting and underfitting, the bias-variance trade-off (137). The relationship is demonstrated in Figure 7.3. The diagram depicts the classic "U" shaped error curve. The best a model can do is find the minimum of the error curve.

Recall that bias can be construed as how "wrong" a model is. Least squares is an example of a high bias model, but it is also a low variance model. Changing a few points in the training set is unlikely to dramatically change the resultant slope. Generally, the more complex a model, the higher the variance and the lower the bias. In the context of ANNs, this is viewed with respect to the number of param-eters, the majority of which are usually weights. The more parameters in a model the greater its capacity to learn. Overfitting is also known as overparameterization.

### 7.2.4    The Bias-Variance Trade-off in Context

The relevance of the bias-variance trade-off to ANNs is currently hotly debated. Many have observed that it does not seem to apply in practice. It is certainly difficult to demonstrate without contriving unrealistic constraints on the ANN, hence the use of a kNN model to demonstrate the concept. An important early work that examined the relationship in the specific context of an ANN is a paper written by Geman et al. (46). They examined the bias-variance trade-off in the context of ML algorithms, including clustering algorithms and ANNs. The authors successfully demonstrated the operation of the trade-off in all the models they examined, except ANNs. They assumed there was a problem with the training, but claimed the trade-off applied to ANNs as well.[2] Later work has shown that bias and variance seem to have a different relationship in ANNs (28); these authors refer to the bias variance trade-off as a dogma in connection to ANNs. Both the bias and the variance can simultaneously go up or down. The authors further suggest an explanation for the problems described in Geman suggesting that their experiments are correct, but their conclusions mistaken. Certainly, extreme caution must be exercised when discussing bias-variance trade-off in the context of ANNs.

More appropriate measures of ANN model performance have been proposed, and they appear to be fruitful areas of research, for example, the theory of "double descent" (10) and effective model complexity (EMC) (72). Whatever the conclusions, ANNs are a field of ML, and ML is sensitive to the bias-variance argument. The debate will doubtless continue, and every practitioner should have a reasonable grasp of the concept. Regardless of the precise relationship between the bias and the variance, overfitting and underfitting are phenomena that are very real and need to be carefully monitored. To produce quality DL models practical methods are required to evaluate generalization.

### 7.2.5    The Test Set

It is clear that meeting a target loss when training a model is not sufficient grounds for accepting a model. A further means to increase confidence in the result is indicated, ideally quantitative and empirical. In this section, we examine how to approximate the generalization error with a *test set*.

Training an ANN is performed with a training set. While it may appear that dataset and training set have been used synonymously, they have not been. The training set comes from the dataset, but not necessarily all of it. Prior to training, it is good practice to divide the dataset in to two disjoint sets, training and test.

---

2 The authors were acting in good faith and behaved correctly. The raw data was presented and the problem discussed openly. The authors believed they had failed when they had actually succeeded in finding something very interesting. It was very good science.

The training set is used to fit the model. The test set is kept in reserve to be used to validate the fitted model following training; its data are never used during training and remain unseen by the model throughout. Assuming the dataset as a whole truly represents the ground truth of the problem domain, then the test set can be used to estimate how the model will really behave when deployed, that is, how it will generalize to unseen data.

The procedure is as follows. The dataset is split between the training set and the test set. The model is fitted to the training set. With the test set, an estimation of the generalization error can now be computed by using the model to perform inference on every datum in said set. As the ground truth is available for the test set, the performance of the model can be quantified. For regressors, the MSE loss is used as the performance metric. The quality of classifiers could also be gauged with their loss function, but typically accuracy is used (percentage correct). The percentage typically ranges between 100% and $(100/K)\%$, where $K$ is the number of distinct classes. A test error of 100% suggests that the model is working very well (if that was the training accuracy overfitting may have occurred). Accuracy of $1/K$ indicates that the model is totally broken. Random guessing is just as accurate; hence, the lower bound. If the test loss, or accuracy, are not tolerable, then the model should be revisited and subsequently retrained.

The ratio of the sizes of test to training sets varies with the size of the dataset as a whole. A training set that consists of circa 100,000 examples or more can be split up as 90:10 training:test. But for smaller datasets, larger proportions of test and training are required. If the training set is small, then an assumption is made that training the model is cheap. In this case, a technique called *folding* is used.

The technique of folding provides for training and validating a model multiple times. This is actually best practice in general, but as fitting models can be expensive there are occasions when it is simply too expensive to train and validate multiple times. The procedure of folding is as follows. The dataset is randomly split in to two disjoint sets, the values of 2/3 training and 1/3 test is a good choice. The random divisions of the data are known as folds. For classification, the proportions of examples for each class should be the same, but this generally happens naturally with uniform sampling. A model is trained with the training set and then its performance with the test set computed. The process is repeated multiple times. The final result is the mean and standard deviation of the accuracies of the individual runs. Following a number of folds, confidence can be had in the hyperparameters that produced the model, which in turn suggests that the model is good.

Finally, overfitting can be avoided with a third division of the data, a *verification* set. A verification set is disjoint from the training set. During training, the model is verified with the verification set following the execution of each epoch. When the model achieves 100% accuracy with the verification set training is halted. This can be expensive, but it is effective.

## 7.3 Classification Performance

Understanding the performance of classifiers can be challenging. Should the test error prove to be 100% accurate, then confidence can be had in the trained model. When the test error is below the required threshold, then it is instructive to examine the results in more detail. An important method is that of the confusion matrix (113), it is a form of Pearson's contingency table (111). An example is presented in Figure 7.4 for the iris dataset. The iris dataset contains 150 entries representing 3 species of iris. There are 50 examples of each of the three species represented in the set. The $k$-fold test method was used on an ANN classifier with a ratio of 1/3 for the test set and 5 folds[3] (the parameter of the folding has nothing to do with the number of classes); so there were 250 predictions made with 5 separate models. The confusion matrix can be used to interpret the results.

Given a classifier with $K$ distinct classes, a confusion matrix is a $K \times K$ matrix of outcomes. The columns are the ground truth, and the rows are the predictions of the model. Given an example from a test set, the model makes a prediction. The confusion matrix is updated by incrementing the entry at, (prediction, target). Ideally, only the diagonal on the matrix would be populated, and all other entries would be zero. Such a result coincides with 100% accuracy. For larger or

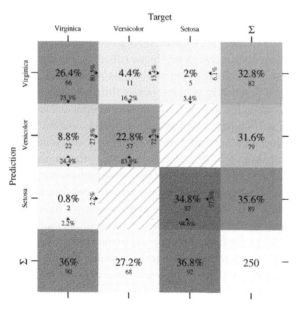

**Figure 7.4** A confusion for the Iris dataset and a trained ANN. As there are 3 species of iris in the dataset the confusion matrix. This is the $3 \times 3$ matrix rooted in the top left of the matrix. Entries include nominal totals and percentages. In addition the lower row and right-most colunm include global summaries.

---

3 The iris dataset is very easy to learn, so training was terminated early to make the confusion matrix "interesting."

complicated problems, this is unlikely. A good model will be diagonally dominant. The confusion matrix captures a great deal of the behavior of a model.

Examination of the confusion matrix suggests that there are four possible outcomes. They are

**True Positive (TP):** A TP is the correct classification. They are found on the diagonal of the confusion matrix. For the species, `virginica`, the entry at $(1, 1)$ represents the TPs, 66.

**False Positive (FP):** A FP is an example that was classified as particular class incorrectly. They are found in the row for a class, excluding the diagonal entry: $FP_i = \sum_{j \neq i}^{K} m_{i,j}$. For `virginica`, $FP1 = 11 + 5 = 16$.

**True Negative (TN):** A TN is an example that is not a member of a class that is not classified as a member of the class. It is the remainder of the matrix that, for class $k$, excludes row $k$ and column $k$, $TN_k = \sum_{i \neq k}^{K} \sum_{j \neq k}^{K} m_{i,j}$. Thus, for `versicolors`, $TN2 = 66 + 6 + 2 + 87 = 161$.

**False Negative (FN):** A FN is a member of a class that was misclassified as another, incorrect, class. For a class, $k$, its FNs are found in the column $k$, excluding the diagonal entry, $FP_j = \sum_{i \neq j}^{K} m_{i,j}$. The FN count for `virginica` is $FN1 = 22 + 2 = 24$.

All four quantities can be computed for each of the $K$ classes of a classifier individually. With these definitions, further definitions can made leading to more insight in the confusion matrix. The quantities defined above are referred to by their acronyms.

*Precision* is defined as $TP/(TP + FP)$. It is a measure of how well a classifier discriminates between a given class and the other classes. For example, medical data is often not as uniformly distributed as the iris dataset. A classifier trained on an experiment looking at serious disease may have far more healthy examples than disease positive examples. A dataset arising from a medical study might contain 95 healthy individuals and only 5 with heart disease. The model could classify all examples in the dataset as healthy yielding 95% accuracy, yet it is clear that the model does not work; it has no value. The precision metric would be infinite for the case of heart disease indicating that the model does not work (the denominator is 0). Accuracy does not tell the whole story. Precision punishes models for making mistakes, not simply giving them credit when they get something right. The highest precision a model can get is 1.0, which occurs when there are no FPs. This can be important, classifying a sick person as healthy is potentially a serious mistake. The opposite, while not ideal, is not as serious.

*Recall* is defined as $TP/(TP + FN)$, where $TP + FN =$ all instances of a class in the test dataset. It is a measure of how well the model "remembers" the class. In the example of the broken model for heart disease, the recall is 0.0, another indicator that the classifier does not work. The best recall possible is 1.0, which occurs when there are no FNs.

A further higher level measure of correctness is the $F1$-score of the matrix. It is a measure of how the model is doing with respect to all of the classes. The per class score is defined as

$$F1_k = 2 \cdot \frac{precision_k \cdot recall_k}{precision_k + recall_k},\qquad(7.4)$$

where $k$ is the class being examined. The best $F1$ score is 1. The precision and recalls have a maximum of 1 so the fractional part of the expression peaks at 0.5. The $F1$ is scaled by a factor of 2 to make it a normal metric. It can be interpreted as the covariance of precision and recall.

For the `virginica` class we have, precision $= 66/(66 + 16) = 0.805$, and the recall $= 66/(66 + 24) = 0.733$. This gives $F1 = 0.767$. Whether this value is acceptable is based on the application. For disease detection, this is probably far too low.

The scores can be combined to sum up the performance of the model. The $F$ score for each class is first computed. The final step is to combine the individual $F1$ scores into a single score for the entire matrix. The two most popular methods are variants of the arithmetical mean. The simplest method is that of the arithmetic mean of the $F$-scores for a confusion matrix,

$$F_{total} = \frac{1}{K}\sum_{i}^{K} F_i.\qquad(7.5)$$

The second method is simply a weighted version. The terms are weighted by the percentage of the test set it represents. The weighted mean is not always appropriate. For example, if used with the healthy-skewed medical dataset, the heart disease class is the most important class, and we do not want it overwhelmed by weighting the healthy people. The weightings can be synthesized to increase the importance of the disease positive cases.

There are many different measures possible when examining a confusion matrix. The Matthews correlation coefficient (MCC) takes better account of the FNs in multiclass models (14). For important applications where coverage and efficacy are really important, it can make sense to employ a framework incorporating many aspects of classification performance. The restrictedness and bias-dispersion are just two metrics used in a complete framework to quantify correctness and incorrectness of models by the authors of class dispersion (37). There are many possibilities. The correct choice depends on the requirements of the application. Metrics are a double-edged sword. Goodhart's law states that any metric becomes useless as soon as it is stated. What he meant was that people tend to lose sight of what they are trying to measure, instead they focus on the optimizing the number. A framework of metrics can slow the effect down.

## 7.4   Regularization

A serious problem when training models is the phenomenon of overfitting. This is of particular concern in larger and deeper networks. One means of addressing the problem is with *regularization*. Regularization is the act of calibrating models such that overfitting is less likely. The particular technique that we describe in this section is called neuron dropout, it is also known as dilution.

An important technique in ML is known as the ensemble method. To increase the accuracy of a system multiple models are trained. Together, all the trained models form a set of models, or an ensemble. When performing inference, the entire ensemble of models is used and some means of aggregating their responses is taken, that is, all the models cast a vote for the final result (e.g. the arithmetic mean of their responses). While effective, this technique is impractical for the larger neural networks where the memory, training time, and inference time may be prohibitive. A method to realize some of the benefits of ensemble methods in a single large neural network was developed called dropout (68; 144; 157).

When used with ANNs, the training infrastructure requires some minor modification. Up until now, the forward pass of an ANN was the same regardless of training or inference. Dropout requires different forward passes for both cases. The forward pass is different when training. The training infrastructure needs to inform the ANN when training has stopped and started. The remainder of the section describes dropout for all phases of use.

### 7.4.1   Forward Pass During Training

The dropout idea is both straight forward and elegant. Prior to training, every neuron in the network is assigned a probability, $p_{dropout}$, that determines its probability of being included in a given forward pass of training; typically, the dropout probability is the same for an entire layer. The coarser granularity of specification is easier to manage, and there is no real advantage to varying the probabilities within a layer. Prior to performing a forward pass in a dropout layer, we determine which neurons are present. Inclusion in the forward pass is determined by sampling the uniform distribution; this is done for each neuron in the layer. Those neurons which are determined not to be present are not included in the forward pass. Thus, each forward pass during training is in a network that is a subset of the original full network, and we have approximated an ensemble. There are exponentially many possible subnetworks that can be embedded in the original network, see Figure 7.5. If there are $n$ neurons, then there are $2^n$ possible subgraphs. Once training has been completed, inference always includes the full network. Dropout is performed for each element in the training set (the forward pass) during training, but only during training. Dropout is easily implemented by simply adding a

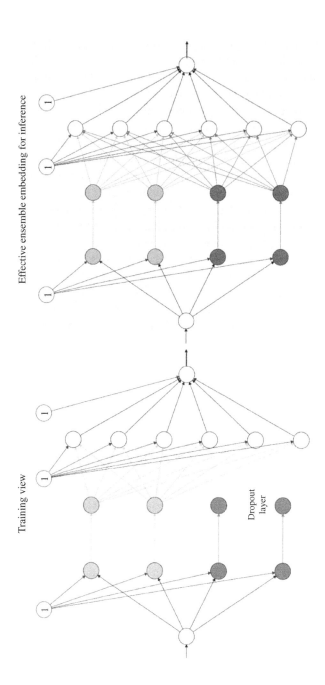

**Figure 7.5** An example of an ANN with a dropout layer. The left side shows a possible configuration with a dropout of 0.5. The right side shows the logical ensemble resulting from training. The subnet changes for every element of the training set.

step to normal layer computation. The modification is shown in Algorithm 7.1. Layers compute their usual output. The list of dead neurons is computed for this forward pass and their states are set to 0.0.

---

**Algorithm 7.1** Dropout for a Dense Layer's Training Forward Pass

1: **procedure** DROPOUTTRAININGFORWARD
2:  $\bar{z} \leftarrow \sigma(Wx + b)$
3:  $\bar{\beta} \leftarrow U(M_\ell)$ ▷ vector uniformly sampled $[0, 1]$ for each neuron.
4:  $\beta \leftarrow \bar{\beta} > p_{dropout}$ ▷ vector of True/False (1/0)
5:  $z \leftarrow \beta \otimes \bar{z}$ ▷ Element-wise multiplication
6: **end procedure**

---

### 7.4.2 Forward Pass During Normal Inference

The forward pass for normal inference needs to be modified to accommodate an ANN trained with dropout. During training, the forward pass only used subnets of the complete graph, the result of dropout. The forward pass during normal inference does not use dropout. Every neuron is always on. Recall the initial dot product for a neuron's state,

$$u = \sum_{i}^{M_{\ell-1}} x_i w_i. \tag{7.6}$$

A problem arises if $\ell - 1$ used dropout during training. $u$ will be smaller during training than during inference. Some percentage of the $x_i$ will be zero during training resulting in consistently smaller dot products. All of the weights deeper in the network will be calibrated for weaker signals. Turning all the neurons on again results in propagating stronger responses than deeper layers observed during training. Once training has terminated layers beneath a dropout layer need to adjust how they compute their state. The expectation of a neuron's dot product during training is

$$\mathbb{E}(u) = \sum p_i x_i w_i, \tag{7.7}$$

where $p_i$ is assigned per layer, the previous layer. Then we can rewrite it as

$$\mathbb{E}(u) = p_{\ell-1} \sum x_i w_i. \tag{7.8}$$

Note that it is the deeper layer accounting for the shallower layer's dropouts. This suggests that the deeper layer's vector of dot products can be performed as

$$u_\ell = p_{\ell-1} W_\ell z_{\ell-1}, \tag{7.9}$$

where we have simply scaled the usual computation with the $p_{dropout}$ of the shallower layer. The resulting signal has been attenuated and will produce more consistent behavior deeper in the ANN.

### 7.4.3 Backpropagation of Error

Just as the forward passes required some modifications so does the backward pass. The backpropagation of error only requires a minor modification. The dropout step needs to be accounted for in the backward pass. Only those neurons that were included in the forward pass should be included in the back propagation. The gradient cannot flow along paths that are dead ends. Dropout is differentiable, and so it can be easily incorporated in the backward pass. This is confirmed as follows:

$$\frac{\partial L}{\partial \bar{z}_i} = \frac{\partial L}{\partial z_i} \cdot \frac{\partial z_i}{\partial \bar{z}_i} = \frac{\partial L}{\partial z_i} \cdot \beta_i, \tag{7.10}$$

where the $\beta_i$ was computed during the forward pass. Consequently, entries in the vector will be only be 1 if the neuron was included in the forward pass, zero otherwise. The resulting gradient is zero for dead neurons.

A potentially onerous drawback of this form of regularization is the different methods of computing the forward pass of an ANN when training and performing inference. As described thus far, a training step involved the normal forward pass of an ANN followed by a backward pass. The forward pass is the same whether training or performing inference. Dropout requires a mechanism, sometimes called "freezing," where the model is informed that training has terminated and the inference version of forward computation is required. This requires more infrastructure in a software implementation.

On a practical note, many implementations use "inverted dropout." During training, the responses are scaled so that learning is not affected by dropout. Then normal inference can be used. This still requires a different code-path for the forward pass during training, but the inference forward pass remains unchanged. Inverted dropout isolates the changes to the layer that is using dropout. The deeper layer does not need to know anything about its immediate predecessor, and that is very desirable. The updated algorithm is specified in Algorithm 7.2.

---

**Algorithm 7.2** Inverted Dropout for a Dense Layer's Training Forward Pass

---

1: **procedure** DROPOUTTRAININGFORWARD
2:     $\bar{z} \leftarrow \sigma(Wx + b)$
3:     $\bar{\beta} \leftarrow U(M_\ell)$          $\triangleright$ vector uniformly sampled $[0, 1]$ for each neuron.
4:     $\beta \leftarrow \bar{\beta} > p_{dropout}$          $\triangleright$ vector of True/False (1/0)
5:     $z \leftarrow \frac{1}{p_{dropout}} \cdot \beta \otimes \bar{z}$          $\triangleright$ Element-wise multiplication
6: **end procedure**

---

Despite the potential difficulties, the essence of the method is relatively simple so dropout is a popular means of regularizing models. There are two ways to implement the technique efficiently. One way is to retrofit it to existing implementations

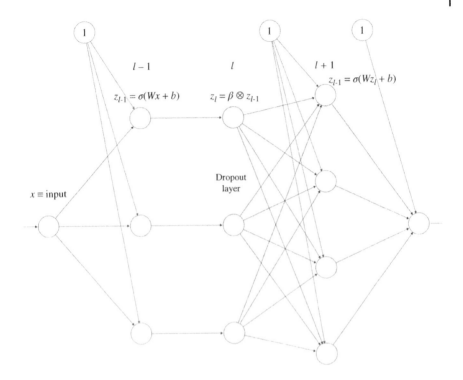

**Figure 7.6** The architecture of a dropout implementation. The dropout logic is interposed in an isolated layer. The layer deals with the implementation while keeping the other implementations ignorant of what is happening.

of layers, which has been described. The most popular way, however, is to introduce a specialized dropout layer. The dropout layer is placed immediately deeper to the target dense layer. A specialized layer has two advantages. The particulars of dropout are encapsulated entirely and isolated in one place. An encapsulated layer makes code reuse easy. The dropout layer does not have to be retrofitted to every type of layer in the library; all existing layers in the library get dropout for free. An example architecture is shown in Figure 7.6. A dedicated dropout layer can be placed as the deeper neighbor in a model beside any type of layer that needs to be regularized. The latter does not even know, effectively creating the illusion that the shallower layer is a dropout layer. Dropout layers form an important tool for regularizing DL models. They are, however, used sparingly, for example, as the final layer in a deep ANN prior to softmax. It is rare to see a dropout layer following every dense layer in a model.

Figure 7.5 gives an example of training with dropout. A specialized dropout layer performs the regularization. During training, the dropout layer decides which neurons will participate, they are light, and which ones to drop, the dark neurons. This happens for every example in the training set. The connections between the regularized layer and the dropout layer are 1:1, not dense. The two dense layers are oblivious to the regularization. The dropout layer accepts the output of the shallower layer and zeros out the entries for the excluded neurons. The new result vector is then passed on as usual, all:all. The dropout layer has no effect on back-propagation phase of the training step. The gradient is received by the dropout layer, and the entries for the precluded neurons are zeroed. The dropout layer then passes the gradient back to the shallower layer.

Regularization is important for training DL models. The learning capacity of an ANN is proportional to the number of neurons. Selecting the right number is difficult. Underfitting is relatively easy to detect, but overfitting it more difficult. Adding neurons to fit the model is common response, and dropout layers help keep the potential overfitting at bay. A software implementation should be verified with the technique of differencing equations presented in Section 3.7

## 7.5 Advanced Normalization

In Section 3.1, it was argued that preprocessing data by normalizing was critical for successful training. Normalizing the training set produces desirable numerical and statistical effects for the input layer. Hidden layers also have the same problems. While preprocessing ameliorates potential numerical problems for the input layer, the hidden layers do not necessarily benefit.

Consider the input layer. It accepts the normalized training data and then produces its response. The signals produced by the input layer will probably be distributed very differently from the normalized training data that produced them. In general, the input for a layer is distributed very differently from its output. This is especially true at the start of training when the weights are random. All the arguments for normalizing training data apply to hidden layers as well. Moreover, following weight updates at the end of each training epoch the distributions change. Indeed, the weight updates are based on the $\frac{\partial L}{\partial w}$s, which *approximates* the *instantaneous* rate of change for the loss function at the precise point, $Loss(\mathbf{w})$, where Loss is the global objective function and $\mathbf{w}$ is the vector of every weight in the ANN. Changing one entry in $\mathbf{w}$ changes $L$, which in turns changes all the $\frac{\partial L}{\partial w}$s. Changing all of them simultaneously has an even stronger effect. This effect retards the training and in consequence the hidden layers are chasing a "moving" target as each epoch changes what they observe. The effect is demonstrated in Figure 7.8. The difference between epochs is clearly visible.

Interlayer normalization attempts to address the problem by introducing normalization between the layers in the ANN. There is, however, a significant challenge. In contrast to the static training set, where the normalization parameters of mean and standard deviation need only be computed once, layer outputs change with every training epoch. Following the weight updates, the distributions of signals emitted by the layers are inflected. This implies that a per-layer normalization scheme needs to update itself following every training epoch. The following presents two approaches in order of both chronological conception and feasibility.

### 7.5.1  Batch Normalization

Batch normalization is a technique developed to address the problem of shifting layer response distributions. The insight behind the idea is that normalization can take place inside the ANN, not just prior to the input layer with the pre-processing of the training set (75; 133). Batch normalization is effected by interposing a layer that implements the normalization of the signals between the layers.

The object of interposing a normalization layer is the same as preprocessing the training set. There are, however, more difficulties. Unlike preprocessing of the training set, which only needs to be done once, the batch normalization has to be done following every training epoch. This is because each training epoch produces different weights and consequently a different distribution of signals. An important restriction is that whatever transformation is interposed, the transformation must be differentiable to fit in to a back-propagation scheme.

All of the excellent arguments for encapsulating dropout in a self-contained layer hold for batch normalization as well, so we will assume that it is the implementation. A batch normalization layer, $\ell$, normalizes the signal from $\ell - 1$. The neurons between the two are connected 1:1. The batch normalization layer has the same number of neurons, and they are directly connected, $M_{\ell-1} = M_{\ell}$. The output of the normalization layer is fully connected to the deeper layer, $\ell + 1$. The arrangement is depicted in Figure 7.7.

Batch normalization does the same job as preprocessing the training data, but in a layer. The batch normalization layer will need statistics for centering and Z-scoring, so it needs the mean and the standard deviation of $\ell - 1$'s signals for the epoch. The mean is computed per neuron over the all the data in the training epoch:

$$\forall \text{neuron}_i \in \ell, \mu_i = \frac{1}{N} \sum_j^N z_{i,j},$$

(7.11)

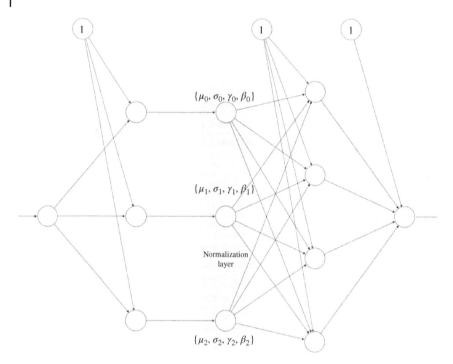

**Figure 7.7** An ANN with a batch normalization layer. The 1:1 links correspond to the per neuron normalization statistics.

and the standard deviation is

$$\sigma_i = \sqrt{\frac{1}{N}\sum_{j}^{N}(z_{i,j} - \mu_i)^2}.\tag{7.12}$$

This is done on a per neuron basis, that is, we have $M_{\ell-1}$ neurons so there are $M_{\ell-1}$ pairs of $\{\mu_i, \sigma_i\}$ in layer $\ell$. Assuming $N$ elements from the training set are in the training epoch, then we need to buffer them to compute the statistics required to perform the normalization. With the statistics calculated layer $\ell - 1$'s, signals are normalized with:

$$\hat{z}_{\ell-1} = \frac{z_{\ell-1} - \mu}{\sigma}.\tag{7.13}$$

While the normalized data will be better behaved, there is a danger that normalization may limit what the $\ell - 1$ layer can represent. To ensure that $\ell - 1$'s ability to learn is not infringed upon there is one final step. The batch normalization layer's final output, $z_\ell$, is computed with two learnable parameters as

$$z_\ell = \gamma \cdot \hat{z}_{\ell-1} + \beta.\tag{7.14}$$

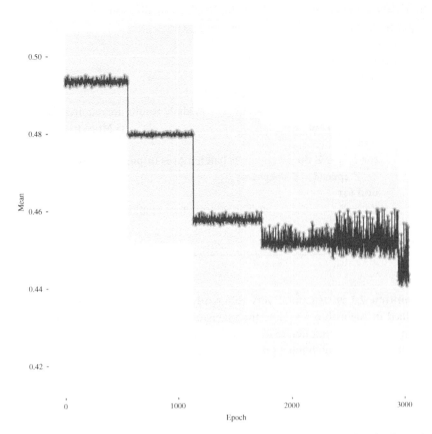

**Figure 7.8** The unnormalized means ribboned with the standard deviation for 5 epochs of training LeNet-5 at layer C5. The epochs are clearly delineated. The weight updates in the deeper layer will have to adapt to a distribution of signals that it has never seen before every epoch.

Both gamma and beta are trainable parameters learnt during fitting of the model. If need be, training can force the parameters to undo the normalization by learning $\gamma = \sigma$ and $\beta = \mu$.

Batch normalization requires all $N$ outputs from its immediately shallower layer before it can compute the statistics. It follows that $\ell$ must buffer $\ell - 1$'s signals. If $\ell - 1$ has $M_{\ell-1}$ neurons, and the training epoch is processing $N$ samples from the training set, then a buffer of size of $M_{\ell-1} \cdot N$ will be required. This leads to a new algorithm for processing a training epoch.

---

**Algorithm 7.3** Training Forward Pass for Batch Normalization

---

1: **procedure** BatchNormalizationForwardPass
2:     $Z \leftarrow$ Training Set
3:     **for** $\ell \in \mathscr{L}$ **do**
4:         **if** $\ell$.isBN **then**
5:             $Z = \ell$.BatchNormalize(buffer)
6:             $Z_\ell \leftarrow Z$          ▷ The intermediate results are required for BPG
7:             **continue**                          ▷ Move to next layer
8:         **end if**
9:         **for** $z_{\ell-1} \in Z$ **do**          ▷ batch moves through the ANN en masse
10:            Z.append $= \ell$.compute($z_{\ell-1}$)
11:        **end for**
12:        $Z_\ell \leftarrow Z$          ▷ The intermediate results are required for BPG
13:    **end for**
14: **end procedure**

---

Algorithm 7.3 is structured very differently than the earlier training epoch described in Algorithm 3.1. Note the inversion of the loops. The batch normalization version does not iterate over the training set, but rather, the layers of the ANN, as the entire batch must progress through the ANN as a whole. The earlier version of a training epoch used to iterate over the training set. A forward pass was immediately followed by a backward pass, ping pong style, and there were $N$ executions of each pass. The batch normalization version only has one forward pass; the training set moves through the ANN together. While it is not necessarily slower, it is roughly doing the same amount of work, merely in a different order, it does consume more memory. The individual $Z_\ell$s must be retained as they are required to compute the $\frac{\partial L}{\partial z}$s during the backward pass (they are used to propagate the gradient between layers). The requirement is far more onerous when processing an entire training batch at once. Back propagation must also proceed in a batch-oriented fashion; the backward pass cannot proceed until the forward pass has completed. Back propagation through a batch normalization layer must also proceed as a batch. This follows from differentiating a path through the normalization.

Backpropagation must go through the normalization layer so its derivatives are required. Batch normalization is differentiable, but messy. The derivatives are separated into two sets, or phases. They need to be evaluated in the order presented as there are dependencies. Notice the derivatives of the variance and the mean involve sums over the entire batch. The first set of derivatives is required to propagate the gradient through the layer. The computation of the gradient needs the following derivatives (reproduced from the paper):

$$\frac{\partial L}{\partial \hat{z}_{\ell-1}} = \frac{\partial L}{\partial z_{\ell}} \cdot \gamma, \tag{7.15}$$

$$\frac{\partial L}{\partial \sigma^2} = \sum_i^N \frac{\partial L}{\partial \hat{z}_{\ell-1}} \cdot (z_{\ell-1} - \mu) \cdot \frac{-1}{2} (\sigma^2 + \epsilon)^{\frac{-3}{2}}, \tag{7.16}$$

and,

$$\frac{\partial L}{\partial \mu} = \left( \sum_i^N \frac{\partial L}{\partial \hat{z}_{\ell-1}} \cdot \frac{-1}{\sqrt{\sigma^2 + \epsilon}} \right) + \frac{\partial L}{\partial \sigma^2} \cdot \frac{-2}{N} \cdot \sum_i^N (z_{\ell-1} - \mu). \tag{7.17}$$

Finally, with the above values computed, the expression below is the gradient that is propagated to the shallower layer:

$$\frac{\partial L}{\partial z_{\ell-1}} = \frac{\partial L}{\partial \hat{z}_{\ell-1}} \cdot \frac{1}{\sqrt{\sigma^2 + \epsilon}} + \frac{\partial L}{\partial \sigma^2} \cdot \frac{2(z_{\ell-1} - \mu)}{N} + \frac{\partial L}{\partial \mu} \cdot \frac{1}{N}. \tag{7.18}$$

With the latter derivative, the gradient can be pushed to the shallower layer. Observe that only layer outputs need to be retained as claimed. The intermediate $\hat{z}_{\ell-1}$ values do not appear, just their derivatives, which can be easily computed.

The second set of derivatives is required to update the learnt parameters, $\gamma$ and $\beta$. They too are sums over the entire batch.

$$\frac{\partial L}{\partial \gamma} = \sum_i^N \frac{\partial L}{\partial z_{\ell}} \cdot \hat{z}_{\ell-1}, \tag{7.19}$$

and

$$\frac{\partial L}{\partial \beta} = \sum_i^N \frac{\partial L}{\partial z_{\ell}}. \tag{7.20}$$

Bear in mind that these expressions are per neuron in the normalization layer. There will be $M_{\ell-1}$ of them, as dictated by the preceding shallower layer.

When training is terminated, the model is ready to be used for inference, and the layer will have learnt the $M_{\ell-1}$ pairs of $\gamma$ and $\beta$, but there is still a requirement for the $\{\mu_i, \sigma_i\}$. During inference, there are tuples of $\{\mu_i, \sigma_i, \gamma_i, \beta_i\}$ required. The easiest solution is to retain the $\{\mu_i, \sigma_i\}$ computed during the last training epoch.

While promising experimentally, batch normalization is not widely implemented. The problems far out-weighed the advantages. The memory requirements can be prohibitive. Using SGD does address the memory requirements to some extent. The method also introduces a great deal of potential numerical instability, the above derivatives represent many opportunities for overflow, underflow and NaN. The algorithm is also difficult to retrofit into existing training libraries as it required a new data flow during training. Batch normalization did, however, inspire a more practical form of interlayer normalization that forms the subject of the Section 7.5.2.

## 7.5.2 Layer Normalization

While batch layer normalization has been shown to be efficacious, its drawbacks are clear. It consumes a great deal more memory than a general training epoch and in addition requires a different flow of the data during training. The latter can lead to what is in essence a complete reimplementation of the supporting software. In an attempt to realize the advantages of batch layer normalization while addressing its drawbacks layer normalization was developed (7; 166).

The central challenge when developing interlayer ANN normalization is computing the required statistics. The key innovation of layer normalization was discarding the separation between neurons in the normalization layer. Preprocessing the data for the input layer per feature makes sense; there are genuine intrafeature relationships that are important and need to be preserved. Once the input layer has computed its scaler products, however, the "features" have been melded together; treating the resulting features separately, it was posited, may not be important.

The insight led to the following, instead of normalizing per neuron across a training batch, layer normalization normalizes the response vector instead. This results in normalizing per training example. Normalization takes place across the vector by computing the mean and standard deviation element-wise of a single vector. This approach leaves the data flow in a training epoch unchanged. Layer normalization can be encapsulated entirely in an interposed layer so nothing outside the layer is aware that it is taking place. When a response, $z_{\ell-1}$, arrives, its mean and standard deviation are computed immediately. No buffering is required, and the normalized response can be passed on straight away. With batch normalization, where the vector, $z_{\ell-1} \in \mathbb{R}^{M_{\ell-1}}$, has $M_{\ell-1}$ neurons, an epoch produced $M_{\ell-1}$ pairs of statistics, and only once per training epoch with the buffered vectors. Layer normalization produces $N$ pairs of statistics, one for each training example in the forward pass, and they are discarded as soon as they have been used. There is no buffering required. The mean is computed with,

$$\mu = \frac{1}{M_{\ell-1}} \sum_{i}^{M_{\ell-1}} z_{\ell-1}[i], \tag{7.21}$$

and the standard deviation is

$$\sigma = \sqrt{\frac{1}{M_{\ell-1}} \sum_{i}^{M_{\ell-1}} (z_{\ell-1}[i] - \mu)^2}. \tag{7.22}$$

The derivatives for layer normalization are the same, except the sums are across the vector instead of the batch. They are reproduced below to account for the different summations.

$$\frac{\partial L}{\partial \hat{z}_{\ell-1}} = \frac{\partial L}{\partial z_\ell} \cdot \gamma \tag{7.23}$$

$$\frac{\partial L}{\partial \sigma^2} = \sum_i^{M_{\ell-1}} \frac{\partial L}{\partial \hat{z}_{\ell-1}} \cdot (z_{\ell-1} - \mu) \cdot \frac{-1}{2}(\sigma^2 + \epsilon)^{\frac{-3}{2}}, \tag{7.24}$$

and,

$$\frac{\partial L}{\partial \mu} = \left( \sum_i^{M_{\ell-1}} \frac{\partial L}{\partial \hat{z}_{\ell-1}} \cdot \frac{-1}{\sqrt{\sigma^2 + \epsilon}} \right) + \frac{\partial L}{\partial \sigma^2} \cdot \frac{-2}{M_{\ell-1}} \cdot \sum_i^{M_{\ell-1}} (z_{\ell-1} - \mu). \tag{7.25}$$

The above computed the gradient is propagated with,

$$\frac{\partial L}{\partial z_{\ell-1}} = \frac{\partial L}{\partial \hat{z}_{\ell-1}} \cdot \frac{1}{\sqrt{\sigma^2 + \epsilon}} + \frac{\partial L}{\partial \sigma^2} \cdot \frac{2(z_{\ell-1} - \mu)}{M_{\ell-1}} + \frac{\partial L}{\partial \mu} \cdot \frac{1}{M_{\ell-1}}. \tag{7.26}$$

And for the trainable parameters:

$$\frac{\partial L}{\partial \gamma} = \sum^{M_{\ell-1}} \frac{\partial L}{\partial z_\ell} \cdot \hat{z}_{\ell-1}. \tag{7.27}$$

$$\frac{\partial L}{\partial \beta} = \sum^{M_{\ell-1}} \frac{\partial L}{\partial z_\ell}. \tag{7.28}$$

Training is performed with the standard SGD training algorithm. A layer normalization layer is interposed between dense layers where required and is completely encapsulated. This is a very attractive feature. Software infrastructure does not need to change to accommodate it, and memory demands are not increased either. The numerical stability of the derivatives is also far better than full batch normalization. Sums over a vector are better behaved than over an entire training set.

To demonstrate the advantages and the dynamics of layer normalization, a comparison between with and without layer normalization for an ANN classifier for the iris dataset is presented. The graph in Figure 7.9 shows the distribution of the means for a layer over two attempts to train a model. The model was initialized with the same weights for both runs. The differences between the distributions are striking. Layer normalization has a tighter distribution. The deeper layer will have an easier time of converging as a result. Without normalization, the distribution drifts creating difficulties its deeper neighbor.

When implementing algorithms such as layer normalization, it is a very good idea to verify the resulting code with the technique of differencing equations introduced in Section 3.7. If the derivatives are not implemented correctly, they will have pernicious effect on convergence; this can be hard to detect without direct

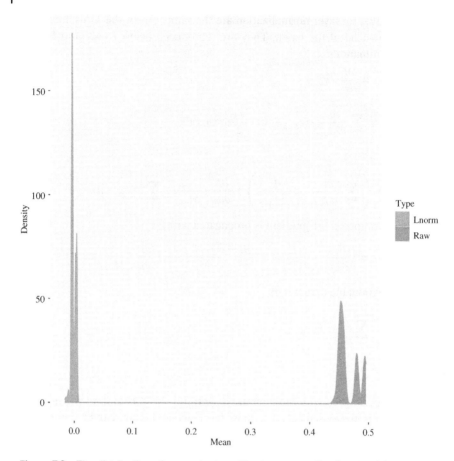

**Figure 7.9** The distribution of means by type. The layer normalization densities are far more predictable over time, hence the deeper layer can learn faster. The weight updates do not confuse it.

confirmation of correctness. The differencing technique will quickly identify the underlying problem.

## 7.6 Summary

Evaluating the quality of a trained model is challenging. The applications for models require them to perform inference on unseen data, and unseen data is unknown data. The performance of a model with unseen data is the generalization error. There is a great deal of theory in ML to analyze generalization error for ML, but the jury is out on its relevance to ANNs. Nonetheless, overfitting and underfitting are genuine phenomena. Regularization techniques are used to address overfitting, and neuron dropout is one of the most important techniques to address it. Normalization accelerates convergence by making interlayer signals more predictable.

## 7.7 Projects

The projects below rely on notebooks that can be found here, https://github.com/nom-de-guerre/DDL_book/tree/main/Chap07.

1. The Python notebook iris07.ipynb contains an implementation of an iris classifier. Plot a graph of the classifier's bias versus variance by experimenting with different topologies.
2. The Python notebook MNIST07.ipynb contains an implementation of an MNIST classifier. Measure the accuracy difference between the dropout version and the control version of the model.
3. Implement a confusion matrix with the MNIST classifier in the previous project.

# 8

# Design Principles for a Deep Learning Training Library

This chapter describes how to design and implement a software library for building deep learning (DL) models. Models are built with software libraries. This is the software that applications use to define, assemble, and train models. The design principles are all demonstrated in a software library called the Realtime Artificial Neural Tool (RANT). RANT is an artifact developed for use with DL experimentation and embedded applications. The source code is available online.[1] The library is written in C/C++ for efficiency, but it does include Python bindings. Some might question why Python was not used. The answer is that most implementations of DL training routines are written in a lower level language. For example, libraries such as TensorFlow are implemented in C/C++ and exposed in Python. Python is implemented in C. To understand how to *implement* a DL library, we need to work in a low-level language. Demonstrating how to *use* a DL training library would be appropriate in Python; again, even Python implementations generally call down into C/C++ code to the workhorse routines.

Many indulge in dogma when prescribing computer languages, but it is important to bear in mind that computer languages are like any other tool, saws, hammers, and kitchen blenders. It is important to use the right tool for the job. All computer languages have strengths and weaknesses. Selecting the appropriate language for a task is an exercise in objectively examining the trade-offs that are appropriate for the task at hand. Many students do not understand statements such as, "Python is slower, but more productive." Such a claim is laden with information for a computer scientist, and we examine it here, in the course of which the use of C/C++ for low-level routines will be motivated.

---

1 https://github.com/nom-de-guerre/RANT.

*Demystifying Deep Learning: An Introduction to the Mathematics of Neural Networks,*
First Edition. Douglas J. Santry.
© 2024 The Institute of Electrical and Electronics Engineers, Inc. Published 2024 by John Wiley & Sons, Inc.

## 8.1 Computer Languages

Computer languages are as old as computers themselves. Every generation of computers tends to be accompanied with a new generation of languages. As computers grow more powerful, the number of abstractions and services offered by computer languages grows. The realized increase in hardware compute power over earlier generations increases the "budget" for using computers to ensure their own self-correctness with more abstract computer languages.

The earliest form of programming digital computers involved writing the machine code, the actual numbers that a computer understands as commands, in raw form. The first machines built with vacuum tubes simply did not have the capacity to be programmed any other way. In the earliest instance, this involved sitting at a console, individually setting the bits of a machine word with toggle switches, and then sending the word to a memory location one at a time; this had to be done for every word in the program! This was a time consuming process. Once the memory had been set up the program could run. Debugging was a nightmare.

Writing central processing unit (CPU) operation codes and operands in numeric form is difficult and prone to mistakes. The introduction of assembly language was an enormous improvement. Computer commands (machine instructions) were assigned human readable mnemonics and translated into machine understandable numbers with software, the assembler. We may view it as extraordinarily primitive today, but it was a big step forward. Assembly code was still prone to bugs, time consuming, and not portable. Programs had to be rewritten every time a new computer was purchased. Assembly language was, however, far more productive. Programmers could write and debug code faster.

Consider the following example for the IBM 701.[2] To add the contents of memory location 6 to the accumulator register the assembler code is, -ADD 6. The binary representation had to be coded by hand prior to the advent of assemblers, 101001:000000000110. The assembler turned the mnemonic into the machine code reducing errors and increasing the speed of software development.

In 1954, IBM introduced FORTRAN, a high-level language for scientific computing. FORTRAN faced a great deal of resistance initially as it was considered far too inefficient compared to assembler code; computers were so slow that squeezing every last operation out of them was paramount. The resistance was short lived. The exorbitant cost of rewriting programs for every new computer architecture quickly led to FORTRAN's adoption. The portability of the code between architectures, faster development time, and fewer bugs more than made up for any speed degradation. Soon important routines were written once and packaged up as

---

2 The IBM 701 Mainframe was a landmark machine whose introduction led to IBM's dominance in the following decades.

libraries. The code had been debugged to the point of total reliability and sharing it further increased productivity. Libraries of important scientific and engineering routines made writing new applications easier. Every new missile guidance system no longer began with rewriting the basic matrix and linear algebra routines that were required. The FORTRAN language took off and is still widely used today.[3]

FORTRAN is terse and was designed for scientists and engineers. It was designed for high-performance scientific computing. The business community had different requirements and users. Business problems are more concerned with data flow (processing customer records and bills, etc.), code readability, and documentation to support maintenance and extensions. FORTRAN was not suitable so a new language, COBOL, was introduced in 1959. COBOL was more data record oriented, and more like English (to the point where the earliest specification was so ambiguous that COBOL code was not portable, it depended on compiler behavior. As portability was a primary goal this was a gross error). These early languages did not stray far from the machine architecture they were originally designed to run on. The computers they were designed for could barely add and subtract, there was no compute head room for abstraction (multiplication was usually a software routine, not a machine instruction). The choice between COBOL and FORTRAN was a trade-off, usually dictated by the application. The number of languages available quickly proliferated in the 1960s as computers became more powerful, cheaper, and more widely available.

Of note, before we fast forward to today is the C language. It was introduced in 1972 with version 2 of the UNIX operating system. UNIX was designed on a new class of computer, the mini-computer,[4] and was developed on a DEC PDP-7. It was fast, simple, and made pointers a first class language element. It is still an important language today for systems programming because it is low level. To understand the utility of C, we need to examine how it works. It will explain why some basic machine learning routines are still written in C++ today, even if they are exposed for use in higher level languages such as Python.

An application is a program of instructions for a CPU to execute; the term of art, program, has precisely the same meaning in lay English. Computer instructions are numbers specifying primitive operations such as add the contents of memory location x to the contents of memory location y and store the result in z. Some CPU architectures can do that with one instruction. Others might require 4 instructions, load [x] into the CPU, load [y] into the CPU, add the values, and store in [z]. High-level languages abstract these primitives and leave the details to

---

3 FORTRAN programs are still used to benchmark and rank the world's fastest supercomputers.
4 Mini-computers were scaled down mainframes and made possible by the recent invention of integrated circuits. The Intel 8088 would be introduced 7 years later in 1979 setting off the PC revolution.

| C | ×86 | | M1 (ARM) | |
|---|---|---|---|---|
| main () | pushq | %rbp | sub | sp, sp, #16 |
| { | movq | %rsp, %rbp | mov | w8, #5 |
|    int x = 5; | xorl | %eax, %eax | str | w8, [sp, #12] |
|    int y = 7; | movl | $5, -4(%rbp) | mov | w8, #7 |
|    int z = x + y; | movl | $7, -8(%rbp) | str | w8, [sp, #8] |
| } | movl | -4(%rbp), %ecx | ldr | w8, [sp, #12] |
| | addl | -8(%rbp), %ecx | ldr | w9, [sp, #8] |
| | movl | %ecx, -12(%rbp) | add | w8, w8, w9 |
| | popq | %rbp | str | w8, [sp, #4] |
| | retq | | mov | w0, #0 |
| | | | add | sp, sp, #16 |
| | | | ret | |

**Figure 8.1** A C program and the resultant assembly code following compilation to two popular architectures. Both architectures make direct use of the stack to store the automatic variables. A C programmer would expect the stack to be utilized in that way, have complete access to the addresses of the identifiers, and understand the results are only valid in that stack frame. Note that just because the ARM version is longer does not mean that it is slower, the individual machine instructions can be faster.

the compiler. A C compiler will accept a statement such as z = x + y and turn it into the correct program of machine instructions (the machine code). Moreover, C statements will often roughly correspond to machine instructions, and that is the fastest a program can run. A good C compiler's optimizer will produce code that does not even touch memory unnecessarily vastly speeding up execution. An example is given for a snippet of C code and the resultant assembler code in the table depicted in Figure 8.1. C makes direct use of a CPU's hardware stack (most modern CPUs directly support a hardware stack). Observe how different the output is between CPU architectures. Writing per platform code with an assembler was both time consuming, riddled with bugs and had to be done every time a new computer was purchased. The idea of compiling high-level languages was an enormous step forward.

A C/C++ programmer needs to understand[5] memory usage very well and manages it directly and completely. It is precisely this control, coupled with inexperience or lack of knowledge, that routinely leads to bugs with C/C++ programs. The heap can be confused with the stack, double free, writing over freed memory, the list is endless, but the list of C/C++ memory bugs is a foreign language to many modern programmers trained on languages such as Python. The power of C/C++ is useful for systems programming, such as writing an operating system kernel or a graphics processing unit (GPU) device driver for machine learning. It is also useful, even necessary, for libraries that are called frequently and need to be performant.

---

5 Sadly, programmers often do not posses the necessary understanding, hence dangerous bugs and security flaws in low-level code written in C.

As computers grew more powerful, the computer itself could be used to increase correctness. Computers now have sufficient power to run programs and provide many run-time ancillary services. Languages such as Java and Python offer little or no correspondence between the machine and the language. Java is compiled to an intermediate assembly language for a Java virtual machine (JVM). Python is interpreted. Both languages offer memory management. Allocating and freeing memory are not concerns for a Python programmer. There is, however, a cost. When Python evaluates z = x + y, it does not correspond to a series of machine instruction but rather a sequence of high-level language operations that in turn execute many machine instructions. This is not necessarily a bad thing. Speed of implementation (productivity) and eliminating an entire class of memory bugs are well worth the price on modern CPU architectures, but too often students are not aware of the trade-off much less the cost.

C/C++ are low-level languages giving them direct access to hardware primitives and hardware. This includes control over the IEEE 754 rounding method. There are four modes, and they are exposed in C/C++ via FLT_EVAL_METHOD (float.h). There are also many platforms where performance is still paramount. Mobile phones and embedded devices are very sensitive to memory usage and CPU consumption. Apple uses Swift and Android uses Java (and Kotlin).

Table 8.1 gives an indication of the differing performance. The Python program creating a classifier with the Iris dataset is using Keras and Tensorflow. Consequently, it is eventually calling down into C/C++ code. The comparison between loops was done with for, which is sympathetic to Python as the difference between while loops is known to be wider. A Python programming rule of thumb is to use for instead of while where possible because it is faster.

An examination of the relative energy requirements of computer languages concluded that C is the most energy efficient language, and Python was ranked at #73 (112). The authors also demonstrate that Python consumes a great deal more memory. This can be an important consideration for embedded applications and mobile devices.

**Table 8.1** Comparison of Performance Between C++ and Python.

| Language | Count to 1,000,000 (For Loop) | 100 Epochs Learning Iris |
| --- | --- | --- |
| C++ | 3 ns | 0.05 s |
| Python | 1628.4 ns | 26.09 s |

a) Comparison of values computed with backpropagation of error and differencing. The ratio suggests good agreement between both methods suggesting correctness of the BPROP implementation.

The energy footprint, and the related metric of carbon footprint, has for the most part been ignored in the machine learning community. Research tends to focus on increases of accuracy and capability. This is not necessarily a bad thing, but some attention will probably fall on the cost of training as models grow increasingly hungry for energy. Efforts such as DAWNBench (23) are a step in the right direction. The benchmark includes metrics such as time to accuracy, which implicitly admits of an energy efficiency interpretation. It is not much of a leap to refine the metric to explicitly measure performance in terms of Joules. Competitions such as JouleSort (125) make a more explicit connection to energy efficiency. Sorting algorithms are evaluated with respect to speed *and* energy usage. The DL community can learn from such efforts. Spiking neural networks are an attempt to build models with lower energy requirements (69), but they do not perform well (47).

A powerful compromise to gain the productivity of Python and the power of C/C++ is the Python package, ctypes. Routines and libraries are written in C/C++ and then exposed higher up in Python. Numpy and Tensorflow are two examples of this approach. Applications can then be written in Python that call the performant code, or access devices such as a GPU, by calling the Python bindings.

It must be made very clear, and this section was not an anti-Python polemic. Python is a very productive language. Implementing a computer language requires selecting a point in the design space dictated by what the language is trying to achieve. The trade-offs adopted by the language constitute the niche that the language occupies. The list of modern computer languages is endless. C/C++ and Python are different languages trying to achieve different things. Python dominates its niche because it is a great language. Python's eco-system of libraries, support and documentation are unparalleled for machine learning and ANNs. The abstractions it offers also yield tremendous productivity. It can, however, be useful to understand what is happening under the hood of the implementation of a language. This is not just abstract, and it can lead to writing better Python code too.

## 8.2   The Matrix: Crux of a Library Implementation

Having motivated the adoption of C/C++ as an appropriate implementation language, the next step is to propose sound design principles for implementing ANN libraries. The first step is to select the basic abstractions that form a sound basis upon which to build an overall architecture. Artificial neural networks are assemblies of synthetic neurons (perceptrons). When implementing an ANN library, it is natural to consider selecting the neuron as the unit of abstraction. Defining a neuron class would encapsulate its weights and connections, and it makes sense. While esthetically pleasing it would perform very badly. It makes more sense to designate the layer as the unit of abstraction. A layer's connections are easily managed with a single matrix of weights (a row per neuron, a column per incoming connection). The algorithms presented thus far have all been matrix-centric, and this is one of the reasons.

Training Neural Networks involve two phases: a forward pass and a backward pass. Both operations are performed, depending on the nature of the problem, hundreds or even tens of thousands of times; it is all that training an ANN does. We have seen in previous chapters how both phases are represented with 3 matrix operations, a matrix vector product in the forward phase, or inference, and a transpose matrix vector product followed by a vector outer product in the backward pass. The performance of an implementation will depend very much on how well these basic operations are implemented. Before one can understand how to best implement these operations, a brief review of computer architecture is required.

A note on the scale of the DL models is in order here. Models vary in size and scale. The algorithms presented so far are correct, but writing down an algorithm is very different from realizing the implementation of one in a computer. The trade-offs and design for an implementation that can handle models with billions of learnable parameters and smaller million parameter models are different. The most challenging problems today require multiple GPUs to train in a practicable time frame (29). Training language models can take days. The techniques developed and presented below are for CPU-based implementations.

## 8.2.1 Memory Access and Modern CPU Architectures

Two important pieces of a modern computer are the CPU and memory (DRAM). Computer programs, and their data, are stored in DRAM. Before a CPU can operate on the contents of memory, data, a datum must be loaded into the CPU and stored in a CPU's register. The CPU loads data from DRAM over a memory bus. Reading and writing memory is one of the slowest operations that modern CPU's perform. It is important to understand how it works. Memory is divided up into bytes and can be thought of as an enormous array (we elide the interposition of virtual memory as it is not required here). The basic architecture is presented in Figure 8.2. The CPU loads a variable by requesting data from the DRAM array with the variable's memory address.[6] This is what the two examples of assembly code spend most of their time doing, accessing memory (the stack) in Table 8.1. There are two salient architectural points to note when reasoning about memory. Both are invisible to the programmer, even at the assembly code level. Nevertheless, these architectural features are extremely important to the performance of programs.

---

6 In C/C++ a memory address is called a pointer. Java and Python do not grant direct access to memory. They offer the safer "reference" abstraction.

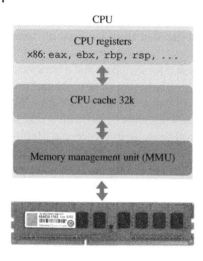

CPU

**Figure 8.2** Detail of the memory hierarchy. The DRAM DIMM at the bottom is where the data lives. To operate on data, the CPU must load it into a CPU register (Intel ×86 architecture depicted). The memory management unit (MMU) loads data from DRAM into the CPU cache, and from the CPU cache, it can be loaded into a CPU register. Source: Kjerish/Wikimedia Commons/CC BY-SA 4.0.

The first point is the existence of a quantum unit of access to memory by the CPU. It is called the CPU cache line. Even if memory is addressable at the granularity of the byte the CPU must access memory, that is, read and write, in units of the cache line size (e.g. 64 bytes on Intel CPUs and 128 bytes for M1 SoCs). A cache line is fetched from DRAM and stored in the CPU cache. The CPU accesses are also aligned on cache line size. For example, if a program reads byte 438, an M1 will load 128 bytes from offset 384 and store it in the CPU cache; the desired byte is the 54th byte in the cache line. Once the cache line is loaded, the actual byte that has been requested will be fetched into the core's register. In the course of loading, the cache line it will evict a cache line that is already in the CPU's cache. This happens invisibly and is managed entirely by the CPU. Note that in this example the program only needs 0.78% of the data that was loaded from memory into the CPU cache.

The number of CPU cycles required to access DRAM is circa 100 clock ticks. The number of cycles required to perform an operation, such as addition, is circa 10 clock ticks. The ratio of time to fetch a datum versus the operation is enormous. Programmers and compilers do not need to be aware of the details of memory access, but it is important to understand it when writing high-performance code. The speed mismatch is observable and easily measurable. When a CPU has to wait for a memory fetch, it is *stalled* and does no work.[7] A CPU clocked at 3.2 GHz could conceivably execute operations on data at that rate, but rarely gets close owing to memory fetches.

---

7 Stalling is such a serious problem that the SPECTRE family of security bugs, etc. was inevitable.

$$A = \begin{pmatrix} 1 & 2 & 3 \\ 4 & 5 & 6 \\ 7 & 8 & 9 \end{pmatrix}$$

| ... | 205 | 206 | 207 | 208 | 209 | 210 | 211 | 212 | 213 | ... | |
|-----|-----|-----|-----|-----|-----|-----|-----|-----|-----|-----|-----|
| | 1 | 2 | 3 | 4 | 5 | 6 | 7 | 8 | 9 | | Row order $A$ |
| | 1 | 4 | 7 | 2 | 5 | 8 | 3 | 6 | 9 | | Column order $A$ |

**Figure 8.3** Two options for the physical memory layout of a matrix, $A$. The base address of the matrix is 205 in DRAM. Row order provides for the rows to be laid out contiguously in memory. Column order is the opposite. CPUs access memory in units of cache lines so the choice is important.

The second important point relating to physical memory is memory layout. Physical computer memory, DRAM, is just a linear array. To support higher dimensional objects, such as a two dimensional matrix, we have to superimpose some abstractions on the linear memory. While we may access the object with a (row, column) pair in a high-level language, the two coordinates must be mapped to a linear address at the machine code level. The matrix, no matter how it is represented higher up, will be laid out linearly in memory. There are two feasible configurations for scientific computing,[8] see Figure 8.3 for an example. They are called row order and column order.

Row order is the arrangement of each row laid out contiguously in memory, one row after another. To access element $(i, j)$ it must be converted to a linear address as address = base + $i \times$ ncolumns + $j$ (e.g. the address of $A(1, 2) = 205 + 1 \times 3 + 2 = 210$, so the content of $A(1, 2)$ is 6). The data can be laid out in column order as well, which is just the opposite of row order. The choice is not arbitrary and very important. Row ordered is favored for matrix vector products, and column order is favored for transpose products and vector decompositions (as a column is contiguous a single pointer encapsulates the vector). With this knowledge, an informed decision can be taken respecting how to lay out the weight matrices.

The most frequent operation over a model's life time is inference. Inference is a recurrence equation encapsulated with matrix–vector multiplications. Matrix–vector products favor row-order layouts. The $W_{\ell+1}z_{\ell}$ product benefits from the row-order layout as it is repeatedly multiplying the rows in $W$ with an ante-layer vector output. Vectors are always contiguous as they are effectively 1-dimensional. When the CPU loads a row from DRAM, it is fetching entire cache lines of data and using 100% of the data that was loaded. Some CPUs can detect the serial access of memory and prefetch cache lines (rows). In this instance, the memory subsystem is streaming data from memory to the CPU cache as fast as

---

8 When the performance of iterating over the entire matrix is not critical, then a matrix can be synthesized by abstracting it. One method is to build a binary tree or hash table of rows or columns. The interposition of abstract data structures over linear arrays is not considered here as the matrix products would be infeasibly slow.

possible. An additional advantage is the data is only loaded once. For $W \in \mathbb{R}^{n,m}$, the number of memory fetches is $n \cdot m \div$ cache line length. If the matrix was laid out in column order, then the number of memory fetches would be $n \cdot m$. In both cases, there are $n \cdot m$ multiplications and $n \cdot (m - 1)$ additions, but the expensive operation is the memory access, and memory access will dominate. The effect is pernicious and easily measured. This is one of the reasons why Python's Numpy library is written in C. Fine-grained control of the memory is crucial for performance. A further advantage to streaming the data is the opportunity for compilers to detect the contiguous memory multiplications. Many CPUs can multiply 4–8 products in parallel. Compiler optimizers that detect contiguous operations can use native CPU vector instructions.

### 8.2.2 Designing Matrix Computations

Careful design of matrix operations is important. They are at the heart of an imple-mentation. Informed by how data moves between a CPU and memory, the design of the matrix operations can now be elucidated.

The algorithms have been implemented and are available as part of the RANT Deep Learning library. The interested reader will find the matrix code encapsu-lated in the type, NeuralM_t. The class is implemented in NNm/NeuralM.h. The class implements all of the operations required to implement an ANN. It is not a general implementation of a matrix. Most matrix operations are missing; they are not required.

The design is optimized for usage on a CPU. The matrices are stored in row order. The three operations that an ANN implementation requires are

1. $u_\ell = W_\ell z_{\ell-1} + b_\ell$: ante-activation neuron state, it is a GAXPY (general $Ax$ plus $y$)
2. $\frac{\partial L}{\partial z_\ell} = W_{\ell+1}^T \delta_{\ell+1}$: interlayer gradient transmission, a transpose matrix–vector multiplication
3. $\Delta W_\ell = \Delta W_\ell + \delta_\ell \cdot z_{\ell-1}^T$: per weight error, a vector outer product to update the net $\frac{\partial L}{\partial w_i}$ s.

The row-order layout renders the implementation of GAXPY straight forward. For $W \in \mathbb{R}^{n,m}$, we can iterate over the $n$ rows to compute the $n$ dot products in the output vector. As the rows and the vector, $z$, are contiguous in memory perfor-mance will be good:

$$\begin{pmatrix} b_1 & w_{1,1} & w_{1,2} & w_{1,3} \\ b_2 & w_{2,1} & w_{2,2} & w_{2,3} \\ b_3 & w_{3,1} & w_{3,2} & w_{3,3} \end{pmatrix} \begin{pmatrix} z_1 \\ z_2 \\ z_3 \end{pmatrix} = \begin{pmatrix} b_1 + \sum_i z_i \cdot w_{1,i} \\ b_2 + \sum_i z_i \cdot w_{2,i} \\ b_3 + \sum_i z_i \cdot w_{3,i} \end{pmatrix}. \tag{8.1}$$

The `NeuralM_t` class includes an extra column for the bias. The GAXPY for $u_\ell = W_\ell z_{\ell-1} + b_\ell$ is implemented in Algorithm 8.1.

---

**Algorithm 8.1** GAXPY for a Neural Matrix

---

1: **procedure** GAXPY($W, x, u$)
2:    index $\leftarrow 0$
3:    **for** $i$ in rows **do**
4:       $u[i] \leftarrow W[\text{index}]$            ▷ the bias
5:       index $\leftarrow$ index $+ 1$
6:       **for** $j$ in columns **do**         ▷ The dot product
7:          $u[i] \leftarrow u[i] + x[j] \cdot W[\text{index}]$
8:          index $\leftarrow$ index $+ 1$    ▷ sequentially stream $W$
9:       **end for**
10:   **end for**
11: **end procedure**

---

The second operation, the transpose multiplication, presents more of a challenge. It can be implemented by physically transposing the matrix, which is a copy, and then using the normal GAXPY routine, but this is both slow and consumes memory. It can be efficiently implemented by logically transposing the weight matrix with a specialized multiplication routine. Moreover, to maintain cache line efficiency the transpose product works on the original matrix, $W_\ell$, and loads the data in row order, but instead of computing a complete dot product per iteration (the $i$th row producing the $i$th entry in the product vector) we compute one term for each of the $n$ dot products simultaneously:

$$\begin{pmatrix} w_{1,1} & w_{1,2} & w_{1,3} \\ w_{2,1} & w_{2,2} & w_{2,3} \\ w_{3,1} & w_{3,2} & w_{3,3} \end{pmatrix}^T \begin{pmatrix} \delta_1 \\ \delta_2 \\ \delta_3 \end{pmatrix} = \begin{pmatrix} \delta_1 \cdot w_{1,1} + \delta_2 \cdot w_{2,1} + \delta_3 \cdot w_{3,1} \\ \delta_1 \cdot w_{1,2} + \delta_2 \cdot w_{2,2} + \delta_3 \cdot w_{3,2} \\ \delta_1 \cdot w_{1,3} + \delta_2 \cdot w_{2,3} + \delta_3 \cdot w_{3,3} \end{pmatrix}. \tag{8.2}$$

The `NeuralM_t` class includes an extra column for the bias. The gradient propagation, defined as $\frac{\partial L}{\partial z_\ell} = W_{\ell+1}^T \delta_{\ell+1}$, is computed in routine 8.2.

The final operation, the outer product, consists of $\Delta W_\ell = \Delta W_\ell + \delta_\ell \cdot z_{\ell-1}^T$, where we are updating a dense matrix. The previous operations are products of a matrix and a vector producing a vector. The outer product is different. The matrix being updated is accumulating the net gradient on a per weight basis. The factors in the product, two vectors, are not the determiners in this operation. The product is a dense matrix and determines the efficient way to proceed. Proceeding along the rows in the product the updated matrix is streamed into, and out of, the CPU. The priniciples described are demonstrated in Algorithm 8.2.

---

**Algorithm 8.2** Gradient Transmission for a Neural Matrix

1: **procedure** BPROP($W_\ell, g_{\ell-1}, \delta_\ell$)
2:    $g_{\ell-1} = 0$                          ▷ assign the null vector
3:    index ← 0
4:    **for** i in rows **do**
5:       index ← index + 1               ▷ skip over the bias
6:       **for** j in columns **do**
7:          $g_{\ell-1}[j] \leftarrow g_{\ell-1}[j] + W_\ell[\text{index}] \cdot \delta_\ell[i]$
8:          index ← index + 1       ▷ sequentially stream $W$
9:       **end for**
10:   **end for**
11: **end procedure**

---

$$\Delta W_\ell = \Delta W_\ell + \delta \cdot z_{\ell-1}^T$$

$$= \Delta W_\ell + \begin{pmatrix} \delta_1 \\ \delta_2 \\ \delta_3 \end{pmatrix} \cdot \begin{pmatrix} z_1 & z_2 & z_3 \end{pmatrix}^T$$

$$= \begin{pmatrix} \Delta w_{1,1}+ = \delta_1 z_1 & \Delta w_{1,2}+ = \delta_1 z_2 & \Delta w_{1,3}+ = \delta_1 z_3 \\ \Delta w_{2,1}+ = \delta_2 z_1 & \Delta w_{2,2}+ = \delta_2 z_2 & \Delta w_{2,3}+ = \delta_2 z_3 \\ \Delta w_{3,1}+ = \delta_3 z_1 & \Delta w_{3,2}+ = \delta_3 z_2 & \Delta w_{3,3}+ = \delta_3 z_3 \end{pmatrix}. \tag{8.3}$$

With efficient implementations of these matrix operations, a sound basis for the implementation of a training library is created. A great deal of work has been done to make matrix operations efficient for CPUs. One approach is to extract all of the performance possible by writing assembly routines optimized for a particular CPU (52). Matrix operations are highly parallelizable, which lends them to concurrent computation. A library can be written to compute the individual dot products in parallel resulting in vast increases in speed (142).

### 8.2.2.1 Convolutions as Matrices

An important activity of CNN filters is computing the kernels (Section 6.3). The kernels can be construed as matrix multiplications. Efficiently computing the kernels is effected by transforming the input image to a matrix of kernels. The new matrix is amenable to high-performance matrix multiplication. High-performance matrix libraries that implement general matrix multiplication (GEMM) (9), or a tuned implementation such as those described in Section 8.2.2, can then be used. The process is depicted in Figure 8.4.

Producing the intermediate matrix can be expensive. While building the intermediate matrix, the kernels are available, why postpone the kernel computation?

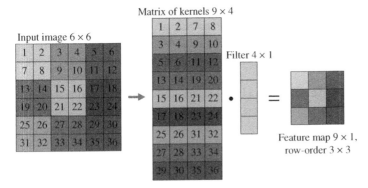

**Figure 8.4** The physical layout of the input matrix is on the left. The matrix of kernels is to the right. The feature map is computed with a matrix multiplication. The kernel is 2 × 2, and the stride is 2.

The answer is the CPU's floating point implementation. On some CPUs, it may not make sense, but for many, the scaler multiplication instruction is expensive. Apple M1s and Intel x86 have limited, but useful, vector instruction. They can compute 4–8 multiplications in parallel, so it is worth the memory copying. On a GPU, the win is far greater.

The matrix of kernels is also useful for backpropagation. Reconstructing the matrix of $\delta$s as a vector then a weight's derivative is the dot product of a column in the kernel matrix and the $\delta$ vector. A similar technique can also be used for transmission of the gradient through the feature layer.

One means of producing a matrix of kernels is with Im2Col (17). Im2Col will generate a matrix of kernels, one kernel per row. The scheme can also be directly implemented. The RANT library includes a simple example.

## 8.3 The Framework

Efficient matrix operations form the kernel of a performant DL library. Matrices alone are not, however, sufficient for a Deep Learning framework. There are some critical missing pieces. From the matrices flow, the higher level abstractions that produce the necessary components. Matrices are used by layers, and layers are synthesized to produce models. It is the latter two pieces that form the study of this section.

The object of a DL software library is to support applications that need to train models and perform inference. The models examined thus far have been feed-forward and fully-connected ANNs. They were described, and specified, in terms of layers. The specification has been in terms of types of layers and their widths. It is the layer that encapsulates the weight matrices. A DL model is comprised of multiple layers, by definition, and so a means of encapsulating layers is also required. In turn, the layers must be aggregated. Collecting the layers falls to the model. It assembles the individual layers and presents them as a whole.

A model can be implemented as a list of layers. The list is responsible for keeping the layers in the correct order and in an iterable format. The model accepts the input, pushes the data through the graph, and retrieves the output. The intervening steps between the input and output are calls to the forward pass of the layers. A list is well suited to such a sequential flow of operations. We have seen that there are many types of possible layers. Dense, convolutional and dropout just to name a few. To make the work of the model tractable, every layer must implement certain functions. The required functions are

1. **Initialize**: Set up initial state, including learnable parameters.
2. **Forward Pass**: Accept $z_{\ell-1}$ and return $z_\ell$.
3. **Gradient Transmission**: Accept $g_{\ell+1}$ and return $g_\ell$. Performs BPG on all learnable parameters.
4. **Update Weights**: Informs the layer that an epoch is over. Update learnable parameters and reset.

To enforce the implementation of the required functionality, layers must inherit from a base class. The base class defines the correct functions. Implementations of a layer overrides the default behavior with the functionality that defines it. The **Forward Pass** routine will be very different in a dense layer and a dropout layer. In C++, this can be done with an abstract class. An abstract class consists of virtual functions equal to zero. The layers inherit from the abstract class and implement the interface, that is, fill in the function definitions. As all layers have the same interface, it is trivial to connect them up as a model. The ANN does not know anything about the layers that are being invoked so any type of layer can be seamlessly included.

A model consists of a list of the abstract class type. The forward pass is implemented by iterating from the start of the list and propagating the results of the **Forward Pass** method. The abstract class ensures a clean and consistent interface. The loop simply iterates over the layers regardless of the composition the model.

Layers and models have been implemented in the RANT library to demonstrate these principles. The abstract class that RANT layers inherit is called `stratum_t`. RANT models are encapsulated in the `NNet_t` class. The architecture is demonstrated in Figure 8.5 for the RANT library. The interested reader is encouraged to peruse the source code.

**Figure 8.5** The representation of an ANN graph. Layers are implemented by inheriting from the `stratum_t` type. The model is an array of pointers of type `stratum_t`. Forward and backward passes are trivially implemented as loops over the list invoking the relevant method for the direction of travel.

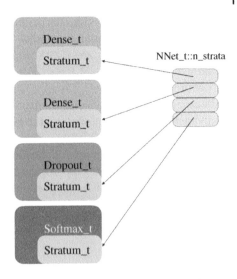

Stitching layers together is potentially fraught with peril. The model enforces sanity by verifying and enforcing correct shape transitions through the model. Two dense layers can neighbor each other with no trouble. But a CNN filter with $n$ features needs to have a deeper neighbor of the same shape, or a flatten layer. The shape checks are performed at model creation time as the layers are added. The model can reject an improper layer addition and return an error.

## 8.4 Summary

Computers languages are designed with different objectives. Designing a computer language involves selecting a design point in a large design space. The niche the language is addressing dictates the trade-offs. Machine learning libraries are often implemented in C/C++ because it produces high-performance code. The libraries are exposed in higher level languages, such as Python, that offer safety and high-level language abstractions. The RANT library can be exposed to Python or R, but is also well suited to real time and embedded applications with demanding requirements and a dearth of resources.

## 8.5 Projects

The projects below use the Python notebook MNIST08.ipynb that can be found here, https://github.com/nom-de-guerre/DDLbook/tree/main/Chap08. Use the notebook to verify your work is both correct and performant.

1. Matrix multiplication is trivially parallelizable. Extend RANT's `NeuralM_t` class to perform multiplication in parallel. Two widely available options for implementing concurrency are POSIX pthreads and libdispatch. Choose one and alter the method NeuralM_t::MatrixVectorMult to perform all the row and vector dot products in parallel.

2. Measure the performance of your parallel implementation of `NeuralM_t` by verifying that it scales linearly with the number of threads. Time the performance of the changes with MNIST08.

3. Implement matrix vector multiplication with column order layout. This can be done by simply changing the loops in NeuralM_t::MatrixVectorMult. The results will not be correct and training will not converge, but it will demonstrate performance issues. Graph row order and column order times as a function of the size of the first dense layer in MNIST08.

# 9

# Vistas

The subject of this book is the introduction to the canonical concepts underpinning deep learning ANNs. The central ideas have been presented, but only the surface has been scratched in the field of deep learning. The discipline of deep learning is a very rich and fertile area of research and commercial application. There are many directions for research and areas of specialization. Armed with a sound grounding in backpropagation, advanced topics come into view. This chapter presents some of the more interesting directions in which deep learning is currently moving. As the sections below will show, the roles of ANNs have far more potential than as regressors and classifiers.

## 9.1    The Limits of ANN Learning Capacity

The ANNs presented so far in this book comprise examples of regression and classification. The latter must learn decision boundaries to correctly classify input. It was argued that the boundary could be extremely nonlinear and an ANN will still learn it. It is intuitive that the more layers and neurons comprising an ANN, the greater the capacity of an ANN to learn. But are there any limits to what an ANN can learn? Are there any fundamental constraints? This section examines the question and points the interested reader to some formal results.

The question of constraints on the ability of ANNs to represent functions has been of interest from their inception. Moreover, an attempt to answer the question formally in 1969 by Minksy and Papert (131) set a pall over ANN research for a long period. They concluded that there were indeed very restrictive constraints on what ANNs could learn. Their conclusion was based on the assumption that ANNs could only learn simple linear decision boundaries. Image recognition and natural language processing, the grand challenges at the time, were deemed

*Demystifying Deep Learning: An Introduction to the Mathematics of Neural Networks,*
First Edition. Douglas J. Santry.
© 2024 The Institute of Electrical and Electronics Engineers, Inc. Published 2024 by John Wiley & Sons, Inc.

beyond the scope of what ANNs could master. Their most famous argument showed that a perceptron could not learn XOR. The conclusions that followed were controversial and seemed to contradict Rosenblatt's earlier formal results. Rosenblatt had already examined the question of convolutions of linear decision boundaries and concluded the opposite in his famous Existence Theorem (129). The debate has moved on since then. Non-linear algorithms and the exponential growth in the power of computers have resulted in new assumptions. ANNs have broken free of their linear shackles. Nonlinear learning has led to enormous renewed interest in ANNs, yielding the current state of the art.

Modern work has been done on the question based on new assumptions leading to many promising results. In the theory of ANNs there are many results providing for the capabilities of what ANNs can represent ("learn"). Such results are known as *universal approximation theorems*. They are concerned with the following, consider some function, $f$, unknown and perhaps (usually) unknowable, can it be approximated, ANN $\equiv \hat{f} \approx f$? The answer is, with some weak assumptions, yes, in many cases.

As has been shown, for the ANNs presented in this book, ANN topology has two hyperparameters, and they are depth and width. This is a two-dimensional hyperparameter space. Universal approximation theorems can usually be classified as either an arbitrary depth argument or an arbitrary width argument. A seminal paper written by George Cybenko in 1989 showed that an ANN of arbitrary width and using the sigmoid activation function can approximate many functions (27). This was an exciting result as the ANN community was emerging from the linearly constrained stupor of 2 decades. Since then, there have been many further results. Hornik showed in 1991 that the choice of activation function is not important so much as the depth of the network (70): a deep learning theorem. Thus theory exists supporting expanding an ANN in any hyperparameter dimension and expressing general functions.

Examination of the problem continues today, and recently, Kidger and Lyons showed in 2020 that for modern network topologies (i.e. deep learning), bounded width and arbitrary depth also yield a universal approximator (82). While all of the results are theoretical and do not necessarily lead to implementation insights, they do provide a sound theoretical basis for ANNs and their training.

Universal approximation theorems also motivate the construction that was placed on ANNs in Section 1.3. They create the connection between the analogy of the raw clay of an untrained model alluded to earlier and the final molding of the clay into any desired shape, that is, a trained model. Clay can be molded to any shape desired, and universal approximation theorems suggest that ANNs can be too. ANNs were originally motivated biologically, but we see now that their use can be motivated more generally: to paraphrase a celebrated mountaineer, "because they work." ANNs can be viewed as programmable functions, and we can program them to represent almost anything. It is this power that has led to so many more applications for deep learning, and we briefly survey a few in the following sections.

## 9.2  Generative Adversarial Networks

The general form of the ANN regressor and classifier has been framed in Chapter 2, and indeed, they are very important applications of Anns. Both forms of Anns share a property: inference is performed by accepting a valid input and producing a verifiable result. They are subject to ground truth. Generative Anns are completely different models. They produce material that is not necessarily "wrong" or "right"; they have no ground truth per se. Evaluating their results can be more subjective.

Generative models produce output that resembles examples from their training domain. The domain is specified with a dataset. A generative ANN produces novel material, and it does not classify an input. A trained generative ANN should produce output that is indistinguishable from an example in its training set. The roles of model and human are reversed in the sense that it is the human that classifies the model's output (is it good enough), as opposed to a model classifying a datum for a human. Consider the problem of learning how to draw a hand-written 2 in the style of the MNIST dataset. Figure 9.1 shows the intermediate stages of a generative ANN trying to learn how to draw a 2. Learning to produce an image that looks like a hand-written 2 is different from training a model to recognize one. But the concepts are related. Both models must have some idea of how to represent two.

Of particular interest of late is the *generative adversarial network* (GAN). GANs were described in 2014 by Goodfellow et al. (50). They were later combined with CNNs to produce the deep convolutional GAN (DCGAN) (119). This innovation proved fruitful, and soon GANs were producing photorealistic images (94). StyleGAN (80) soon followed producing images of human faces that were indistinguishable from real faces. The realistic images led to the coining of the

**Figure 9.1**  An example of generating twos. During training, 4 sample twos were generated every 25 epochs of training. The progression starts from the left and goes to the right.

phrase, "deepfake." GANs can now generate realistic images for anything that has a dataset to represent it such as impressionist paintings, aardvarks, or Rolling Stones albums (81). There are examples of entire videos being produced from a single photograph of a real person. The GAN is a fascinating innovation in that it can produce output that has never been seen before.

Figure 9.1 shows a trivial example of teaching a GAN to learn twos from the MNIST dataset. Over time the twos become more distinct. They were generated with code that is available on the book website (see Section 9.7). An Apple M1's GPU took 5.6 seconds per epoch, and over 200 epochs consumed 18 minutes. To limit the computational resources required to train the GAN the model was kept simple. The training set consists of selecting a single digit from MNIST. The example on the website is simpler; MNIST 2s have been downsampled to 14 × 14 to make it more accessible to notebook computers.

### 9.2.1   GAN Architecture

The crux of the GAN idea is to train two models simultaneously, but adversarially; the two independent models *compete* with each other. Their names are the generator and discriminator. The generator and discriminator can be thought of as the forger and the verifier, respectively. The discriminator is trained with a dataset from the target domain. For example, if images of dogs are desired then the training set will consist of photographs of dogs. They do not need to be labeled. The discriminator is trained to recognize images of dogs. The generator produces fake images of dogs. During training, the generator tries to fool the discriminator with its faux images. Their respective loss functions force both models to improve. The generator and the discriminator are perpetually in a race to get ahead of each other. This construct is a classic example of a zero-sum game.

Following the conclusion of training, the two models are divorced and only the forger is retained. The product of training is a model, the generator (forger), that produces output that is indistinguishable from the training set.

A rough sketch of the GAN training algorithm is as follows. The generator fabricates an example that it hopes will fool the discriminator. The discriminator accepts the fake from the generator and an example from the training set. The dataset can be considered the ground truth, and the generator a forgery, but once the generator is producing quality output, that line is blurred. The discriminator learns to distinguish between the real examples and the fakes from the generator. The generator improves as it learns from the discriminator detecting its forgeries. Thus both models improve in tandem competing with one another. Once training is completed, the discriminator can be discarded. The generator is the product of training. The architecture of the GAN is presented in Figure 9.3. The dataset in Figure 9.2 was used. The GAN is learning to draw a 2.

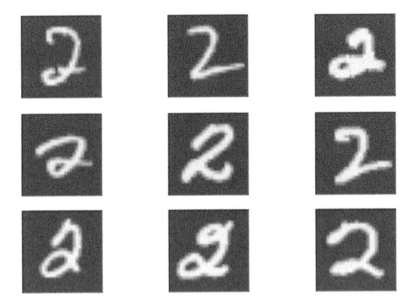

**Figure 9.2**    A selection of hand-written 2's from the MNIST dataset.

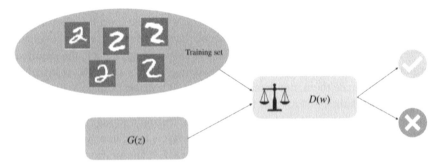

**Figure 9.3**    The GAN game. The generator, $G$, produces fakes and attempts to fool the descriminator, $D$. $D$ is learning how to recognize the real article from the training set. $G$ learns from $D$.

Two models are required. CNNs can be used for both models (making it a DCGAN). Let the discriminator be $D$, then its job is to act as a gatekeeper and only pass exemplars from the domain training set. The exclusivity is maintained by rejecting the fakes proposed by its opponent, the generator. The function $D$'s range is then $\mathbb{K} = \{\text{Real}, \text{Fake}\}$. It is the discriminator's task to learn the hidden structure of the exemplar dataset. Let $x \in \mathbb{T} \subset \mathbb{U}$ where $\mathbb{T}$ is the training set. Then $x$ is an example from the training set. For $D(x) : \mathbb{U} \to \mathbb{K}$ the answer should only be Real if $x$ really is from the training set. A perfect $D$ would perform as follows:

$$D(w) = \begin{cases} \text{Real} \equiv 1 & w \in \mathbb{T} \\ \text{Fake} \equiv 0 & w \notin \mathbb{T}. \end{cases} \tag{9.1}$$

Of course, $D$ will only approximate Eq. (9.1) or the generator would not be very useful, it merely represents the ideal. The discriminator is clearly a binary classifier (see Section 4.3.1). Any ANN that can learn the domain training set can be used as a discriminator. For example, the discriminator used to create the examples in Figure 9.1 was a CNN designed to learn how to recognize MNIST 2s.

Generators present more of a challenge. The immediate complication lies in the fact that ANNs require input. Generators are no different, and a means of generating input is required in addition to producing output. Let the generator be $G$. $G$ must produce its own input and learn to produce sensible output. The first problem is solved easily; the arguments to a generator are sampled from a random distribution. The two most popular distributions are the normal and uniform distributions, the former usually being used.

A vector of samples is obtained, $z \in \mathbb{R}^d$, by sampling one of the distributions. The connection between $\mathbb{R}^d$ and $\mathbb{U}$ is not dictated by the range. $G$ must learn the distribution of $\mathbb{T}$ in $\mathbb{U}$. It is the task of $G$ to map the sampled vector to something sensible in its range, $G(z) : \mathbb{R}^d \to \mathbb{U}$. Not even the shape is important, but a vector is convenient. It is the learnable parameters in $G$ where the sport lies; they do the work. Using transposed convolutions and dense layers, the sample vector is shaped to the desired output dimensions while simultaneously mapping it to the required output distribution. In contrast to the classifying CNN, a DCGAN, is learning features to produce them, not detect them. Like all training problems, fitting the parameters is challenge. Provided that $G$'s CNN has the capacity to learn the distribution of $\mathbb{T}$ the transformation can be learned. During training the parameters in the convolutions (projecting filters) and dense layers learn how to turn random noise into desirable output. Returning to Figure 9.1, it shows the evolution of a generator learning to map $\mathbb{R}^{100} \to \mathbb{R}^{28 \times 28}$ such that it produces what looks like hand-written twos. It is the learning capacity of $G$ that does the work, not the input.

## 9.2.2 The GAN Loss Function

GANs can be trained just like any neural network, with backpropagation of error, but there are two models. The models are in competition. The first piece that is required for a training regime is the definition of a differentiable loss function. The generator is trying to fool the discriminator. The discriminator needs to protect itself from the deceit of the generator. This is a zero-sum game; knowing the outcome for one of the parties completely determines the outcome of the other.

The loss should capture the adversarial relationship between the models. Once the loss functions are available, both models can be trained with SGD and backpropagation of error.

The discriminator can be construed as a binary classifier; see Section 4.3.1. Framing the discriminator problem solely as a classifier does not quite capture the winner take all nature of the exercise. The loss function needs to quantify the cost of losing. Unlike a normal classifier, which can just be "wrong," the discriminator has not simply misclassified an input, and it has lost a game; there is a real cost attached to a mistake. We begin with the definition of a binary classifier:

$$loss_{binary} = -[p \cdot \log(\hat{p}) + (1 - p) \cdot \log(1 - \hat{p})]. \tag{9.2}$$

The discriminator has two inputs which lead to,

$$loss_D = \sum_w^{x \cup G(z)} loss_{binary}(w) = loss_{binary}(x) + loss_{binary}(G(z)). \tag{9.3}$$

The two cases can be treated separately and then recombined later. For the case of $x \in \mathbb{T}$ then $D(x)$ is,

$$loss_x = -[1 \cdot \log(D(x)) + (1 - 1) \cdot \log(1 - D(x))] = \log(D(x)). \tag{9.4}$$

and for the fake attempt,

$$loss_{G(z)} = -[0 \cdot \log(D(G(z))) + (1 - 0) \cdot \log(1 - D(G(z)))] = \log(1 - D(G(z))). \tag{9.5}$$

Combining the two yields Goodfellow et al.'s famous loss function for a GAN. It was framed as a zero-sum game:

$$\min_G \max_D [\log(D(x)) + \log(1 - D(G(z)))]. \tag{9.6}$$

The first term reflects the fact that examples from the training set should produce 1, and the second term reflects the desire to return 0 for the fakes. The subtraction of 1 turns the minimum problem into a maximum problem, so the entire expression needs to be maximized with respect to the discriminator. The generator wants to minimize the expression as its interests are in direct conflict to those of the discriminator. In practical implementations, the minimization and the maximization are broken out, and the generator uses the loss function,

$$\min_G - \log(1 - D(G(z))). \tag{9.7}$$

By making Eq. (9.6) negative, the usual gradient descent can be used; it is the standard loss minimization problem. When used with SGD the losses are summed and scaled by the mini-batch size.

Algorithm 9.1 demonstrates the basic steps when training a GAN. The training routine loops for the specified number of steps. For clarity of exposition the

---

**Algorithm 9.1** Generative Adversarial Network Training

---

1: **procedure** TRAININGLOOP(*N steps*)
2:     **for** $i \in 1 : N$ *steps* **do**
3:         *fake* ← Generator()
4:         *genuine* ← random from Training Set
5:         $D_{fake}$ ← D(*fake*)
6:         $D_{genuine}$ ← D(*genuine*)
7:         ▷ The first argument to binary cross entropy is the ground truth
8:         $loss_D$ ← xEntropy(1, $D_{genuine}$) + xEntropy(0, $D_{fake}$)
9:         $loss_G$ ← xEntropy(1, $D_{fake}$)
10:         ▷ With the losses computed back-propagation of error is initiated.
11:         BackPropagation ($D, loss_D$)
12:         BackPropagation ($G, loss_G$)
13:         UpdateWeights (D)
14:         UpdateWeights (G)
15:     **end for**
16: **end procedure**

1: **procedure** GENERATOR
2:     $z$ ← random from $\mathbb{R}^d$
3:     *fake* ← G($z$)
4:     **return** *fake*
5: **end procedure**

---

mini-batch size is set to 1. Larger mini-batches would be used in a real implementation. An inner loop that excludes the weight updates would achieve this.

The game is designed to be adversarial, but it appears that the models really cooperate. The generator needs to learn the distribution of the domain dataset, and the information that it needs is obtained from the discriminator. It is the discriminator that propagates the information that informs the generator where it went wrong. By evaluating the generator's output and sharing the loss the generator learns to counterfeit the exemplar dataset's distribution. More details can be found in Goodfellow's tutorial (51).

Finally, it is not clear how to specify a condition for termination. The loss functions are not good guides. As the generator and discriminator compete the losses bounce around without really representing the quality of the generator. For output intended to be consumed by people then, human inspection can be used to gauge the number of required steps to produce a satisfactory generator. Training is often calibrated by a human observing the number of steps required to produce acceptable results.

GANs were not the first models to generate content, nor do they constitute the sole means of doing so. Other approaches are possible. Models trained to make predictions or learn features can be used to go in reverse. If a model has learnt the features of its training set, then there is potential to leverage that knowledge to generate data. Many models that are sequential and predictive can be reversed to produce output instead of consuming it. A technique proposed for nonlinear dimensional reduction, auto-encoders (87), can be used for generative purposes (85). Employing CNNs in combination with recurrent-neural networks (RNN) (20) can also be used for generative purposes. An early example of drawing MNISTesque digits with an RNN can be found here (56). CNNs have also been used, not just the DCGAN (95). The larger DCGANs can suffer from the vanishing gradient problem. An attempt to address the problem with a stronger loss function in the form of least squares was described in (100).

## 9.3 Reinforcement Learning

A powerful branch of machine learning that is rapidly growing in importance is reinforcement learning (RL). RL is a form of unsupervised machine learning. While strictly speaking, RL constitutes a rich field of study in its own right, ANNs and RL have been combined with such success of late that the study of RL is to be commended to all practitioners. A compelling example of ANN and RL complementary success is that of ChatGPT, best documented in the description of InstructGPT (108). RL techniques can be used on their own to solve problems, or they can be used to train neural networks. RL models can also be used in conjunction with ANNs as a component of a larger model. RL has roots in control theory, game theory, and Markov processes. All of these topics are fundamental in engineering, economics, and operations research, to name a few, so RL has wide application. In this section, a cursory outline of RL is presented, including a trivial but fully worked example available on the book's website (see (9.7)). For a full introduction to RL, the reader is directed to the excellent and approachable book (115).

The insight behind RL lies in the intuition of how biological animals behave. Animals, including humans, dislike pain, and hunger. What animals do enjoy are pleasure and the satisfaction of satiation. These feelings are strongly aligned with natural selection. When the behaviors attendant to pleasure and pain are aligned with the selective forces in an environment, animals do well. Animals tend to behave such that they seek pleasure and they avoid pain. An animal with a genetic mutation that leads to it enjoying the feeling of hunger will probably not reproduce, and the genetic mutation will die with the individual. Animals that dislike being hungry and eat to ward it off are more likely to reproduce. This is known as positive reinforcement. Humans can train, or domesticate, some animals by using positive reinforcement. Rewarding the desired behavior of an animal with food will reinforce the desired behavior in the animal. The insight that led to the use of positive reinforcement in machine learning is that these phenomena can be modeled mathematically.

RL is fundamentally different from the ANN methods that have been presented thus far. The model that results from training an ANN with a training set can be interpreted geometrically. ANNs are trained with supervised learning techniques; the datasets include the ground truth – the labels. The dataset with the ground truth defines a high-dimensional space. The object of training is to find a suitable approximation of the decision boundaries in this high-dimensional space. In the literature, this is also known as searching for structure. The means of training is the repeated presentation of points in the high-dimensional space. The object is to perform inference with the trained model, that is, given a point that is not in the training set, the ANN is expected to place the new tuple inside the correct decision boundary. This system works very well for classification. The experience that results in learning, in this case, is the repeated exposure to correct examples used to compute loss functions.

For the problem of training a model to learn a behavior, consider a robot learning to pick up a book, different techniques are required. This particular problem is known as dextreous manipulation. The problem of teaching a model how to pick up a bottle, or walk, is intractable when attempted with supervised learning techniques. Consider the size of the training set, or even how to generate it. This problem is clearly very different: the object is to teach a behavior, not discover structure.

For a more concrete example, consider the game of chess depicted in Figure 9.4. It is black's move, and an experienced human player would immediately recognize that is an opportunity to employ the Sicilian Defence. Consider training a model to play the game. Supervised learning techniques would be extremely awkward when applied to this scenario. The number of possible states for chess is very large (the number of valid board configurations). An effective training set, labeled, is not a tenable solution. RL is well suited to addressing exactly this kind of problem. RL models are, however, trained differently. ANNs require a labeled training set and a differentiable loss function. RL models do not learn by example, but rather, by *interaction* with an environment, in this example, by *playing* chess. The problem is to teach an agent how to behave, and this is done with positive reinforcement and negative reinforcement. In the chess example the environment is the state of the board and the desired behavior is to select a winning move.

A final note on employing supervised learning in this context. If a training set for learning chess was generated, then the trained model would probably not play *better* than the process that generated the training set (probably a human). A desideratum may well be to produce something that is superior to human capabilities. The human-curated training set connotes no scope for improvement – it is a theoretical bound on achievement. RL offers the opportunity to create something that is better at a task than the model's creator.

**Figure 9.4** A chess game following the opening moves of both players. Blue went first, it is thus the black player's turn to move.

### 9.3.1 The Elements of Reinforcement Learning

RL is an unsupervised machine learning technique. All of the training methods that have been presented thus far had the twin components of labeled data and a loss function. Training consisted of verifying the output of a model with a known answer (the ground truth) and emending the model with a differentiable loss function. RL is different. It does not require labeled data, or even data per se.

The central abstraction in the RL world is called an *agent*. The agent learns by blundering about in an *environment*. Learning occurs through interacting with the environment. The agent interacts with the environment seeking rewards that reinforce the desired behavior. Over time the agent improves and learns how to perform a task. To train an agent with RL there are some basic components required that are now defined. Let us now examine the environment and reward more formally.

An agent learning how to behave in an abstract environment can be trained with RL. The environment is provided by the people training the agent. The environment represents the problem domain. For example, if training an agent to play chess, the environment must accept a move from the agent and update the state of the game appropriately. The environment must also detect wins, losses, and draws. By interacting with the environment, i.e. making chess moves, the agent learns how to play. To learn, there must be reinforcement, both positive and negative. Losing discourages bad moves and winning encourages good moves.

A task is accomplished by performing actions in an environment. An agent interacts with an environment by sending it actions to change the state. An environment is the set, $S$, of all possible states for the problem under consideration. The set can be infinite if continuous, such as a robot learning to walk, or the set can be finite if it is discrete. A game such as checkers, which has $\approx 10^{40}$ valid board configurations, has a finite, if large, state space. At time $t$ the system is in the state, $s_t \in S$, where $s_t$ is the state at that time. The system advances to a state, $s_{t+1}$, when the agent sends an action to environment. The agent must grow adept at selecting a good action to transition to a desirable new state.

An agent has a set of possible actions that it can take in the environment, $A$. Of particular importance is the set, $A(s_t)$, which is the set of all possible *valid* actions when in the state, $s_t$. To change state, that is, transition from state $s_t$ to $s_{t+1}$, an agent must select and execute an action, $a \in A(s_t)$, that should ideally be an improvement. The action selected and executed is, $A_t$. This leads to the notion of a *reward* function. Interacting with the environment results in a reward function attaching a measure of "goodness" or "badness" to the action. High rewards are sought after and low rewards avoided.

This leads directly to the notion of best, and what is meant by it. A metric is required for quantitative comparison. The means employed is a reward function, $R(s) \in \mathbb{R}$. The reward must be computable for every action, but it does not have to be defined. The reward function looks like, $R : S \to \mathbb{R}$. At time $t$ one action will be selected, $A_t$, resulting in a new state and its reward, $R_{t+1}(s_{t+1})$.

The object of training is to produce a policy, $\pi$, that the agent can follow to navigate the environment. The role of the policy is to select the actions that the agent executes. To change state, an agent must select and execute an action, $a \in A(s_t)$. The actions are selected by $\pi$, and it looks like $\pi : S \to A$. As $\pi$ is the policy it is responsible for selecting the "best" action. The action selected by $\pi$ is $A_t$. Sending the action to the environment will result in the new state, $s_{t+1}$ and the reward, $R_{t+1}$. The agent navigates through the environment producing the sequence of states, $\{s_0, s_1, \ldots, s_t\}$ and their attendant rewards, $\{R_0, R_1, \ldots, R_t\}$. The sequence of states is known as a trajectory.

The outlines of an algorithm are now emerging. An agent employs a policy, $\pi$, that when in state $s_t$ selects an action, $A_t$, such that it maximizes $R_{t+1}$. More formally, in $s_t$ the policy $\pi$ assigns a probability of success to each action. The problem of selecting an action is simply that of choosing the highest probability.

### 9.3.2 A Trivial RL Training Algorithm

There are many ways to train using RL. One approach is to model the problem as a Markov Decision Process (MDP). Training an agent for a MDP problem results in a policy that reduces the MDP to a Markov Chain. There are a number of means of doing so, and this section presents the dynamic programming approach (11).

Figure 9.5 depicts an example of a trivial MDP. Figure 9.5a is the full MDP. The states and actions are: $S = \{S_0, S_1, S_2, S_3\}$ and $\mathcal{A} = \{a_0, a_1, a_2, a_3, a_4\}$. Black arrows lead from states to actions. Light arrows lead from actions to the next state. Light edges are labeled with the relevant probability of it being traversed if the

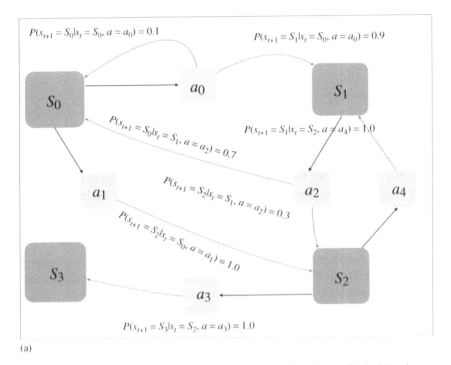

(a)

**Figure 9.5** (a) Markov Decision Process and (b) the resulting Markov Chain following computation of a policy, $\pi$, and applying it. Black arrows lead to actions and light arrows lead to possible results of the actions. In the Markov Chain there is at most one black arrow emanating from a state. This is the result of applying a policy to the MDP.

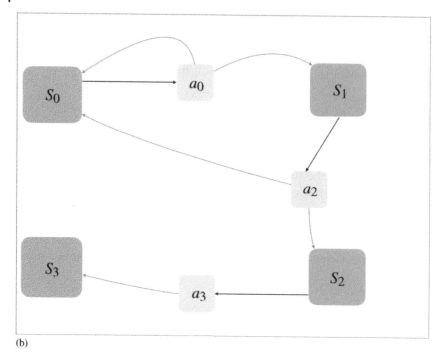

(b)

**Figure 9.5** *(Continued)*

action is selected. Note that a particular action does not necessarily produce a predictable result. For example, when in state $S_0$ and executing action $a_0$ there are two possible outcomes. Some of the states have multiple actions available to them. The policy is responsible for selecting the action. Training an agent to produce a policy result in the solution depicted in Figure 9.5b. The MDP has been reduced to a Markov Chain as the policy has decided which action to take when in a given state, e.g. $\pi(S_0) = a_0$. Consequently there is only one black arrow starting from any state in the diagram; the policy chose the surviving arrows.

Training an agent with RL produces a policy, $\pi$, that performs a task to an acceptable level. To motivate the method about to be presented, the initial state of training must be presented. This will motivate the algorithm while demonstrating a fundamental trade-off when training with RL. To this end, we introduce a more concrete example in the form of the game of tic-tac-toe.

The game of tic-tac-toe[1] consists of drawing a $3 \times 3$ matrix. Two players take turns placing either an **x** or an **o** on the board. The object of the game is for a

---

1 Tic-tac-toe is also known as noughts and crosses in some countries.

player to place 3 of their pieces in sequence. Diagonal, horizontal, and vertical series of 3 are all valid. This is an example of a zero-sum game; the winner takes all. The game can be modeled as an MDP. Every valid board configuration is a state in the MDP diagram (the game's set, $S$). The actions are the valid moves in a configuration. A player cannot place their piece in a square that is already occupied, $A(s_{t+1}) = A(s_t) - A_t$. The set of actions consists of placing a piece in one of the 9 possible squares on the board, $A = \{(1, 1), (1, 2), (1, 3), (2, 1), ..., (3, 3)\}$, where the moves index the $3 \times 3$ board. Finally, the reward function is defined as:

$$R(s) = \begin{cases} 1.0 & s = \text{win} \\ 0.5 & s = \text{draw} \\ 0.0 & s = \text{loss.} \end{cases} \tag{9.8}$$

To initiate training, and assuming the agent goes first and plays **x**, the first problem is to select one of the 9 possible moves. A problem immediately presents itself, and there is no $A_0$ such that $R_1$ is defined, that is, one cannot win, lose, or draw with an opening move. More information is required. The problem is known as the *sparse rewards* problem, and not every move yields a reward. A mechanism is required to communicate rewards received later in the game to earlier states so that the policy can account for them. This idea is related to the following important concept when training with RL techniques.

As the agent navigates its environment (plays the game) it moves from state to state as the policy reacts to the opponent's moves by selecting the action in a given state with the highest reward. This is known as greedy action selection. When the training algorithm accepts the greedy choice of the policy, it is known as *exploitation*. During training, the object is to discover good behaviors, that involves exploring *new* behaviors, experimenting with actions. Executing an action that is not the best known at the time is an act of *exploration*. Exploration presents the opportunity to discover unknown behaviors that may be superior to those already observed. To achieve this, the policy is modified such that during training $\pi$ accepts the best *known* action with probability, $1 - \epsilon$. $\epsilon$, a hyperparameter for training RL, is the probability of randomly exploring. If the greedy action is rejected, then one of the remaining valid actions is randomly selected. How to select $\epsilon$ is discussed below. Exploration is the mechanism employed to learn about unseen phenomena in the environment. A training algorithm employing exploration is known as $\epsilon$-greedy. $\epsilon$ can be viewed as the level of curiosity of the agent.

The tension between exploitation and exploration derives from the understanding that instant gratification, the immediately optimal option, is not always the best option in the long term. Postponing gratification in the hope that there is something better in the future is clearly related to the problem of sparse rewards. A means of accounting for the total reward along a trajectory (a path through the

MDP graph) is required. This is captured with the idea of a *value* function. Value functions are derivatives of reward functions, but not in the Calculus sense of the word. The reward function is the instant gratification of an action. A value function is based on the reward function, but it is a longer-term view of the reward function. Value functions differ from reward functions in their time-scale and reflect planning. For most people, surgery is painful and has a low reward. Its value, however, is high. In the long run, it can increase life span or may increase the baseline of a reward function by fixing a chronic problem such as back pain or cataracts. One way to compute value is to calculate the expectation of reward with respect to a given action and state tuple, $(s_i, a_j)$:

$$Q_{n+1} \mid (s_i, a_j) = \mathbb{E}(R) = \frac{R_1 + R_2 + \cdots + R_n}{n}, \tag{9.9}$$

$Q$ defined in Eq. (9.9) is the *action value* function. It captures the long term payoff of pursuing the action in the state. Note that $n$ and the subscripts are not time, they are the number of observations, that is, the number of times during training the action was executed in that state. During training, a game will be played many times. For example, the opening move of the agent in tic-tac-toe might be to place an **x** in (2, 1), then Eq. (9.9) is computing the expectation for that particular move for an empty board. In the initial state of tic-tac-toe all moves are valid so the agent would maintain 9 action values, one for each move, to learn the best move. As defined $Q_n$ is not suitable for computation as it requires storing far too much data (even for a trivial game such as tic-tac-toe, which has 19,683 valid states, ignoring symmetry). A different form of the equation is required that is more suitable for implementation:

$$
\begin{aligned}
Q_{n+1} &= \frac{1}{n} \sum_{i=1}^{n} R_i \\
&= \frac{1}{n} \left( R_n + \sum_{i=1}^{n-1} R_i \right) \\
&= \frac{1}{n} \left( R_n + \frac{n-1}{n-1} \cdot \sum_{i=1}^{n-1} R_i \right) \\
&= \frac{1}{n} (R_n + (n-1) \cdot Q_n) \\
&= \frac{1}{n} (R_n + n \cdot Q_n - Q_n) \\
&= Q_n + \frac{1}{n} (R_n - Q_n).
\end{aligned}
\tag{9.10}
$$

Equation (9.10) is an example of a *temporal difference* equation. It is far more suitable for a practical implementation. The equation requires the storage of two values, $Q_n$ and $n$ (number of times the action was executed in that state). A law of large numbers argument suggests that as the number of training runs increases (9.10) will converge to the correct action value for the action.

Armed with a means of computing the value of actions and a reward function the training of an agent to learn tic-tac-toe can be presented. It is a table-driven approach. When training every valid state has a table of action values. The policy selects the action with the highest value. Ties are broken by selecting one randomly. The proposed action is executed leading to the next state. The opponent simply chooses an action randomly (skill does not matter, it makes the value functions more accurate as all permutations are executed, or an agent can play itself). The cycle is repeated recursively until a reward is obtained. In the case of tic-tac-toe a training run can have a maximum trajectory length of 9 states. When a terminal state is reached the reward is consumed by the action that actuated it by updating its action value for that state. The updated *value*, not the reward, is then passed to the immediate predecessor agent state in the trajectory.

Figure 9.6 demonstrates the core ideas for a simple game such as tic-tac-toe. There is a global dictionary, Policy, that returns the per state policy, Z, which is $\pi_s$. Z includes the per action value for the state and the number of times that each action has been invoked. They are called Qn and n, respectively. The reward function was designed such that it can be interpreted as a probability and the expectation definition preserves that property. Selecting the highest value can be interpreted as choosing the action with the highest probability of winning.

The routines in Algorithm 9.2 demonstrate some of the principles of training with RL. They are used by Algorithm 9.3 to learn how to play tic-tac-toe. It must be emphasized that tic-tac-toe is a trivial problem, but there were still challenges. The required pieces were the environment and the reward function. It is argued

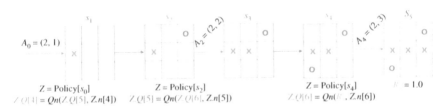

**Figure 9.6** An example training run for tic-tac-toe. The progression of the game is from left to right. The agent's moves are labeled with the action, $A_t$. The result of this game is a win for the agent. $A_4$ results in $s_5$ and $R_5 = 1.0$. The reward is consumed and values are updated backward through the trajectory of moves. The linear indices for Z are *row · 3 + column*.

---

**Algorithm 9.2** Implementation of a Policy for Tic-Tac-Toe

1: **procedure** $\pi(s)$
2:    $Z \leftarrow Policy(s)$
3:    $index \leftarrow \underset{index}{\arg\max}\ Z.Qn[index]$          ▷ Greedy selection
4:    $a_{greedy} \leftarrow \mathcal{A}(index)$
5:    $explore \leftarrow (\text{sample} \in [0, 1]) \leq \epsilon$
6:    **if** *explore* **then**
7:        **return** random $(\mathcal{A}(s) - a_{greedy})$     ▷ Try anything but the best action
8:    **end if**
9:    **return** $a_{greedy}$
10: **end procedure**

---

that unsupervised training techniques are easier as a training set does not need to be curated. It is clear, however, that it merely substitutes one problem for another, and the challenge should not be underestimated. The reward function for tic-tac-toe is very simple and intuitive. For a trivial zero-sum game a reward function is relatively easy to construct. The reward function for a robot learning to stand, or a hand learning to grasp a glass bottle is far more complicated (and not obvious). Games with deeper game trees may have to address the problem of sparse rewards. Google's Go implementation did manage to train with a zero-sum terminal reward function (139), but it is not always possible. The $19 \times 19$ board used in their implementation can have trees that are $10^{48}$ moves deep. For complicated tasks the reward function itself can be learnt. Apprentice learning describes itself as inverse RL as it attempts to recover a reward function from a solved system (2). Stochastic approaches, such Hindsight Replay, have also been successful (5).

The representation of the policy for tic-tac-toe is expensive. The table driven approach provides for the explicit storage of the $\pi_s$ and is simply not feasible for any interesting problem. Q-Learning is one solution (160) as it takes better advantage of the MDP property of the problem and does not require tables. Action values make sense for simple applications, but for more complicated problems *state value* functions, $V$, are used.

RL is a powerful technique for building machine learning models. It is particularly useful when there is no training set available and the desired outcome is more behavioral. It should not be viewed in isolation from ANNs. The two fields are very much intertwined and growing ever more so. RL can be used to train neural networks and neural networks can be used to train RL models. This mutually supporting relationship is only set to grow. This section was a necessarily brief introduction, but it is hoped that the essence of the paradigm has been conveyed.

---

**Algorithm 9.3** Learn a Policy to Play Tic-Tac-Toe

---

1: **procedure** TRAIN AGENT($N$)
2:     **for** $i \in N$ **do**                ▷ Training consists of playing $N$ times
3:         RunGame ()
4:     **end for**
5: **end procedure**

1: **procedure** RUNGAME
2:     $s_0 \leftarrow$ Empty Board
3:     *trajectory* $\leftarrow \emptyset$
4:     **for** $i \in 1{:}9$ **do**
5:         $A_t \leftarrow \pi(s_t)$
6:         trajectory.push $(s_t, A_t)$
7:         $s_t \leftarrow$ Execute $(A_t,$ Agent$)$
8:         **if** $R_t \leftarrow$ Reward $(s_t)$ **then**
9:             **break**
10:         **end if**
11:         $t \leftarrow t + 1$                         ▷ The opponents turn
12:         $a_{opponent} \leftarrow$ random $(\mathcal{A}(s_t))$
13:         $s_t \leftarrow$ Execute $(A_t,$ Opponent$)$
14:         **if** $R_t \leftarrow$ Reward $(s_t)$ **then**
15:             **break**
16:         **end if**
17:     **end for**
18:     $Q_i \leftarrow R_t$
19:     **while** trajectory $\neq \emptyset$ **do**
20:         $s, a \leftarrow$ trajectory.pop ()
21:         $Z \leftarrow$ Policy $(s)$
22:         index $\leftarrow$ index $(a)$
23:         Z.Qn[index] $\leftarrow$ Z.Qn[index] $+ \frac{1}{Z.\text{n[index]}} \cdot (Q_i - Z.\text{Qn[index]})$
24:         Z.n[index] $\leftarrow$ Z.n[index] $+ 1$
25:         $Q_i \leftarrow$ Z.Qn[index]
26:     **end while**
27: **end procedure**

---

## 9.4 Natural Language Processing Transformed

This section presents transformers in the context of natural language process-ing (NLP). Transformers are the basis of most natural language processing applications today. They were presented in a landmark paper that described transformers in their current form, "Attention is all You Need" (155). The authors showed that a well-known technique, attention, could be used by itself to address the problem of relationships between words in language. Transformers have wider application, but it is the problem domain of natural language that they have had the biggest impact. The paper described a refinement of attention called self-attention implemented with a transformer. Transformers not only perform better than previous methods, but they overcome the inherent sequential nature of earlier methods and naturally support parallel processing, an important consideration when using GPUs. The output of transformers is vital for use in "heavy" NLP applications that consume it downstream in the text processing pipeline. ANNs consume the output of transformers when they are training for NLP domain problems. Transformers process text that can then be used for classification, regression, and generative purposes. Since its publication self-attention has been wildly successful and arguably set off off the current NLP revolution.

An important challenge facing AI is to facilitate communication between computers and humans. The ideal is for computers to learn how humans speak, not vice versa. Currently, humans are subject to the strictures that computers impose on them when they interact. The onus is on people to comport their practices to those of computers; the machines dictate to the humans. Computers are dumb calculators and do not grasp the intricacies of human language. NLP is the field of teaching computers to competently deal with human modes of language. The subject of NLP is worthy of a volume in its own right and any attempt to present it in a single section can only scratch the surface. For a thorough treatment of NLP the reader is directed to (77).

Humans employ a different class of language when communicating with each other than they do with computers. The problem arises from the inherent differences between the natures of computers and people. Computers only understand numbers represented as binary integers. Human language consists of words and context. Despite the differences the gap has been partially bridged. There are many examples of computer languages that humans can employ to instruct a machine: C, Python, Rust, Lisp, Swift, Smalltalk, Pascal, Basic, Java... the examples are legion. The list is by no means exhaustive. There are thousands. Humans have instructed computers using computer languages for decades, but they are *special* languages. The field of computer languages, also referred to as programming languages, is an active and important area of computer science research. Humans can communicate with computers, but any programmer would agree, only in a very superficial and exhausting way. Computers languages are a different type of language than human language, and are specially designed. Programming languages are *context free* grammars. Human languages have context and ambiguity.

### 9.4.1 The Challenges of Natural Language

Natural language presents two specific challenges to a computer. Computers are "dumb"; a computer is effectively a mathematical automaton. Human languages consist of words and grammar, and both are minefields for a computer that is incapable of inferring context.

Words in human languages can have multiple senses and the sense meant is inferred from implicit contextual information. Homonyms also give computers trouble; the sense meant is not explicit in a sentence. The words meat and meet are problematic for speech recognition software. In written text lie can mean either horizontal or a conscious untruth. Humans have little trouble dealing with either situation because the context usually makes the meaning clear, but even humans can disagree over what a sentence means. In contrast computer programs are unambiguous and have a single and provable interpretation.

Humans derive the context from many means, including body language, intonation, and emphasis.[2] NLP concentrates on grammatical cues. A word's sense may depend on its position in a sentence (spatial dependency). The semantic meaning of word in a sentence may be modified by words in other clauses in the sentence. This can be ambiguous linguistically and people use context to infer what is meant. Consider the following examples:

1. `The person did not cross the road because it was tired.`
   From the context, it is clear that the person was tired. Roads do not get tired.
2. `The person did not cross the road because it was wide.`
   From the context, it is clear that the road was wide. People are not wide.
3. `The person did not cross the road because it was busy.`
   Even for a human, this sentence is ambiguous. Either noun could reasonably be considered busy and so the sentence has multiple semantic meanings.

Human language relies on context. Context is important when determining the full import of a sentence. Synonyms and homonyms are (usually) easily handled by the humans. Computers have trouble extrapolating meanings sensibly. The challenge of NLP is to surmount these obstacles. The resulting software and models are infinitely more complex than a C++ compiler or a Python interpreter.

### 9.4.2 Word Embeddings

A fundamental abstraction ubiquitous in modern NLP is the word embedding. Word embeddings form the basis of almost all NLP systems. It is the abstraction,

---

2 Hence the joke, Teacher: "A double negative makes a positive, but not vice-versa." Student: "Yea, right."

the basic building block, that higher level NLP tools are built with. This section motivates and outlines their use.

Sentences are comprised of words, but computers only understand numbers. The first task is to convert a word to something that a computer program can handle. A trivial means of accomplishing this is called tokenizing. A static dictionary can map a word, and its inflections (e.g. take and took), to a unique integer. The representation can be augmented by attaching the part of speech as well. This is not a very good system as homonyms break it immediately. There is also no information contained in the numeric representation. More than a token is required. In addition to the token, the meaning of the word must be captured. This would seem to lead to a catch-22. The definition of a word is yet more words leading to more definitions. A means of representing the meanings of words mathematically is clearly indicated.

A powerful means of representing words are *vector semantics*. Words can be represented with vectors. The vectors are embeddings of words in a vector space that captures the semantic meaning of a word; the vector space is called a semantic space. The method is known as word embeddings; the meanings of words are embedded in the semantic space. The vectors are the means of encapsulating words for use by an NLP system. The word embeddings are vectors that encapsulate the meaning of a word, and they are numerical. Computers are good at dealing with vectors, and indeed that is why such a representation was selected. Representing words as vectors implies that the full force of mathematics can be brought to bear on them.

A word embedding should have certain properties. For the embeddings and mathematical operations to be useful the linguistic value must not be lost. The mathematical operations should makes sense linguistically in the word space. The vectors are elements of a vector space so a measure of distance can be defined for them. The measure should reflect linguistic relationships. Dog, cat, tea, and coffee are all different words so they will have unique embeddings. Let $x_{word}$ be the embedding of *word*. The following relations should hold: $x_{dog} - x_{cat} < x_{dog} - x_{tea}$ and $x_{tea} - x_{coffee} < x_{dog} - x_{tea}$. And further, $x_{mammal} - x_{cat} < x_{mammal} - x_{soda}$. The distance between word embeddings is known as similarity, and a good word embedding will define a useful measure that captures similarity. It should naturally capture synonyms and conceptual relationships.

Word embeddings can be implemented as static dictionaries. The dictionaries are surprisingly easy to generate. An NLP application has a text domain of concern, a corpus (e.g. 10,000 legal opinions), and the corpus can be treated as a training set. Words that occur close to each other are usually related, this is called the distributional hypothesis, and forms the basis of learning an embedding. The word, judge, is more likely to be in the same sentence with lawyer, opinion, or judgment than soup or beetle, and this is naturally reflected in the corpus. This property is called self-supervising, and does not require explicit labels. Processing the text it becomes clear that the word judge is connected with lawyer, but not giraffe. An application developer chooses the dimension of the embedding, $\mathbb{R}^d$, and then trains the dictionary. Once trained the dictionary is used by calling it with a word's token. The dictionary returns the word embedding, which is a vector: $\text{dict(judge)} \rightarrow x_{judge}$. The vector is real-valued and dense. Word2vec is the canonical example of this approach (104). Once the embeddings have been computed they can be used with a model; they are the input that can be used with an ANN. The dimensionality of the word embeddings does a better job of capturing the multiple senses of a word, but it is not ideal. Nor does an embedding give any indication of which sense is meant in the current sentence or its effect on other words.

Word embeddings are typically required to produce vectors that are normalized, $\|x\| = 1$. The set of embeddings describe the surface of a hypersphere, that is, a sphere in $d$ dimensions. Recall that the dot product is defined as,

$$x \cdot y = \|x\| \cdot \|y\| \cdot \cos(\theta), \tag{9.11}$$

where $\theta$ is the angle between the two vectors. The dot product is the projection of $x$ on to $y$. When dot products are used with normalized vectors the result is the cosine of the angle between them. This property applies to word embeddings. Word embeddings are normalized so the dot product is the cosine of the angle between the embeddings. Word embeddings can be designed to make the cosine meaningful. It is often the cosine that is used as a measure of similarity, not the difference used in the example above. The method is called cosine similarity. Similar words will have similar embeddings. The angle between them will be small. As the angle grows smaller the cosine approaches 1. Large angles connote little similarity and cosine approaches $-1$. The intuitive interpretation and the range of cosine $\leq \pm 1$ make cosine similarity very attractive mathematically.

Word embeddings makes it possible to encode text such that computers can make sense of it. A sentence of length $n$ is a sequence of tokens, $t_1, t_2, \ldots, t_n$. The sentence is processed in sequence from 1 to $n$ producing the set of embeddings,

$$\{x_1 = \text{dict}(t_1), \ldots, x_n = \text{dict}(t_n)\}. \tag{9.12}$$

Given a sentence with $n$ words, a matrix can be built by placing each word embedding row-wise in a matrix (the transpose of the vectors, $x_i^t$):

$$E = \begin{pmatrix} x_1^T \\ x_2^T \\ \vdots \\ x_n^T \end{pmatrix}. \tag{9.13}$$

The embeddings matrix can be used to multiply one of the word's embedding,

$$Ex_i = s_i. \tag{9.14}$$

The result is a vector of the similarities between the word and all of the words in the sentence. $s_i$ is the projection of the word $x_i$ onto the rest of the sentence. Moreover, $EE^T = S$, is a matrix of the similarity vectors for all the words in a sentence, column wise. The diagonal will be exclusively 1s as self-similarity has a cosine of 1, $\theta = 0$. This property is very useful for NLP systems, especially those that are matrix based, such as ANNs.

Word embedding is a very powerful tool for dealing with natural language applications. They do, however, leave something to be desired. Recall the list of contextual sentences above. The meaning of some words depended on words in other parts of the sentence. A sentence must be examined simultaneously in its entirety to encapsulate it fully. A static mapping from a word to its vector does not account for context. The word's relation to other words in a sentence is important when determining its meaning, or even the value of its contribution to the sentence.

Representing words with vectors that account for context is a *language model*. A language model can also be predictive, that is, produce the distribution of tokens: $P(t_i \mid t_{i-1})$. Predictive language models can be turned around and made generative. If the model can predict tokens well then in reverse it can also produce them. Word embeddings are sufficient for many applications, but applications that must really understand or mimic human language require language models. Language models are the basis for chatbots such as ChatGPT (GPT is the name of the language model) and many others. The current state of the art for building language models is the transformer. It is the transformer that forms the subject of the Section, 9.4.3.

### 9.4.3 Attention

Attentive processes are operations that prioritize a subset of information. They can be thought of as providing focus on a particular aspect of a problem. Recalling the embeddings in Eq. (9.12), there is a clear limitation. The individual word embeddings have not utilized any information about other words in the sentence; each embedding was performed in isolation.

For a token, $t_i$, how does the model handle the information latent in some token, $t_j$, that has already been seen but is now forgotten ($j < i$) or is yet to be observed ($j > i$). Moreover, processing a sentence is sequential, and the job of a language model is to predict the $j > i$. Accounting exclusively for earlier tokens in the sentence is of particular importance and is called causal. There are two related problems when attempting to incorporate relationships between words. The first is producing a means of detecting the relationships between words in a sentence. The second problem is the question of how to represent the relationships.

Relating words in a sentence is known as *attention*. Attention increases the importance some items and decreases the importance of others; it focuses attention on the most important subset of information.

A simple method to produce attention is to compute a vector of weights that can be applied embeddings,

$$a = (\alpha_1, \dots, \alpha_n).$$ (9.15)

The weights have the following property:

$$\sum_{i}^{n} \alpha_i = 1, \alpha \geq 0,$$ (9.16)

where all the weights are nonnegative. In the case of accounting for only those tokens already seen up until $t_i$ a modification is required:

$$\sum_{j=1}^{i} \alpha_j = 1.$$ (9.17)

The weights are computed at inference time, so they are called *soft weights*. The idea of computing weights during inference was introduced in a generative text setting (53), but it quickly proved useful for comprehension as well. This is in contrast to normal weights, parameters of a model, which are fixed following the conclusion of training. The attentional soft weights can be used in a dot product with the sentence to attenuate the elements appropriately. One means of computing attention is to employ the embedding matrix to compute the similarities. The similarities are then construed as importance and used for attention.

$$a_i = \text{softmax}(Ex_i).$$ (9.18)

Equation (9.18) produces the vector of attentional weights, $a_i$, for the word $x_i$. The softmax function ensures that the similarities meet the constraints defined in Eq. (9.16). By computing the attention with the entire sentence words are connected across distance. A new embedding can now be computed that accounts for attention with the soft weights,

$$y_i = \sum_{j=1}^{i} \alpha_j \cdot x_j,$$ (9.19)

where the $\alpha_j$ is the $j$th entry in the attention tuple, a scaler. The new embedding is a convex linear combination of nearby words scaled by their attention scores. The resulting embedding accounts for the importance of other words in the sentence by incorporating their similarities in its embedding.

The use of similarity for attention is an improvement over static word embeddings, but it is not ideal. In particular, it assumes quality word embeddings and a useful measure of similarity. A further refinement described by Vaswani et al. in their attention paper is *self-attention*. They proposed a scheme that employed *learned* matrices. The computation of attention was decomposed and abstracted presenting the opportunity to introduce multiple learned matrices in the computation. The matrices are trained with backpropagation of error and SGD. This is the idea that is the basis of the transformer.

### 9.4.4 Transformer Blocks

Transformers are made up of transformer blocks stacked on top of one another. The output of one transformer block is the input to the next. To understand how transformers work transformer blocks need to be described. A transformer block consists of two pieces. The input layer performs a computation that is similar to attention just described, and the output uses a neural network.

Further abstraction of the process of computing attention is required to understand transformers. The word embeddings in Eq. (9.14) play many roles. It is useful to examine each one in isolation. The argument to the embedding matrix, the vector being projected (multiplied), can be viewed as a *query*. The computation is being carried out with respect to the query vector. The embedding vector $x_i$ is the current focus of attention (hence the name, self-attention). The rows of the embedding matrix are similar to those of *keys*. Keys map the query to potential candidates that may be of use. The query was projected onto the keys with Eq. (9.14). The resulting vector was normalized with Eq. (9.18) to produce the attentional vector. The attentional vector was used in Eq. (9.19) with a *value* vector to produce the final embedding (in this case, the value vector was $x_i$). The keys are used to map a query to a value. Learning can be introduced into the problem by using learned matrices of parameters for each of the three tasks. The three roles in a transformer block computing self-attention are performed by:

$$q = W^q x$$
$$k = W^k x$$
$$v = W^v x, \tag{9.20}$$

where three learned matrices of weights have been introduced. They are, in order of the enumeration in (9.20), query, key, and value. The superscript denotes their identity. The weights matrices are used to multiply the input word embedding to produce the vectors required for self-attention. For a predictive model only those tokens already seen are included. When processing token $i$ Eq. (9.20) are applied to all $x_j, j \leq i$. Laying out the resulting vectors row order in matrices produces matrices that look like,

$$Q_i = \begin{pmatrix} (W^q x_1)^T \\ (W^q x_2)^T \\ \vdots \\ (W^q x_i)^T \end{pmatrix}. \tag{9.21}$$

For $x \in \mathbb{R}^d$, $Q_i$ is a $i \times d$ matrix. The same is done to produce a keys matrix, $K$, as well as a values matrix, $V$. Continuing with the computation the next step is to find the attentional weights. The weights are calculated with the query and key matrices,

$$a = \text{softmax}\left( \frac{K_i q_i}{\sqrt{d}} \right), \tag{9.22}$$

where the weights vector, $a$, will have $i$ entries. The dot product has been scaled by dividing by $\sqrt{d}$ where $d$ is the dimension of the input vectors. The similarity computations based on normalized vectors produced cosine of angles, which are between $\pm 1$. The new learned matrices can produce arbitrarily large dot products and so the scaling is required to ensure the numerically stable operation of softmax. With the weights computed the final attention can be computed with the value vectors.

$$\bar{y}_i = \sum_{j=1}^{i} \alpha_j \cdot v_j, \tag{9.23}$$

where the $\alpha_j$ are scalers. The new vector is a linear combination of the value vectors scaled by the weights. The final operation of the self-attentive layer is to apply a residual connection and then to normalize.

$$y_i = layerNorm(\bar{y}_i + x_i). \tag{9.24}$$

Layer normalization is described in Section 7.5.2. The residual connection transmits information deeper into a network by jumping over an intermediate, parallel layer. It also helps with training as the gradient will be stronger as it skips the same component in the backward direction (64). Following the self-attention layer the final result of the transformer block is produced by using an ANN.

$$z_i = layerNorm(ANN(y_i) + y_i). \tag{9.25}$$

The result is residually connected and then normalized to produce the final output.

The exposition so far has been vector-centric; the focus was on computing the self-attention for a single token. There is no reason why more than one token cannot be processed at once. Indeed, for a sentence of length $n$ all the computations can be performed in parallel with matrix multiplications. A matrix of the input vectors is used instead of the individual vectors. $X$ is composed by stacking the $x_i^T$ in row order. As they are in row order the parameter matrices are the right-side factors in the multiplication.

$$Q = XW^q$$
$$K = XW^k$$
$$V = XW^v. \tag{9.26}$$

The matrix formulation that results can be efficiently implemented with matrix software for either CPUs or GPUs.

$$\text{SelfAttention}(Q, K, V) = \text{softmax}\left(\frac{QK^T}{\sqrt{d}}\right)V. \tag{9.27}$$

The result is a self-attention matrix. The matrix product, $QK^T$ will need the upper triangle marked as $-\infty$ to ensure that they do not contribute to the softmax operation. This preserves the property that self-attention calculations only use previously seen tokens for each token position.

A transformer consists of stacking the transformer blocks (the original paper used 6). The architecture is presented graphically in Figure 9.7. Input arrives and it percolates through the transformer blocks in sequence. The output of a block forms the input to the next. After the final transformer block has finished the result is a matrix with the new embeddings. The result has the same dimensions as the input matrix. A transformer block has four trainable pieces. They are the three weights matrices and the ANN.

Algorithm 9.4 illustrates the complete process for self-attention. It is invoked with text, e.g.: `Transformer` ("Transformers are powerful tools."). The first step

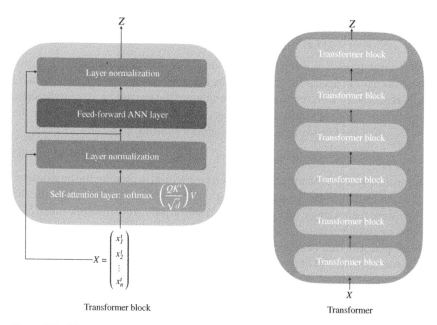

**Figure 9.7** The transformer architecture. The figure on the left depicts the transformer block. The block consists of 4 layers. A transformer consists of stacking the discrete blocks to form a composition.

---

**Algorithm 9.4** Self-Attention Transformer

---

1: **procedure** TRANSFORMER(Sentence)
2:     $n \leftarrow$ length(Sentence)
3:     **for** $i \in 1 : n$ **do**
4:         $X[i] \leftarrow (\text{dict}(i, \text{Sentence}[i]))^T$          ▷ Initial Word Embedding
5:     **end for**
6:     $Z \leftarrow X$
7:     **for** $Tb \in Transformer$ **do**          ▷ Done with every transformer block
8:         $Q \leftarrow Z \cdot Tb.W^q$
9:         $K \leftarrow Z \cdot Tb.W^k$
10:         $V \leftarrow Z \cdot Tb.W^v$
11:         $\bar{Y} \leftarrow \text{softmax}\left(\frac{QK^T}{\sqrt{d}}\right)V$          ▷ self-attention
12:         $Y \leftarrow \text{layerNorm}(\bar{Y} + Z)$
13:         $\bar{Z} \leftarrow \text{ANN}(Y)$
14:         $Z \leftarrow \text{layerNorm}(\bar{Z} + Y)$
15:     **end for**
16:     **return** $Z$
17: **end procedure**

---

is to preprocess the text. The text is tokenized followed by a static word embedding. Both tasks are performed by dict. This produces the initial set of vectors for the transformer. The embedding includes positional information in the sentence, hence $i$ is passed into dict as well as indexing the sentence. The initial embeddings are then passed on to the transformer. The data percolates through each transformer block until the last one is reached. Each block computes the self-attention and then runs it through an ANN. After the data exits the transformer, it is ready for use by a downstream model.

An important implementation note. Each transformer block has its own set of learned matrices, and the dimensions are fixed at training time. A real transformer prescribes $n$. The original attention paper used a value of 512. This means that 512 tokens need to be passed in at a time. The initial vector, $X$, will have a dimension of $n \times d$. If less than $n$ tokens are available then it needs to be padded with a special "null" embedding that will not contribute to the self-attention. The matrix product, $QK^T$, has $n^2$ entries. It grows quadratically with the length of the input. Selecting the size of $n$ needs to be done carefully to avoid excessive memory consumption. The more usual problem is the opposite of an insufficient number of tokens, but rather, having a document that is too long. When there are too many tokens for a single invocation the transformer is invoked multiple times with $n$-sized subsets.

## 9.4.5 Multi-Head Attention

The weight matrices in the transformer blocks are learned. During training, they attempt to discover relationships between tokens. Transformers work well, so they do learn, but it is not always clear *what* they are learning. Recall the motivation for multiple convolutional filters for detecting features in images in Section 6.2. It was argued that it is useful to detect multiple features to increase the chances of classifying images correctly. A filter layer consisted of multiple filters applied in parallel with dedicated feature maps. This led to learning more relationships in the data and made the model more accurate. The same argument holds for transformer blocks.

To capture as many useful linguistic patterns as possible multiple sets of query, key, and value weight matrices can be trained. The result is called multi-head self-attention. Each set of weight matrices is considered a head. A transformer block with $h$ heads has a set of $h$ weight triples of the form, $\{\{W_1^q, W_1^k, W_1^v\}, \ldots, \{W_h^q, W_h^k, W_h^v\}\}$. The $h$ sets of parameter matrices are used to compute self-attention in parallel (and on the appropriate hardware concurrently). Multi-head transformer blocks are similar to multi-filter CNN layers. Following the $h$ parallel self-attention calculations the $h$ vectors are stitched together with concatenation,

$$\overline{Y} = \overline{Y}_1 \oplus \cdots \oplus \overline{Y}_h \in \mathbb{R}^{n \times h \cdot d}. \tag{9.28}$$

The concatenation is row-wise, that is, the number of columns increases. A problems arises respecting the dimensions of $\overline{Y}$. It does not conform to the dimensions of the input vector or the expected output vector. It has $d \times h$ columns. The input and the output of transformers, hence also transformer blocks, must have the same dimension. Transformer blocks can be stacked arbitrarily so the dimensions of input and output must be in agreement. To address the mismatch another step is introduced in the transformer blocks to shrink $\overline{Y}$ down to the required dimensions. The concatenated vector is projected to produce the final vector of the correct dimensions. The projection is effected with a learned vector, $W^o \in \mathbb{R}^{h \cdot d \times d}$, that has the correct dimensions,

$$Y^p = \overline{Y} W^o \in \mathbb{R}^{n \times d}. \tag{9.29}$$

Only one $W^o$ is required per transformer block. It can be construed as learning how to weight the various heads, or discovered linguistic features, in the block. The projection is performed prior to invoking a block's ANN. The final output of the multi-head transformer block thus produces the correct size vector. Multi-head self-attention transformer blocks are stacked as usual to produce a multi-head transformer. Figure 9.8 displays the resulting layout of a single transformer block.

**Figure 9.8** The transformer block for multi-head attention. The changes are confined to the self-attention portion. There are now multiple computations of self-attention. The learned matrix $W^o$ projects them in preparation for the final step, layer normalization with the residual connection.

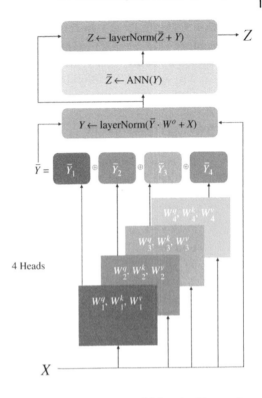

The complete algorithm is presented in Algorithm 9.5. Multi-head self-attention is powerful because it is learnt. Analogously to CNN filters many heads can be trained to learn features in the training set corpus. Natural language is complex and so multiple layers are required to extract the linguistic features.

## 9.4.6 Transformer Applications

Transformers are used to build language models. Language models are used in turn to build applications. The output of a language model can be fed to a downstream model that specializes in the language model for a task, such as a chatbot or an email scanner. Transformers and self-attention led to enormous improvements in NLP. Almost all language models are now transformer based. Google's attention paper was followed with a publication describing their language model, BERT (33). Google's conversation technology, LaMBDA (149) is based on BERT. Amazon's Alexa uses transformers (143). OpenAI's GPT family of libraries are based on transformers (118). The ChatGPT chatbot is based on GPT (108), so it is a transformer-based model. Apple has invested heavily in transformer technology (6). The Microsoft and NVIDEA collaboration Megatron-Turing is a

---

**Algorithm 9.5** Multi-Head Transformer

---

1: **procedure** TRANSFORMER(TextBlock)
2:   **for** $i \in 1 : N$ **do**                        $\triangleright$ The length is a model parameter
3:     $X[i] \leftarrow (\text{dict}(i, \text{TextBlock}[i]))^t$          $\triangleright$ Initial Word Embedding
4:   **end for**
5:   $Z \leftarrow X$
6:   **for** $Tb \in Transformer$ **do**          $\triangleright$ Done with every transformer block
7:     $\bar{Y} \leftarrow \emptyset$
8:     **for** $head \in Tb$ **do**             $\triangleright$ Done for each head in a block
9:       $Q \leftarrow Z \cdot head.W^q$
10:       $K \leftarrow Z \cdot head.W^k$
11:       $V \leftarrow Z \cdot head.W^v$
12:       $\bar{Y} \leftarrow \bar{Y} \oplus \text{softmax}\left(\frac{QK^t}{\sqrt{d}}\right)V$      $\triangleright$ self-attention concatenated
13:     **end for**
14:     $Y^p \leftarrow \bar{Y} \cdot Tb.W^o$
15:     $Y \leftarrow \text{layerNorm}(Y^p + Z)$
16:     $\bar{Z} \leftarrow \text{ANN}(Y)$
17:     $Z \leftarrow \text{layerNorm}(\bar{Z} + Y)$
18:   **end for**
19:   **return** $Z$
20: **end procedure**

---

transformer-based system (141). While there are concerns that language models are growing too powerful, (12), there is too much at stake and the relentless race to build better ones will almost certainly continue. Switch-C is setting the stage for trillion+ parameter language models (40).

The applications of language models are legion. Anything that involves natural language is a potential application. Language translation performance has dramatically improved with transformer technology. Legal document summarization saves a great deal of money. It is sufficiently accurate for some applications that paying lawyers to read routine material is no longer required. NLP agents that monitor news feeds keep abreast of enormous quantities of news automatically, and reliably. News monitoring is important to many organizations such as governments and the trading floors of banks, and it can take many forms. Televisions monitors or online news feeds such as Reuters and Bloomberg create automatic alerts and executive summaries. Routing emails reliably saves hiring personnel to monitor group mailboxes. ChatGPT has been acknowledged as an author on scientific papers (146). The latest OpenAI technical report on GPT-4 acknowledged ChatGPT for producing summaries of text and as a copy-editing tool (1).

Of significance is the wide availability of pretrained language models based on transformers. While they are available as commercial products, there are also some that are open source. The ability to download and use pretrained language models have led to an enormous increase in the power of even simple derivative models. Training transformers requires more resources than are generally widely available. The Attention paper reported 3.5 days for training on an 8 GPU system. A pretrained language model can be downloaded then attached to a downstream ANN that consumes its output. Only the downstream ANN requires training, or "fine tuning." The ANN ingesting the output of the language model is specialized for the desired application. The resources required are modest as the language model is already trained. Pretrained models can be used to train applications on even a modest notebook computer. The wide availability of pretrained models has dramatically increased access and facilitates NLP research and pedagogy that would otherwise be impossible.

It is difficult to understate the impact of transformers on NLP tasks, and since their introduction in 2017, there has been tremendous progress in many NLP problem domains. They continue to attract a tremendous amount of mind share. In terms of investment and research money, the commitment to transformer based technology only seems to be accelerating. Transformers clearly have a bright future, and they have only just started their journey. Finally, it is suggested that the Turing Test is probably too dated for use as a test for artificial intelligence. Transformers have moved the goal posts.

## 9.5 Neural Turing Machines

We conclude with another approach to learning tasks. Section 9.3 demonstrated how to use RL to build agents that learn how to perform tasks. Neural Turing Machines (NTM) attempt to train models to learn a program to perform a task (54). The difference between RL and an NTM lies in how the task is expressed. Training an agent to perform a task with RL produces a policy. Training an NTM produces a program. As the name implies, the program is learnt in the context of a Turing Machine, a simple yet powerful model of computation.

An exhaustive introduction to the Turing machine[3] is beyond the scope of this book, but a brief review is indicated to understand the approach of the NTM. A Turing Machine is a mathematical abstraction conceived by Alan Turing in 1936. His object was to design a model of computation with which to examine fundamental theoretical questions connected to computability. The Turing Machine's enduring importance lies both in its simplicity and power.

---

[3] Turing called them *a-machines*, Turing machine was coined by his PhD supervisor, Alonso Church.

A Turing machine is a finite-state automaton. It has a finite set of states, $\{q_0, q_1, \ldots, q_n\}$. The automaton processes an infinitely long tape that represents persistent external state. The tape consists of a string of records. Each record is precisely one symbol from a finite alphabet, $\{s_0, s_1, \ldots, s_m\}$. The tape is accessed by a head that can read and write the tape. One record can be accessed at any given moment, that is, in any given state; the record under the tape head. The tape can be moved one record at a time, either to the left or to the right. Taken together, the automaton and the tape can be viewed as a computer. The automaton is the CPU controlling the I/O with the tape. The machine reads a record, changes state, and then acts on that state, e.g. writing a symbol, $s_i$, to the tape or moving the tape. A Turing machine has been shown to possess the capacity to execute most algorithms, and in fact is the standard for determining the computing capability of a system (e.g. a programming language). This is done by showing that the system under consideration can simulate a Turing Machine. A system that can simulate a Turing Machine is considered "Turing Complete." For a thorough treatment see (24).

The object of the NTM is to simulate a Turing machine with ANNs, but not slavishly. The NTM model is based on a Turing machine, but does not pedantically follow it. A Turing Machine is the framework for the NTM model. An NTM might lie somewhere between a Turing Machine and a Von Neumann Machine. There are two components of a Turing Machine, the automaton and the tape. They serve very different functions. An NTM needs to simulate those pieces, and this is how the analogy to a Turing Machine arises. An NTM is an amalgamation of two distinct models, an ANN that acts as the automaton, called the *controller*, and a second model that acts as the tape, known as the *memory*. The architecture is interesting in its own right in that it is an example of the synthesis of specialized functions with distinct responsibilities. The result is greater than the sum of its parts. Animal brains have similar layouts with dedicated regions responsible for specific tasks. This is different from a CNN, where individual layers might be different, but the layers are all contributing to the single task of the CNN; it only has one function. Indeed, it is not difficult to imagine including a CNN in an NTM as a distinct component to help the NTM interact with the world. An NTM has distinct components assigned very different functions contributing to higher-level capabilities.

The training of a NTM is really training the program that the NTM will run. The result of training is stored in the NTM's memory. Unlike the pure Turing Machine, the NTM views its memory as random access. Consequently, the NTM's memory must provide associative recall. The memory is implemented as an array with addressing logic placed on top of it. The controller accesses the memory through the addressing logic. It is the addressing logic that is trained, not the memory per se, which is a flat array. Unlike a Turing Machine's tape, which only has a single cell accessible at any moment, the cell under the tape head, all of an NTM's memory is directly connected to the controller through the addressing mechanism. The addressing model is interposed between the controller and the memory, and it acts as the tape head. Attentional methods[4] are used to access an individual memory location by focusing on the address of the desired memory location. Read and write operations are always the same size, but the addressing model ensures that only the desired portion of the data has any effect.

A few ANN architectures were examined to act as the controller, but the best-performing architecture was found to be a feed-forward ANN. Because the FF ANN had access to the memory bank, it was able to mimic an RNN better than an RNN could. The NTM is differentiable from end-to-end, that is, from addressing logic through to the complete controller. This means that an NTM could be trained with a loss function and gradient descent. The NTM was able to learn how to read, write, and copy strings.

A more ambitious effort followed the NTM called a differentiable neural computer (DNC) (147). The DNC had a much improved attentional mechanism producing more efficient memory accesses. This permits the DNC to learn how to handle more difficult tasks, such as graph queries. The DNC was able to find the shortest path from point A to point B (the authors used the example of a public transport system). It is important to distinguish between memorizing the routes, or some other formulation of the problem, and actually executing a program that was learnt. The DNC learns the program that accepts input and carries out a task.

Research continues and there are now significant resources in the public domain. Details for a practical implementation of a NTM were published (120). The authors released the code with an opensource license. There is a great deal of "secret sauce" to train an NTM, so it is an important artifact.

The NTM has led to the general class of ANNs called a Memory Augmented Neural Network (MANN) (78). Providing state for ANNs dramatically increases their power. There are other permutations on the original design. The design of a MANN (49) took end-to-end differentiability to the limit and includes the memory, not just the addressing mechanism between the memory and the controller. The authors reported that less supervision was required during training leading to quicker and more reliable convergence. Ignoring an attention-based addressing mechanism and placing the logic directly in the memory has also been examined (49). In this case, the memory does not have to be densely connected to the controller.

Capturing the temporal dependencies in input data, or more generally spatial dependencies in sequential data, has proven to be problematic for ANNs. MANNs have the potential to address the problem by making the state explicit in the model. RNNs are notoriously difficult to train and are very limited. Providing external and

---

4 These predate the use of transformers and are responsible for the terminology of queries, keys, and values.

programmable memory has opened the door to all kinds of new applications. This includes reformulating problems in a new way. Providing state is arguably taking ANNs from the stateless, functional programming paradigm of Church's Lambda Calculus, to the stateful world of Turing Machines and programming with side effects. Judgment has not yet been passed on the consequences as it is still far too early, but it is an alluring prospect.

## 9.6 Summary

This chapter has examined some of the theoretical limitations of what ANNs can represent, that is, what they can *learn*. With some weak assumptions about the problem, it seems they can learn almost anything. The text has presented the canonical and fundamental algorithms for training deep learning artificial neural networks. The basics of training models with backpropagation of error prepares the reader for more advanced study. ANNs are from a very active research area. Generative adversarial networks can be trained to produce novel content from an exemplar dataset. RL and deep learning are becoming more intertwined producing hybrid systems. Transformers are very deep ANNs with enormous numbers of parameters. They are useful with sequential data, such as natural language and time-series.

## 9.7 Projects

The following projects can be found on the book's website: https://github.com/nom-de-guerre/DDL_book/tree/main/Ch09.

1. The website contains a Python Notebook, SmallGAN.ipynb. The generator's latent space is normally distributed. Experiment with a uniform distribution and determine which latent space is superior.
2. The tic-tac-toe example is available as a Python notebook, Tic-Tac-Toe.ipynb. The reward functions values a draw as 0.5. Experiment with different reward functions, such as valuing a draw as 0.0, and measure the changes to the winning percentage of the agent.
3. The website includes a Python notebook, ClassifyNews.ipynb, that uses a pretrained language model. It is connected to a FFFC ANN. The model is a textual classifier. Vary the ANN's topology (both width and depth) and measure the effect on accuracy. The notebook includes instructions for obtaining the data and the pretrained model.

# Appendix A

# Mathematical Review

This appendix contains a review of some of the basic mathematical concepts required to understand the contents of this book. It is not meant to be an exhaustive reference, nor an introduction, but simply a review of undergraduate mathematical concepts required to understand the book.

## A.1 Linear Algebra

Perhaps the most important mathematical object used in the text is the matrix from linear algebra. The simplest matrix is a vector. A column vector is an important special case of a matrix. The reader is referred to (49) for a full treatment. We begin with the simplest example of a matrix, the vector.

### A.1.1 Vectors

A vector is a matrix, $x \in \mathbb{R}^n$, with multiple rows and only one column. A vector looks like,

$$x = \begin{pmatrix} x_1 \\ \vdots \\ x_n \end{pmatrix}.$$

It has $n$ rows and 1 column. A vector can be multiplied by a scaler,

$$\alpha \cdot x = \begin{pmatrix} \alpha \cdot x_1 \\ \vdots \\ \alpha \cdot x_n \end{pmatrix}. \tag{A.1}$$

Vectors of the same dimensions can be added (or subtracted) as follows:

$$x + y = \begin{pmatrix} x_1 \\ \vdots \\ x_n \end{pmatrix} + \begin{pmatrix} y_1 \\ \vdots \\ y_n \end{pmatrix} = \begin{pmatrix} x_1 + y_1 \\ \vdots \\ x_n + y_n \end{pmatrix}. \tag{A.2}$$

*Demystifying Deep Learning: An Introduction to the Mathematics of Neural Networks,*
First Edition. Douglas J. Santry.
© 2024 The Institute of Electrical and Electronics Engineers, Inc. Published 2024 by John Wiley & Sons, Inc.

The transpose of a vector is created by swapping the each element's row and column, $x^T = (x_1, \ldots, x_n)$. Thus, a transposed vector has 1 row and $n$ columns. The magnitude of a vector is computed with the Pythagorean theorem,

$$|x|_2 = \sqrt{\sum_i^n x_i}. \tag{A.3}$$

A vector can be normalized such that its magnitude is 1 by dividing a vector by its magnitude,

$$x_{normal} = \frac{x}{|x|_2}. \tag{A.4}$$

For vectors, $x, y \in \mathbb{R}^n$ the inner product is defined as

$$x^T \cdot y = \sum_{i=1}^n x_i y_i = \alpha, \tag{A.5}$$

where $\alpha$ is a scaler. An inner product is a vector's dot product. A property of the dot product is that it is zero if the two arguments are orthogonal: $x^T \cdot y = 0 \implies x, y$ are orthogonal. It is related to the dot product with the following equation:

$$x^T \cdot y = |x| \cdot |y| \cdot \cos(\theta). \tag{A.6}$$

Note that the inner product of a vector with itself is $x^T \cdot x = |x|_2^2$, a vector's magnitude squared.

The outer product is the opposite of the inner product. Instead of a scaler it produces a square matrix, $x \cdot y^T \in \mathbb{R}^{n,n}$, and it is defined as

$$x \cdot y^T = \begin{pmatrix} x_1 y_1 & x_1 y_2 & \cdots & x_1 y_n \\ x_2 y_1 & x_2 y_2 & \cdots & x_2 y_n \\ \vdots & & & \\ x_n y_1 & x_n y_2 & \cdots & x_n y_n \end{pmatrix}. \tag{A.7}$$

## A.1.2 Matrices

The general matrix is defined as $A \in \mathbb{R}^{n,m}$

$$A = \begin{pmatrix} a_{1,1} & a_{1,2} & \cdots & a_{1,m} \\ a_{2,1} & a_{2,2} & \cdots & a_{2,m} \\ \vdots & & & \\ a_{n,1} & a_{n,2} & \cdots & a_{n,m} \end{pmatrix}, \tag{A.8}$$

where $n$ is the number of rows and $m$ is the number of columns.

A matrix is a mapping. The Image($A$) is the set of all vectors that are produced by multiplying it with a vector. It is defined as $y \in \text{Image}(A) \Longrightarrow \exists x | Ax = y$.

The Kernel($A$) is the set of vectors that when multiplied by $A$ result in a vector of all zeros: $x \in \text{Kernel}(A) \Longrightarrow Ax = 0$.

Two special matrices of note are the NULL matrix, which has zero's in all of its entries and defined as

$$
\mathbf{0} = \begin{pmatrix} 0_{1,1} & 0_{1,2} & \cdots & 0_{1,n} \\ 0_{2,1} & 0_{2,2} & \cdots & 0_{2,n} \\ \vdots & & & \\ 0_{n,1} & 0_{n,2} & \cdots & 0_{n,n} \end{pmatrix},
\tag{A.9}
$$

and the identity matrix, which has 1's on the diagonal, and 0's in all of the off-diagonal entries,

$$
\mathbf{I} = \begin{pmatrix} 1_{1,1} & 0_{1,2} & \cdots & 0_{1,n} \\ 0_{2,1} & 1_{2,2} & \cdots & 0_{2,n} \\ \vdots & & & \\ 0_{n,1} & 0_{n,2} & \cdots & 1_{n,n} \end{pmatrix}.
\tag{A.10}
$$

A matrix or a vector multiplied by the identity matrix is the original matrix, that is, $IA = AI = A$.

For two matrices, $A, B \in \mathbb{R}^{n,m}$, then matrix addition and subtraction are defined as

$$
A + B = \begin{pmatrix} a_{1,1} + b_{1,1} & a_{1,2} + b_{1,2} & \cdots & a_{1,m} + b_{1,m} \\ a_{2,1} + b_{2,1} & a_{2,2} + b_{2,2} & \cdots & a_{2,m} + b_{2,m} \\ \vdots & & & \\ a_{n,1} + b_{n,1} & a_{n,2} + b_{n,2} & \cdots & a_{n,m} + b_{n,m} \end{pmatrix}.
\tag{A.11}
$$

The number of rows and columns must be equal, that is, the matrices must have precisely the same dimensions.

For a vector, $x \in \mathbb{R}^m$, and matrix, $A \in \mathbb{R}^{n,m}$, matrix-vector multiplication is defined as

$$
Ax = \begin{pmatrix} \sum_{i=1}^{m} a_{1,i} \cdot x_i \\ \sum_{i=1}^{m} a_{2,i} \cdot x_i \\ \vdots \\ \sum_{i=1}^{m} a_{n,i} \cdot x_i \end{pmatrix} = y,
\tag{A.12}
$$

which produces a new column vector, $y \in \mathbb{R}^n$. Each entry in $y$ is the dot product of $x$ with a row in $A$.

For matrices, $A \in \mathbb{R}^{n,m}$ and $B \in \mathbb{R}^{m,p}$, the matrix product $AB = C$ is defined when the number of columns in $A$ equals the number of rows in $B$. The product is, $C \in \mathbb{R}^{n,p}$ (the matrix vector product is not a special case, per se, $p = 1$).

$$
AB = \begin{pmatrix}
\sum_{i=1}^{m} a_{1,i} \cdot b_{i,1} & \sum_{i=1}^{m} a_{1,i} \cdot b_{i,2} & \cdots & \sum_{i=1}^{m} a_{1,i} \cdot b_{i,m} \\
\sum_{i=1}^{m} a_{2,i} \cdot b_{i,1} & \sum_{i=1}^{m} a_{2,i} \cdot b_{i,2} & \cdots & \sum_{i=1}^{m} a_{2,i} \cdot b_{i,m} \\
\vdots & & & \\
\sum_{i=1}^{m} a_{n,i} \cdot b_{i,1} & \sum_{i=1}^{m} a_{n,i} \cdot b_{i,2} & \cdots & \sum_{i=1}^{m} a_{n,i} \cdot b_{i,m}
\end{pmatrix}. \tag{A.13}
$$

Each entry in $C$ is, $c_{i,j} = $ the dot product of row $i$ in $A$ and column $j$ in $B$ (hence the columns and rows must agree in the two operands).

The transpose of a matrix,

$$
A = \begin{pmatrix}
a_{1,1} & a_{1,2} & \cdots & a_{1,m} \\
a_{2,1} & a_{2,2} & \cdots & a_{2,m} \\
\vdots & & & \\
a_{n,1} & a_{n,2} & \cdots & a_{n,m}
\end{pmatrix}, \tag{A.14}
$$

is, for every $a_{i,j}^T = a_{j,i}$ .

$$
A^T = \begin{pmatrix}
a_{1,1} & a_{2,1} & \cdots & a_{n,1} \\
a_{1,2} & a_{2,2} & \cdots & a_{n,2} \\
\vdots & & & \\
a_{1,m} & a_{2,m} & \cdots & a_{m,n}
\end{pmatrix}. \tag{A.15}
$$

A concrete example is

$$
\begin{pmatrix}
1 & 2 \\
3 & 4 \\
5 & 6
\end{pmatrix}^T = \begin{pmatrix}
1 & 3 & 5 \\
2 & 4 & 6
\end{pmatrix}. \tag{A.16}
$$

The transpose affects matrix multiplication as follows: $(AB)^T = B^T A^T$.

### A.1.3 Matrix Properties

Consider a linear system of simultaneous equations, $Ax = b$. This is the problem of finding $x$, which is unknown. The system can be solved by finding the inverse of the matrix, $A$ and it is written, $A^{-1}$. The inverse of a matrix is a matrix such that, $A^{-1}A = I$. It can be used to find the solution to a linear system: $Ax = b \Longrightarrow x = A^{-1}b$.

## A.1.4  Linear Independence

Matrix-vector multiplication can be interpreted as follows:

$$
Ax = \begin{pmatrix} a_{1,1} & a_{1,2} & a_{1,3} \\ a_{2,1} & a_{2,2} & a_{2,3} \\ a_{3,1} & a_{3,2} & a_{3,3} \end{pmatrix} \begin{pmatrix} x_1 \\ x_2 \\ x_3 \end{pmatrix}
$$

$$
= x_1 \cdot \begin{pmatrix} a_{1,1} \\ a_{2,1} \\ a_{3,1} \end{pmatrix} + x_2 \cdot \begin{pmatrix} a_{1,2} \\ a_{2,2} \\ a_{3,2} \end{pmatrix} + x_3 \cdot \begin{pmatrix} a_{1,3} \\ a_{2,3} \\ a_{3,3} \end{pmatrix}. \tag{A.17}
$$

It is a linear combination of the column vectors of the matrix, $A$. If none of the column vectors can be written as a nontrivial (all $x_i \neq 0$) linear combination of the others, then the column vectors are said to be linearly independent.

The dimension of a matrix is different from its *rank*. The rank is the span of the matrix's image. It is the number of linearly independent column vectors. For a matrix, $A \in \mathbb{R}^{n,m}$, if all $m$ of the column vectors are linearly independent, then the matrix is full rank, and $\text{Rank}(A) = m$. A matrix that is not full rank is called rank deficient.

## A.1.5  The QR Decomposition

Any matrix can be decomposed as $A = QR$, where $Q$ is orthonormal and spans $A$. This is the $QR$ decomposition of a matrix. Orthonormal means that every column vector in $Q$ has a magnitude of 1 and is orthogonal with all of the other column vectors. Thus, $Q$ has the useful property that $Q^T Q = I$. $R$ is upper triangular. It has many uses, including solving dense linear systems. In practice, linear systems are never solved by inverting $A$. $Ax = b = QRx \implies Rx = Q^T b$. As $R$ is upper triangular solving for $x$ is trivially performed with backward substitution.

The QR decomposition of a matrix can be computed cheaply and with good numerical stability with either householder reflectors or givens transformations. See (109) for details.

## A.1.6  Least Squares

Consider the problem of analyzing data. Given a set of $m$ unknown parameters or features, and the results of $n$ experiments, the data can be stored in a matrix, $A \in \mathbb{R}^{n,m}$. If we wish to explain the data with respect to some vector $y$, such that $Ax = y$, then usually $n \gg m$. The problem is that $y \notin \text{Image}(A)$ so $Ax \neq y$ for all $x$. The problem then is to find an $\hat{x}$ such that $|A\hat{x} - y|_2$ is a minimum. Pythagoras tells us that the minimum is to be found when the residual vector is orthogonal to all the column vectors of $A$. Multiplying with $A^T$ computes the dot products with all of $A$'s column vectors. This leads to the *normal* equations. The normal equations are

$$A^T(A\hat{x} - y) = 0 \Longrightarrow A^T A\hat{x} = A^T y. \tag{A.18}$$

The normal equations must be equal zero as the residual vector must be at a right angle to the image of $A$. The QR decomposition yields the least squares solution, $R\hat{x} = Q^{-1}y$. See (145) for more details.

### A.1.7 Eigenvalues and Eigenvectors

A special matrix equation is of the form, $Au = \lambda u$. $\lambda$ is a scaler known as an *eigenvalue*, and $u$ is an eigenvector. Eigenvalues can computed with the Francis Algorithm, and their attendant eigenvectors with inverse iteration. Of special note is the eigenvector associated with the largest eigenvalue. The pair can be obtained with the Power Method. It is an iteration of the form,[1]

$$x_{i+1} = \frac{Ax_i}{|Ax_i|}. \tag{A.19}$$

As $i \to \infty$ the denominator approaches the largest eigenvalue and the left-hand side approaches its eigenvector. This is important as this is what occurs in expressions of the form, $A^n x$. The higher the degree the closer to the power method will be the result; this is asymptotically important.

### A.1.8 Hadamard Operations

The Hadamard matrix product is an element wise operation. For two matrices, $A, B \in \mathbb{R}^{n,m}$, it is defined when they have the same number of rows and columns. The operation is defined as

$$A \otimes B = \begin{pmatrix} a_{1,1} \cdot b_{1,1} & a_{1,2} \cdot b_{1,2} & \cdots & a_{1,m} \cdot b_{1,m} \\ a_{2,i} \cdot b_{2,1} & a_{2,2} \cdot b_{i,2} & \cdots & a_{2,m} \cdot b_{2,m} \\ \vdots & & & \\ a_{n,1} \cdot b_{n,1} & a_{n,2} \cdot b_{n,2} & \cdots & a_{n,m} \cdot b_{n,m} \end{pmatrix}. \tag{A.20}$$

A scaler function, $f$, when given a vector as an argument is applied per element to the vector:

$$f(x) = \begin{pmatrix} f(x_1) \\ \vdots \\ f(x_n) \end{pmatrix}. \tag{A.21}$$

---

1 This is the basis of Google's Page Rank algorithm (88).

## A.2    Basic Calculus

In the following expression, $y = f(x) = e^x$, there are some important and distinct elements. $f$ is a function of $x$. $y$ is the value of the function, $f$. $x$ is a member of the domain of $f$, and $y$ is a member of the range of $f$. A function is a mapping from a range to a domain. In this instance, it is written as $f : \mathbb{R} \to \mathbb{R}$.

Functions are a special case of relations. Relations are also mappings, but the mapping can have multiple values. Functions may only have a single value. $y = x^2$ is a function; it only takes on one value. $y = \sqrt{x}$ is a relation; the mapping produces two values.[2] For example, $\sqrt{4} = \pm 2$.

The Calculus is the basis of training neural networks. Some of the more important results are presented here. A thorough treatment can be found in (88). The classical definition of a derivative for a scaler function is

$$\frac{df}{dx} = \lim_{h \to 0} \frac{f(x+h) - f(x)}{h}. \tag{A.22}$$

An important derivative is that for $e^x$, where $e$ is the natural number,

$$e = \lim_{n \to \infty} \left(1 + \frac{1}{n}\right)^n \simeq 2.7182818284590452353..., \tag{A.23}$$

a transcendental number.

The derivative of $e^x$ from the classical definition is

$$\begin{aligned}
\frac{d}{dx}\left(e^x\right) &= \lim_{h \to 0} \frac{e^{x+h} - e^x}{h} \\
&= \lim_{h \to 0} \frac{e^x e^h - e^x}{h} \\
&= \lim_{h \to 0} \frac{e^x(e^h - 1)}{h} \\
&= e^x \cdot \lim_{h \to 0} \frac{e^h - 1}{h} \\
&= e^x.
\end{aligned} \tag{A.24}$$

Calculus is important because nonlinear functions can be optimized with it. A function will have a *stationary point* at its extrema. The derivative will be zero at either a local minimum or a local maximum. By differentiating an equation, setting the result equal to zero and solving, the function is optimized.

### A.2.1    The Product Rule

For more involved functions differentiating is possible with two rules of macro differentiation. The Product Rule: if a function can be written as $f(x) = g(x) \cdot h(x)$,

---

2  Do not confuse the difference between a scaler and a vector with multiple values.

then the derivative can computed as

$$f'(x) = g' \cdot h + g \cdot h'. \tag{A.25}$$

**Example:** $f(x) = \sin(x) \cdot x^2 \implies f'(x) = \cos(x) \cdot x^2 + \sin(x) \cdot 2x.$

## A.2.2 The Chain Rule

**The Chain Rule:** If a function can be written as a composition, $f(x) = f(u(x))$, then its derivative can be computed as

$$\frac{df}{dx} = \frac{df}{du} \cdot \frac{du}{dx}. \tag{A.26}$$

**Example:** $f(x) = \sin(x^2)$, let $u = x^2$, then $f(x) = \sin(u) \implies f'(x) = \cos(x^2) \cdot 2x.$

## A.2.3 Multivariable Functions

For scaler multivariable functions such as $z = f(x, y) = x^2 + xy + y^3$ differentiation must account for the variable of interest. Such functions are differentiated with partial derivatives. To understand how $z$ is changing with respect to $x$, we consider all of the other variables as constants. So,

$$\frac{\partial z}{\partial x} = 2x + y, \tag{A.27}$$

and

$$\frac{\partial z}{\partial y} = x + 3y^2. \tag{A.28}$$

The gradient of a function is a vector function of how the scaler function is changing. It is defined as

$$\nabla z = \begin{pmatrix} \frac{\partial z}{\partial x} \\ \frac{\partial z}{\partial y} \end{pmatrix} = \begin{pmatrix} 2x + y \\ x + 3y^2 \end{pmatrix}. \tag{A.29}$$

Note that the gradient of a scaler function is a vector function. The analog of the chain rule for partial derivatives is

$$\frac{\partial f}{\partial x} = \frac{\partial f}{\partial u} \cdot \frac{\partial u}{\partial x}$$

## A.2.4 Taylor Series

An important tool for approximating functions is a Taylor series. For a full treatment, the interested reader is directed to (126). A Taylor series is useful for approximating a function where an analytic expression is not available. They are often used for analyzing and comparing functions. The general form is

$$f(x + \Delta x) = f(x) + \sum_{i=1}^{\infty} \frac{d^i y}{dx^i} \cdot \frac{\Delta x^i}{i!}. \tag{A.30}$$

They are often truncated to a finite expression and an error term,

$$f(x + \Delta x) = f(x) + \sum_{i=1}^{n} \frac{d^i y}{dx^i} \cdot \frac{\Delta x^i}{i!} + O(\Delta^{n+1}). \tag{A.31}$$

More usually the terms of interest in the finite form are expanded,

$$f(x + \Delta x) = f(x) + \frac{dy}{dx} \cdot \Delta x + \frac{d^2 y}{dx^2} \cdot \frac{\Delta x^2}{2!} + O(n^3). \tag{A.32}$$

An important Taylor series is the series for the exponential function,

$$e^x = 1 + x + \frac{x^2}{2!} + \cdots \tag{A.33}$$

For $x$ expressed in radians the two most common trigonometric functions and their Taylor series functions are

$$\cos(x) = 1 - \frac{x^2}{2!} + \frac{x^4}{4!} - \frac{x^6}{6!} + \cdots \tag{A.34}$$

$$\sin(x) = x - \frac{x^3}{3!} + \frac{x^5}{5!} - \frac{x^7}{7!} + \cdots \tag{A.35}$$

## A.3 Advanced Matrices

For a vector function, $\mathbf{f}$, with domain and range $\mathbb{R}^N \to \mathbb{R}^M$, has a Jacobean that is an $M \times N$ matrix defined as

$$\mathbf{J} = \begin{pmatrix} \nabla^T f_1 \\ \vdots \\ \nabla^T f_M \end{pmatrix} = \begin{pmatrix} \frac{\partial f_1}{\partial x_1} & \frac{\partial f_1}{\partial x_2} & \cdots & \frac{\partial f_1}{\partial x_N} \\ \frac{\partial f_2}{\partial x_1} & \frac{\partial f_2}{\partial x_2} & \cdots & \frac{\partial f_2}{\partial x_N} \\ \vdots & & & \\ \frac{\partial f_M}{\partial x_1} & \frac{\partial f_M}{\partial x_2} & \cdots & \frac{\partial f_M}{\partial x_N} \end{pmatrix}. \tag{A.36}$$

The Jacobean of a vector function can be interpreted as how the function is changing with respect to all of its arguments. A detailed exposition can be found in (88).

## A.4 Probability

Probability is a mathematical means of attaching a quantitative chance of an event occurring during an experiment. The universe of possible events is called the sample space, $\Omega$. An outcome of an experiment is an observation, $\omega \in \Omega$. The probability of a particular outcome, $\omega$ is $P(X = \omega)$, where $X$ is a random variable. Conversely, the probability of not observing $\omega$ is $1 - P(X = \omega)$. A probability has the following properties:

$$0 \leq P(\omega) \leq 1.0, \tag{A.37}$$

and

$$P(\Omega) = 1.0. \tag{A.38}$$

For events, $A, B \subset \Omega$, the events are said to independent if

$$P(AB) = P(A)P(B). \tag{A.39}$$

For independent and disjoint events, $A, B$, the probability of $A$ given that $B$ has occurred is

$$P(A|B) = \frac{P(AB)}{P(B)}. \tag{A.40}$$

Related is the famous Bayes theorem,

$$P(A|B) = \frac{P(B \mid A)P(A)}{P(B)}. \tag{A.41}$$

The expectation for a random variable $X$ distributed discretely is computed with,

$$\mathbb{E}(X) = \sum P(x)x. \tag{A.42}$$

For a random a random variable distributed continuously, we use,

$$\mathbb{E}(X) = \int\limits_{-\infty}^{+\infty} xf(x)dx. \tag{A.43}$$

For further reading see (126).

# Glossary

The following is a glossary of terms and acronyms used in the book. The list is not exhaustive. Many terms and acronyms are overloaded in the literature and in practice so the definitions should not be considered authoritative. The terms can have multiple senses.

| | |
|---|---|
| Activation Function | A function in the layer of a neural network to produce the final output. The role is usually to introduce nonlinearity into the computation. Without an activation function a neural network will convolve to a linear mapping. The activation function is typically applied to each artificial neuron individually. |
| Algorithm | A sequence of unambiguous steps to compute a result or accomplish a task. The steps must be unambiguous and in the case of multiple steps, be they recursive or iterative, it must terminate. |
| ANN | Artificial neural network is a mathematical model of neural assemblies. It is typically modeled as a graph with weighted edges. The vertices are neurons. |
| Back-Propagation of Error | A supervised training technique used to produce trained ANN models. Starting with a differentiable loss function learnable parameters are updated by relating the error with the Calculus' chain rule. |
| Batch | A subset from the training set that is presented to an ANN during training. The examples in the batch are pushed through the ANN, and backpropagation of error is used to compute the error of the learnable parameters. The learnable parameters in the model |

*Demystifying Deep Learning: An Introduction to the Mathematics of Neural Networks,*
First Edition. Douglas J. Santry.
© 2024 The Institute of Electrical and Electronics Engineers, Inc. Published 2024 by John Wiley & Sons, Inc.

|  |  |
|---|---|
|  | are updated following the processing of the elements in the batch. |
| Bias | A fundamental mistake made in model selection. For example, modeling a phenomenon with a parametric distribution that is uniformly distributed with a binomial distribution. The binomial parameter will never be correctly estimated as the underlying process is different from that assumed. It is defined as $y - \hat{y}$, the ground truth minus the inferred quantity. |
| Bias-Variance Trade-off | A theory of fundamental limitations of training machine learning models. It argues that decreasing the bias of a trained model simultaneously increases the variance. One must trade-off one or the other to find the lowest error in the search for the best results of a model. |
| Category | An element in a set of classes (see class). |
| Class | A specific type in a set of types. For example, the set { `dog`, `cat`, `giraffe` } contains 3 types, or classes. |
| Classification | The classification problem is that of accepting an input and assigning it to one of set of classes. |
| CNN (1) | Classifying Neural Network, a neural network trained to classify input into a finite one of a finite set. |
| CNN (2) | Convolutional Neural Network, a neural network that includes convolutional layers. A convolutional layer accepts a matrix and reduces the dimensions of the matrix by applying a filter. The filter contains learnable parameters. |
| Column | A dataset can be viewed as a table of columns and rows. The table represents a set of disjoint observations, or outcomes of experiments. The columns represent the quantities that were measured. For example, perhaps the temperature at a particular location is measured every morning for a year. This would yield a table of 365 rows and one column; the column would contain the measured temperature. |
| Confusion Matrix | A matrix used to understand the quality of a classification model. The rows and columns are both labeled with the categories from the set of possible |

classes, but the rows represent the prediction from the model and column the ground truth. Entries are created by performing inference with a model and a datum. The row predicted by the model and the column dictated by the ground truth is incremented by 1. It can be used to derive further accuracy metrics or interpreted on its own.

| | |
|---|---|
| Covariate | In the context of machine learning, the covariate is the response in the dataset. See response. |
| Convex Set | A set where any two points in the set define a line segment that is also in the set. |
| Convex | A convex function with a range that is a convex set. |
| Convolution | A form of regularizing an ANN layer's input. It applied a kernel to produce an output map. Two common kernels are the Frobenius Product and MaxPooling. |
| Cross Entropy | A loss function for use with categorical problems. |
| Data Set | A collection of data. It can be viewed as describing a generating process. It consists of a number of columns, each of which represents a feature, and a number of rows each of which represents a sample. |
| Decision Boundary | Given a set $S = \bigcup_{k}^{K} S_k$, where each subset represents a complete set of examples for category, $k$, and $S_k$ consists of tuples, $x \in \mathbb{R}^d$, then the boundary between the subsets in the input space, $\mathbb{R}^d$, is the decision boundary. The object of training a classifier is to compute the decision boundary; the resultant model is usually an approximation. |
| Dense | A type of layer in an ANN. Every element in a dense layer is connected to every output in the shallower layer. |
| Deep Learning | An ANN with at least 1 hidden layer. |
| Edge | The connection between nodes in a graph. |
| Epoch | Training an artificial neural network is usually done with a machine learning algorithm. Each step through the algorithm is an epoch. A step includes going through the training data and updating the model. An epoch can either be measured as a step or a complete run though the dataset if multiple steps are required. |
| Feature | A synonym for column (see column). |

| | |
|---|---|
| Feed-Forward | An ANN graph that does not contain a cycle (in graph theory, a tree). All neuron results are propagated forward without ever being used in an earlier neuron. |
| FFFC | Feed-forward and fully connected. See entries for both. |
| Fully-Connected | See dense. |
| GAN | Generative Adversarial Network; a system consisting of two ANNs. One ANN learns the dataset to differentiate between fakes and real examples. The other ANN tries to imitate the training set. The two ANNs compete with each other, the generative ANN attempting to fool the discriminator ANN. The result is a generative ANN that produces novel output. |
| Generalization | During training, a machine learning model learns the training set. Generalization is the measure of how a trained machine learning model performs with respect to unseen data. |
| Gradient | The vector derivative of a multivariable function. See Appendix A. |
| Gradient Descent | Optimizing high-dimensional convex equations can be done by computing its gradient and moving in an appropriate direction (decreasing for minimization problems and increasing for maximization problems). |
| Graph | A mathematical construct consisting of a set of nodes, sometime also referred to as vertices and edges. The edges connect the vertices; graphs are used to represent relationships. A graph is written as $G(V, E)$. Respecting ANNs nodes are neurons and edges are connections between neurons. See Appendix A. |
| Ground Truth | Supervised learning problems require data. The dataset consists of the input to a model, predictors, and the correct response for each tuple of predictors. The correct answer is known as the ground truth. |
| Label | Datasets used for training classifying ANNs with supervised learning training techniques include the "answer," the ground truth. For classification, the answer is known as a label. |

| | |
|---|---|
| Learnable Parameter | A machine learning model contains parameters that need to be trained with respect to a training set. A learnable parameter is any quantity in the model that is improved during training. |
| Learning | See the entry for machine learning. |
| Likelihood | Likelihood is not a synonym for probability. Probabilities make *predictions*. Likelihood explains *observed data*. It is often used to compute the parameters required to calculate probabilities. |
| Logits | The raw output from a classifying ANN. Logits can be passed on to a terminal layer in the form of Softmax to produce the final prediction. |
| Loss Function | Supervised training techniques use a loss function to regulate learning. Supervised training techniques require an empirical measure of "wrong." A loss function accepts the output of an ANN and the ground truth; the difference between the two is quantified and used for the seed of backpropagation. They typically must be differentiable. |
| LSTM | Long Short Term Memory, an ANN that is an example of the RNN. |
| Machine Learning | Machine learning is a technique to realize artificial intelligence in a digital computer. An algorithm can be considered to be a machine learning technique if, using Tom Mitchell's definition, "a computer program is said to learn from experience, E, with respect to some class of tasks, T, and performance measure, P, if its performance at tasks in T, as measured by P, improves with experience E." Put another way, a computer programmed with an algorithm that is capable improving empirically measured performance with increased exposure. |
| Matrix | A mathematical object whose names derives from the Latin mater (they were originally conceived as the "mother" of determinants). It is a rectangular array whose elements can be anything but are typically real numbers or complex numbers. It has well-defined operations including addition, subtraction, and multiplication. |
| MLE | See cross entropy |

| | |
|---|---|
| Model | In the context of machine learning, a model is an object that attempts to mimic a phenomenon. A model makes predictions. |
| MSE | Mean Squared Error, a loss function for use with regression. It is defined as $\sum$. |
| Multiclass | The classification problem formulated for mutually exclusive categories. |
| Multilabel | The classification problem formulated for independent membership in the set of categories. An example can simultaneously be classified in more than one category, and membership in categories is independent. |
| Neuron | The specialized cell that forms animal brains. Neurons are connected to other neurons with a neural synapse. Artificial neural networks model biological neural assemblies with graphs and trained weights. |
| Node | The abstraction that encapsulates a neuron in an ANN graph. See graph. |
| Normalization | In the context of machine learning, normalization refers to the process of transforming data to produce data preserving relationships that are more consistent with respect to scale. |
| Optimization | Given an objective function, that is, a function to make "best," find the minimum or the maximum. Optimizing an ANN by minimizing its loss function is how learning is effected. |
| Parameter | A static quantity required by a function (or model) that determines its behavior. For example, the probability of success is a parameter of a binomial distribution. Parameters are treated as variables during training as they can change as an optimal value for them is computed. They are fixed when used for inference. |
| Perceptron | The most common type of artificial neuron. Its state is computed by a dot product of its weights with its inputs. The resulting scaler then has an activation function applied to produce the final result. |
| Predictor | A synonym for column. See column. |
| Preprocessing (Data) | The act of normalizing input data. See the entry for normalization. |

| | |
|---|---|
| Probability | Probability is a quantitative means of expressing uncertainty. It is a quantity that makes predictions. Any function, $f$, that has the following properties can be construed as a probability: $0 \leq p(x) \leq 1.0$, and for discrete $p(x)$ (mass function), $\sum^{\forall x} p(x) = 1$, and for continuous $p(x)$ (density function), $\int_{-\infty}^{\infty} p(x)dx = 1$. |
| Regression | The act of building a model to explain observed data. The model explains the relationship between continuous dependent variables. |
| Regularization | In the context of machine learning, it is a method to reduce the generalization error of trained model. |
| Residual Connection | An arrangement of an ANN's layers such that a layer transmits its signal to the immediately deeper layer as well as the following layer. For layers A, B, and C, B accepts A's signal. C accepts both B's and A's signals; the residual connection. |
| Response | The response is the value computed by an ANN. Consider, $y = \text{ANN}(x)$, $y$ is the response. For supervised learning, the correct response must be included with the training set. |
| RNN | Recurrent Neural Network, a neural network whose graph contains cycles. They are trained with backpropagation through time to account for the cycles. |
| Sigmoid | A real valued function that maps its input between 0 and 1. It is used as an activation function (see activation function). |
| Signal | A signal can either be the output of an artificial neuron, a layer, or the ANN. |
| Softmax | A vector valued function used to rationalize related outputs as mutually exclusive probabilities. Consider a set of categories, $\mathbb{K}$, and cardinality $K = |\mathbb{K}|$. A tuple, $z$, can be converted to a discrete synthetic probability distribution with, $$\hat{p}_j = \text{Softmax}(z) = \frac{e^{z_j}}{\sum_k^K e^{z_k}}.$$ |
| Stochastic | Randomly determined. A stochastic process evolves randomly. When modeling or simulating stochastic processes pseudo-random number generators are typically used. |

| | |
|---|---|
| Supervised Learning | A technique of training machine learning models. Supervised learning requires the answer to be present in the training set. Learning results from relating a model's computed answer to the answer. |
| SGD | Stochastic Gradient Descent, a means of selecting subsets from the training set to produce mini-batches. It can be construed as sampling the error gradient of a model with respect to a loss function. |
| Test Set | A subset of a dataset reserved to measure generalization. A dataset can be divided into a training set and a test set. The training set is used to train the model. The test is used kept in reserve and only used to test the accuracy of the trained model. The performance of the training model with the test is used as a proxy for a model's generalization error. |
| Training | The act of producing a model that learns a training set. See model and learning. |
| Training Set | The data used to train a model. |
| Verification Set | The data used to verify a model during training. It is a disjoint subset of the dataset and can be interpreted as the generalization error of the model. |
| Weight | A directed edge between two neurons is a connection between the two neurons. A weight is used to scale the signal emanating from the source neuron. Training neural networks is the process of finding good weights so the network can make good predictions. |

# References

**1** Openai (2023). GPT-4 technical report, 2023.

**2** Pieter Abbeel and Andrew Y. Ng. Apprenticeship learning via inverse reinforcement learning. In *Proceedings of the Twenty-First International Conference on Machine Learning*, ICML '04, page 1, New York, NY, USA, 2004. Association for Computing Machinery. ISBN 1581138385. doi: 10.1145/1015330.1015430.

**3** Amirali Aghazadeh, Vipul Gupta, Alex DeWeese, Ozan Koyluoglu, and Kannan Ramchandran. BEAR: Sketching BFGS algorithm for ultra-high dimensional feature selection in sublinear memory. In Joan Bruna, Jan Hesthaven, and Lenka Zdeborova, editors, *Proceedings of the 2nd Mathematical and Scientific Machine Learning Conference*, volume 145 of *Proceedings of Machine Learning Research*, pages 75–92. PMLR, 16–19 Aug 2022. URL https://proceedings.mlr.press/v145/aghazadeh22a.html.

**4** Shun-Ichi Amari, Hyeyoung Park, and Kenji Fukumizu. Adaptive method of realizing natural gradient learning for multilayer perceptrons. *Neural Computation*, 12(6):1399–1409, Jun 2000. ISSN 0899-7667. doi: 10.1162/089976600300015420.

**5** Marcin Andrychowicz, Filip Wolski, Alex Ray, Jonas Schneider, Rachel Fong, Peter Welinder, Bob McGrew, Josh Tobin, OpenAI Pieter Abbeel, and Wojciech Zaremba. Hindsight experience replay. In I. Guyon, U. Von Luxburg, S. Bengio, H. Wallach, R. Fergus, S. Vishwanathan, and R. Garnett, editors, *Advances in Neural Information Processing Systems*, volume 30. Curran Associates, Inc., 2017. URL https://proceedings.neurips.cc/paper/2017/file/453fadbd8a1a3af50a9df4df899537b5-Paper.pdf.

**6** Apple. Deploying transformers on the apple neural engine. https://machinelearning.apple.com/research/neural-engine-transformers, 2022. Accessed: 2023-03-31.

**7** Lei Jimmy Ba, Jamie Ryan Kiros, and Geoffrey E. Hinton. Layer normalization. *CoRR*, abs/1607.06450, 2016.

**8** Alexander Bain. *Mind and Body: The Theories of Their Relation*. D. Appleton and Company, 1873.

**9** Sergio Barrachina, Manuel F. Dolz, Pablo San Juan, and Enrique S. Quintana-Ortí. Efficient and portable GEMM-based convolution operators for deep neural network training on multicore processors. *Journal of Parallel and Distributed Computing*, 167:240–254, 2022. ISSN 0743-7315. doi: 10.1016/j.jpdc.2022.05.009. URL https://www.sciencedirect.com/science/article/pii/S0743731522001241.

**10** Mikhail Belkin, Daniel Hsu, and Ji Xu. Two models of double descent for weak features. *SIAM Journal on Mathematics of Data Science*, 2(4):1167–1180, 2020. doi: 10.1137/20M1336072.

**11** R. Bellman. A Markovian decision process. *Journal of Mathematics and Mechanics*, 6(5):679–684, 1957.

**12** Emily M. Bender, Timnit Gebru, Angelina McMillan-Major, and Shmargaret Shmitchell. On the dangers of stochastic parrots: Can language models be too big? In *Proceedings of the 2021 ACM Conference on Fairness, Accountability, and Transparency*, FAccT '21, pages 610–623, New York, NY, USA, 2021. Association for Computing Machinery. ISBN 9781450383097. doi: 10.1145/3442188.3445922.

**13** Lucas Beyer, Olivier J. Hénaff, Alexander Kolesnikov, Xiaohua Zhai, and Aäron van den Oord. Are we done with imagenet? *CoRR*, abs/2006.07159, 2020. URL https://arxiv.org/abs/2006.07159.

**14** B.W. Matthews. Comparison of the predicted and observed secondary structure of T4 phage lysozyme. *Biochimica et Biophysica Acta (BBA)-Protein Structure*, 405(2):442–451, 1975.

**15** B. Widrow and M. Hoff. Adaptive switching circuits. In *Proceedings WESCON*, pages 96–104, 1960.

**16** Ewen Callaway. It will change everything: Deepmind's AI makes gigantic leap in solving protein structures. *Nature*, 588:203–204, 2020.

**17** Kumar Chellapilla, Sidd Puri, and Patrice Simard. High performance convolutional neural networks for document processing. In *Tenth International Workshop on Frontiers in Handwriting Recognition*. SuviSoft, 2006.

**18** Anna Choromanska, Mikael Henaff, Michaël Mathieu, Gérard Ben Arous, and Yann LeCun. The loss surface of multilayer networks. *CoRR*, abs/1412.0233, 2014. URL http://arxiv.org/abs/1412.0233.

**19** Aakanksha Chowdhery, Sharan Narang, Jacob Devlin, Maarten Bosma, Gaurav Mishra, Adam Roberts, Paul Barham, Hyung Won Chung, Charles Sutton, Sebastian Gehrmann, Parker Schuh, Kensen Shi, Sasha Tsvyashchenko, Joshua Maynez, Abhishek Rao, Parker Barnes, Yi Tay, Noam Shazeer, Vinodkumar Prabhakaran, Emily Reif, Nan Du, Ben Hutchinson, Reiner Pope, James Bradbury, Jacob Austin, Michael Isard, Guy Gur-Ari, Pengcheng Yin, Toju Duke, Anselm Levskaya, Sanjay Ghemawat, Sunipa Dev, Henryk Michalewski, Xavier Garcia, Vedant Misra, Kevin Robinson, Liam Fedus, Denny Zhou, Daphne Ippolito, David Luan, Hyeontaek Lim, Barret Zoph, Alexander Spiridonov, Ryan Sepassi, David Dohan, Shivani Agrawal, Mark Omernick, Andrew M. Dai, Thanumalayan Sankaranarayana Pillai, Marie Pellat, Aitor Lewkowycz, Erica Moreira, Rewon Child, Oleksandr Polozov, Katherine Lee, Zongwei Zhou, Xuezhi Wang, Brennan Saeta, Mark Diaz, Orhan

Firat, Michele Catasta, Jason Wei, Kathy Meier-Hellstern, Douglas Eck, Jeff Dean, Slav Petrov, and Noah Fiedel. PaLM: Scaling language modeling with pathways. *CoRR*, abs/2204.02311, 2022. doi: 10.48550/arXiv.2204.02311.

20 Junyoung Chung, Çaglar Gülçehre, KyungHyun Cho, and Yoshua Bengio. Empirical evaluation of gated recurrent neural networks on sequence modeling. *CoRR*, abs/1412.3555, 2014. URL http://arxiv.org/abs/1412.3555.

21 Alonzo Church. An unsolvable problem of elementary number theory. *American Journal of Mathematics*, 58(2):345–363, 1936.

22 Kirkwood A. Cloud, Brian J. Reich, Christopher M. Rozoff, Stefano Alessandrini, William E. Lewis, and Luca Delle Monache. A feed forward neural network based on model output statistics for short-term hurricane intensity prediction. *Weather and Forecasting*, 34(4):985–997, 2019.

23 Cody Coleman, Daniel Kang, Deepak Narayanan, Luigi Nardi, Tian Zhao, Jian Zhang, Peter Bailis, Kunle Olukotun, Chris Ré, and Matei Zaharia. Analysis of DAWNBench, a time-to-accuracy machine learning performance benchmark. *ACM SIGOPS Operating Systems Review*, 53(1):14–25, Jul 2019. ISSN 0163-5980. doi: 10.1145/3352020.3352024.

24 Mark Collier and Jöran Beel. Implementing neural turing machines. In Vera Kurková, Yannis Manolopoulos, Barbara Hammer, Lazaros S. Iliadis, and Ilias Maglogiannis, editors, *Artificial Neural Networks and Machine Learning - ICANN 2018 - 27th International Conference on Artificial Neural Networks, Rhodes, Greece, October 4-7, 2018, Proceedings, Part III*, volume 11141 of *Lecture Notes in Computer Science*, pages 94–104. *Springer*, 2018. doi: 10.1007/978-3-030-01424-7_10.

25 Committee. IEEE standard for binary floating-point arithmetic, 1985.

26 Thomas Cover and Joy Thomas. *Elements of Information Theory*. Wiley, 2006. ISBN 0471241954.

27 G. Cybenko. Approximation by superpositions of a sigmoidal function. *Mathematics of Control*, 2:303–314, 1989.

28 Yehuda Dar, Vidya Muthukumar, and Richard G. Baraniuk. A farewell to the bias-variance tradeoff? An overview of the theory of overparameterized machine learning, 2021.

29 Jeffrey Dean, Greg S. Corrado, Rajat Monga, Kai Chen, Matthieu Devin, Quoc V. Le, Mark Z. Mao, Marc'Aurelio Ranzato, Andrew Senior, Paul Tucker, Ke Yang, and Andrew Y. Ng. Large scale distributed deep networks. In *NIPS*, 2012.

30 Rina Dechter. Learning while searching in constraint-satisfaction-problems. In *Proceedings of the Fifth AAAI National Conference on Artificial Intelligence*, AAAI'86, pages 178–183. AAAI Press, 1986.

31 Howard B. Demuth, Mark H. Beale, Orlando De Jess, and Martin T. Hagan. *Neural Network Design*. Martin Hagan, Stillwater, OK, USA, 2nd edition, 2014. ISBN 0971732116.

**32** Jia Deng, Wei Dong, Richard Socher, Li-Jia Li, Kai Li, and Li Fei-Fei. ImageNet: A large-scale hierarchical image database. In *2009 IEEE Conference on Computer Vision and Pattern Recognition*, pages 248–255, 2009. doi: 10.1109/CVPR.2009.5206848.

**33** Jacob Devlin, Ming-Wei Chang, Kenton Lee, and Kristina Toutanova. BERT: Pre-training of deep bidirectional transformers for language understanding, 2018. URL https://arxiv.org/abs/1810.04805.

**34** D. Rumelhart and Ronald Williams Geoffrey Hinton. Learning representations by back-propagating errors. *Nature*, 323(6088):533–536, 1986.

**35** John Duchi, Elad Hazan, and Yoram Singer. Adaptive subgradient methods for online learning and stochastic optimization. *Journal of Machine Learning Research*, 12(61):2121–2159, 2011. URL http://jmlr.org/papers/v12/duchi11a.html.

**36** B. Efron. Bootstrap methods: Another look at the Jackknife. *The Annals of Statistics*, 7(1):1–26, 1979. doi: 10.1214/aos/1176344552.

**37** Michael Egmont-Petersen, Jan L. Talmon, Jytte Brender, and Peter McNair. On the quality of neural net classifiers. *Artificial Intelligence in Medicine*, 6(5):359–381, 1994. ISSN 0933-3657. doi: 10.1016/0933-3657(94)90002-7. URL https://www.sciencedirect.com/science/article/pii/0933365794900027. Neural Computing in Medicine.

**38** Tyna Eloundou, Sam Manning, Pamela Mishkin, and Daniel Rock. GPTs are GPTs: An early look at the labor market impact potential of large language models, 2023.

**39** D. Farringdon, S. Waples M. Gill, and J. Agromaniz. The effects of closed-circuit television on crime: Meta-analysis of an English national quasi-experimental multi-site evaluation. *Journal of Experimental Criminology*, 3:21–38, 2007.

**40** William Fedus, Barret Zoph, and Noam Shazeer. Switch transformers: Scaling to trillion parameter models with simple and efficient sparsity. *CoRR*, abs/2101.03961, 2021. URL https://arxiv.org/abs/2101.03961.

**41** G. Forsythe. Pitfalls in computation, or why a mathbook isn't enough, 1970.

**42** Kunihiko Fukushima. Cognitron: A self-organizing multilayered neural network. *Biological Cybernetics*, 20(3):121–136, 1975.

**43** Kunihiko Fukushima. Neocognitron: A self-organizing neural network model for a mechanism of pattern recognition unaffected by shift in position. *Biological Cybernetics*, 36:193–202, 1980.

**44** G. Hinton. Where do features come from? *Cognative Sciences*, 38(6):1078–1101, 2014.

**45** Ofer Gal. *The New Science. The Origins of Modern Science*. Cambridge University Press, 2021. ISBN 978-1316649701.

**46** Stuart Geman, Elie Bienenstock, and René Doursat. Neural networks and the bias/variance dilemma. *Neural Computation*, 4(1):1–58, 1992. ISSN 0899-7667. URL http://portal.acm.org/citation.cfm?id=148062.

47  Wulfram Gerstner and Werner M. Kistler. *Spiking Neuron Models: Single Neurons, Populations, Plasticity.* Cambridge University Press, 2002. doi: 10.1017/CBO9780511815706.

48  Xavier Glorot and Yoshua Bengio. Understanding the difficulty of training deep feedforward neural networks. In *Proceedings of the 13th International Conference on Artificial Intelligence and Statistics*, volume 9, 2010.

49  Gene H. Golub and Charles F. Van Loan. *Matrix Computations.* The Johns Hopkins University Press, 4th edition, 2013.

50  Ian Goodfellow, Mehdi Mirza Jean Pouget-Abadie, David Warde-Farley Bing Xu, Aaron Courville Sherjil Ozair, and Yoshua Bengio. Generative adversarial nets. In *Advances in Neural Information Processing Systems*, 2014.

51  Ian J. Goodfellow. NIPS 2016 tutorial: Generative adversarial networks. *CoRR*, abs/1701.00160, 2017. URL http://arxiv.org/abs/1701.00160.

52  Kazushige Goto and Robert A. van de Geijn. Anatomy of high-performance matrix multiplication. *ACM Transactions on Mathematical Software (TOMS)*, 34(3), May 2008. ISSN 0098-3500. doi: 10.1145/1356052.1356053.

53  Alex Graves. Generating sequences with recurrent neural networks. *CoRR*, abs/1308.0850, 2013. URL http://arxiv.org/abs/1308.0850.

54  Alex Graves, Greg Wayne, Malcolm Reynolds, Tim Harley, Ivo Danihelka, Agnieszka Grabska-Barwińska, Sergio Gómez Colmenarejo, Edward Grefenstette, Tiago Ramalho, John Agapiou, Adrià Puigdomènech Badia, Karl Moritz Hermann, Yori Zwols, Georg Ostrovski, Adam Cain, Helen King, Christopher Summerfield, Phil Blunsom, Koray Kavukcuoglu, and Demis Hassabis. Hybrid computing using a neural network with dynamic external memory. *Nature*, 538:471–476, 2016.

55  Alex Graves, Greg Wayne, and Ivo Danihelka. Neural turing machines. *CoRR*, abs/1410.5401, 2014. URL http://arxiv.org/abs/1410.5401.

56  Karol Gregor, Alex Graves Ivo Danihelka, and Daan Wierstra Danilo Rezende. DRAW: A recurrent neural network for image generation. In *32nd International Conference on Machine Learning*, 2015.

57  Kevin Gurney. *An Introduction to Neural Networks.* Taylor & Francis, Inc., 1997. ISBN 1857286731.

58  M.T. Hagan and M.B. Menhaj. Training feed forward network with the Marquardt algorithm. *IEEE Transactions on Neural Networks*, 5:989–993, 1994.

59  Karen Hao. The two-year fight to stop amazon from selling face recognition to the police, 2020.

60  J.A. Hartigan and M.A. Wong. A k-means clustering algorithm. *JSTOR: Applied Statistics*, 28(1):100–108, 1979.

61  T. Hastie, R. Tibshirani, and J.H. Friedman. *The Elements of Statistical Learning: Data Mining, Inference, and Prediction.* Springer Series in Statistics. Springer, 2009. ISBN 9780387848846. URL https://books.google.co.uk/books?id=eBSgoAEACAAJ.

62  Kaiming He, Xiangyu Zhang, Shaoqing Ren, and Jian Sun. Delving deep into rectifiers: Surpassing human-level performance on imagenet classification. In

*Proceedings of the IEEE International Conference on Computer Vision (ICCV)*, December 2015.

63  Kaiming He, Xiangyu Zhang, Shaoqing Ren, and Jian Sun. Delving deep into rectifiers: Surpassing human-level performance on imagenet classification. In *2015 IEEE International Conference on Computer Vision (ICCV)*, pages 1026–1034, 2015. doi: 10.1109/ICCV.2015.123.

64  Kaiming He, Xiangyu Zhang, Shaoqing Ren, and Jian Sun. Deep residual learning for image recognition. *CoRR*, abs/1512.03385, 2015. URL http://arxiv.org/abs/1512.03385.

65  Donald Hebb. *The Organization of Behaviour: A Neuropsychological Theory*. Wiley, 1949.

66  Kashmir Hill. Wrongfully accused by an algorithm. *New York Times*, 2020.

67  Geoffrey E. Hinton, Simon Osindero, and Yee Whye Teh. A fast learning algorithm for deep belief nets. *Neural Computing*, 18(7):1527–1554, 2006. doi: 10.1162/neco.2006.18.7.1527.

68  Geoffrey E. Hinton, Nitish Srivastava, Alex Krizhevsky, Ilya Sutskever, and Ruslan Salakhutdinov. Improving neural networks by preventing co-adaptation of feature detectors. *CoRR*, abs/1207.0580, 2012.

69  A.L. Hodgkin and A.F. Huxley. A quantitative description of membrane current and its application to conduction and excitation in nerve. *The Journal of Physiology*, 117(4):500–544, 1952.

70  Kurt Hornik. Approximation capabilities of multilayer feedforward networks. *Neural Networks*, 4(2):251–257, 1991. ISSN 0893-6080. doi: 10.1016/0893-6080(91)90009-T. URL https://www.sciencedirect.com/science/article/pii/089360809190009T.

71  Wei Hu, Lechao Xiao, and Jeffrey Pennington. Provable benefit of orthogonal initialization in optimizing deep linear networks. In *Proceedings of ICLR*. ICLR 2020, 2020.

72  Xia Hu, Lingyang Chu, Jian Pei, Weiqing Liu, and Jiang Bian. Model complexity of deep learning: A survey. *Knowledge and Information Systems*, 63:2585–2619, 2021.

73  Christian Igel and Michael Huesken. Improving the rprop learning algorithm. In *Second International Symposium on Neural Computation*, pages 115–121, 2000.

74  Christian Igel, Marc Toussaint, and Wan Weishui. Rprop using the natural gradient. In Detlef H. Mache, József Szabados, and Marcel G. de Bruin, editors, *Trends and Applications in Constructive Approximation*, pages 259–272, Basel, 2005. Birkhäuser Basel. ISBN 978-3-7643-7356-6.

75  Sergey Ioffe and Christian Szegedy. Batch normalization: Accelerating deep network training by reducing internal covariate shift. In *Proceedings of the 32nd International Conference on International Conference on Machine Learning*, volume 37, ICML'15, pages 448–456. JMLR.org, 2015.

76  William James. *The Principles of Psychology*, volume 2. Dover Publications, 1918.

**77** Daniel Jurafsky and James Martin. *Speech and Language Processing: An Introduction to Natural Language Processing, Computational Linguistics, and Speech Recognition.* Prentice Hall, 2008. ISBN 9780131873216.

**78** Lukasz Kaiser and Samy Bengio. Can active memory replace attention? In Daniel D. Lee, Masashi Sugiyama, Ulrike von Luxburg, Isabelle Guyon, and Roman Garnett, editors, *Advances in Neural Information Processing Systems 29: Annual Conference on Neural Information Processing Systems 2016*, December 5–10, 2016, Barcelona, Spain, pages 3774–3782, 2016. URL https://proceedings.neurips.cc/paper/2016/hash/fb8feff253bb6c834deb61ec76baa89.

**79** Eric Kandel and Thomas Jessell James Schwarz. *Principles of Neural Science,* 4th edition. McGraw-Hill, 2000. ISBN 978-083857701.

**80** Tero Karras, Timo Aila, Samuli Laine, and Jaakko Lehtinen. Progressive growing of gans for improved quality, stability, and variation. *CoRR*, abs/1710.10196, 2017. URL http://arxiv.org/abs/1710.10196.

**81** Tero Karras, Janne Hellsten Miika Aittala, Jaako Lehtinen Samuli Laine, and Timo Aila. Training generative adversarial networks with limited data. In *Neural Information Processing Systems (NeurIPS)*, 2020.

**82** Patrick Kidger and Terry Lyons. Universal approximation with deep narrow networks. In Jacob Abernethy and Shivani Agarwal, editors, *Proceedings of Thirty Third Conference on Learning Theory*, volume 125 of *Proceedings of Machine Learning Research*, pages 2306–2327. PMLR, 09–12 Jul 2020. URL https://proceedings.mlr.press/v125/kidger20a.html.

**83** J. Kiefer and J. Wolfowitz. Stochastic estimation of the maximum of a regression function. *The Annals of Mathematical Statistics*, 23(3):462–466, 1952. ISSN 00034851. URL http://www.jstor.org/stable/2236690.

**84** Diederik P. Kingma and Jimmy Ba. Adam: A method for stochastic optimization. In Yoshua Bengio and Yann LeCun, editors, *3rd International Conference on Learning Representations, ICLR 2015*, San Diego, CA, USA, May 7–9, 2015, Conference Track Proceedings, 2015. URL http://arxiv.org/abs/1412.6980.

**85** Diederik P. Kingma and Max Welling. Auto-encoding variational Bayes. In Yoshua Bengio and Yann LeCun, editors, *2nd International Conference on Learning Representations, ICLR 2014*, Banff, AB, Canada, April 14–16, 2014, Conference Track Proceedings, 2014. URL http://arxiv.org/abs/1312.6114.

**86** Donald Knuth. *Seminumerical Algorithms. The Art of Computer Programming.* Addison-Wesley, 2002. ISBN 0201038226.

**87** Mark A. Kramer. Nonlinear principal component analysis using autoassociative neural networks. *Aiche Journal*, 37:233–243, 1991.

**88** Erwin Kreyszig, Herbert Kreyszig, and E.J. Norminton. *Advanced Engineering Mathematics.* Wiley, Hoboken, NJ, 10th edition, 2011. ISBN 0470458364.

**89** Alex Krizhevsky, Ilya Sutskever, and Geoffrey E. Hinton. Imagenet classification with deep convolutional neural networks. In F. Pereira, C.J. Burges, L. Bottou, and

K.Q. Weinberger, editors, *Advances in Neural Information Processing Systems*, volume 25. Curran Associates, Inc., 2012. URL https://proceedings.neurips.cc/paper/2012/file/c399862d3b9d6b76c8436e924a68c45b-Paper.pdf.

90  Nupur Kumari, Richard Zhang, Eli Shechtman, and Jun-Yan Zhu. Ensembling off-the-shelf models for gan training. In *Proceedings of the IEEE/CVF Conference on Computer Vision and Pattern Recognition (CVPR)*, June 2022.

91  Y. LeCun, B. Boser, J.S. Denker, D. Henderson, R.E. Howard, W. Hubbard, and L.D. Jackel. Backpropagation applied to handwritten zip code recognition. *Neural Computation*, 1(4):541–551, 1989. doi: 10.1162/neco.1989.1.4.541.

92  Y. Lecun, L. Bottou, Y. Bengio, and P. Haffner. Gradient-based learning applied to document recognition. *Proceedings of the IEEE*, 86(11):2278–2324, 1998. doi: 10.1109/5.726791.

93  Yann LeCun, Léon Bottou, Genevieve B. Orr, and Klaus-Robert Müller. Efficient backprop. In *Neural Networks: Tricks of the Trade*, 2nd edition, volume 7700 of *Lecture Notes in Computer Science*, pages 9–48. Springer, 2012. ISBN 978-3-642-35288-1.

94  Christian Ledig, Lucas Theis, Ferenc Huszar, Jose Caballero, Andrew P. Aitken, Alykhan Tejani, Johannes Totz, Zehan Wang, and Wenzhe Shi. Photo-realistic single image super-resolution using a generative adversarial network. *CoRR*, abs/1609.04802, 2016.

95  Honglak Lee, Roger Grosse, Rajesh Ranganath, and Andrew Y. Ng. Unsupervised learning of hierarchical representations with convolutional deep belief networks. *Communications of the ACM*, 54(10):95–103, Oct 2011. ISSN 0001-0782. doi: 10.1145/2001269.2001295.

96  Gottfried Leibniz. *Discourse on Metaphysics and Other Essays: Discourse on Metaphysics; On the Ultimate Origination of Things; Preface to the New Essays; The Monadology*. Hackett Publishing Co., 1992. ISBN 0872201325.

97  D.C. Liu and J. Nocedal. On the limited memory BFGS method for large scale optimization. *Mathematical Programming*, 45(3, Ser. B):503–528, 1989.

98  Paul Lodge. Leibniz's mill argument against mechanical materialism revisited. *Ergo*, 2014. doi: 10.3998/ergo.12405314.0001.003.

99  Lu Lu. Dying relu and initialization: Theory and numerical examples. *Communications in Computational Physics*, 28(5):1671–1706, Jun 2020. doi: 10.4208/cicp.oa-2020-0165.

100  Xudong Mao, Qing Li, Haoran Xie, Raymond Y.K. Lau, Zhen Wang, and Stephen Paul Smolley. Least squares generative adversarial networks. In *2017 IEEE International Conference on Computer Vision (ICCV)*, pages 2813–2821, 2017. doi: 10.1109/ICCV.2017.304.

101  James Martens. Deep learning via Hessian-free optimization. In *Proceedings of the 27th International Conference on International Conference on Machine Learning*, ICML'10, pages 735–742, Madison, WI, USA, 2010. Omnipress. ISBN 9781605589077.

**102** James Martens. New insights and perspectives on the natural gradient method. *Journal of Machine Learning Research*, 21(146):1–76, 2020. URL http://jmlr.org/papers/v21/17-678.html.

**103** Scott McKinney, Marcin Sieniek, Varun Godbole, Jonathan Godwin, Natasha Antropova, Hutan Ashrafian, Trevor Back, Mary Chesus, Greg S. Corrado, Ara Darzi, Mozziyar Etemadi, Florencia Garcia-Vicente, Fiona J. Gilbert, Mark Halling-Brown, Demis Hassabis, Sunny Jansen, Alan Karthikesalingam, Christopher J. Kelly, Dominic King, Joseph R. Ledsam, David Melnick, Hormuz Mostofi, Lily Peng, Joshua Jay Reicher, Bernardino Romera-Paredes, Richard Sidebottom, Mustafa Suleyman, Daniel Tse, Kenneth C. Young, Jeffrey De Fauw, and Shravya Shetty. International evaluation of an AI system for breast cancer screening. *Nature*, 577:89–94, 2020.

**104** Tomás Mikolov, Ilya Sutskever, Kai Chen, Gregory S. Corrado, and Jeffrey Dean. Distributed representations of words and phrases and their compositionality. In Christopher J.C. Burges, Léon Bottou, Zoubin Ghahramani, and Kilian Q. Weinberger, editors, *Advances in Neural Information Processing Systems 26: 27th Annual Conference on Neural Information Processing Systems 2013. Proceedings of a Meeting Held December 5–8, 2013*, Lake Tahoe, Nevada, United States, pages 3111–3119, 2013. URL https://proceedings.neurips.cc/paper/2013/hash/9aa42b31882ec039965f3c4923ce901.

**105** Tom Mitchell. *Machine Learning*. McGraw-Hill, 1997. ISBN 9384761168.

**106** M. Minsky and S. Papert. *Perceptrons*. MIT Press, 1969.

**107** Nikolai Nowaczyk, Jörg Kienitz, Sarp Kaya Acar, and Qian Liang. How deep is your model? Network topology selection from a model validation perspective. *Journal of Mathematics in Industry*, 12:1, 2022.

**108** Long Ouyang, Jeff Wu, Xu Jiang, Diogo Almeida, Carroll L. Wainwright, Pamela Mishkin, Chong Zhang, Sandhini Agarwal, Katarina Slama, Alex Ray, John Schulman, Jacob Hilton, Fraser Kelton, Luke Miller, Maddie Simens, Amanda Askell, Peter Welinder, Paul Christiano, Jan Leike, and Ryan Lowe. Training language models to follow instructions with human feedback, 2022. URL https://arxiv.org/abs/2203.02155.

**109** Lawrence Page, Sergey Brin, Rajeev Motwani, and Terry Wino-grad. The PageRank citation ranking: Bringing order to the web. Technical Report 1999-66, Stanford InfoLab, November 1999. URL http://ilpubs.stanford.edu:8090/422/. Previous number = SIDL- WP-1999-0120.

**110** Yudi Pawtan. *In All Likelihood*. Oxford University Press, 2013. ISBN 0199671222.

**111** K. Pearson. *On the Theory of Contingency and Its Relation to Association and Normal Correlation*, volumes 1–4; volume 7 in Drapers' company research memoirs: Biometric series. Dulau and Company, 1904. URL https://books.google.co.uk/books?id=8h3OxgEACAAJ.

**112** Rui Pereira, Marco Couto, Francisco Ribeiro, Rui Rua, Jácome Cunha, João Paulo Fernandes, and João Saraiva. Ranking programming languages by energy efficiency. *Science of Computer Programming*, 205:102609, 2021. ISSN 0167-6423. doi:

10.1016/j.scico.2021.102609. URL https://www.sciencedirect.com/science/article/pii/S0167642321000022.

**113** S. Madeh Piryonesi and Tamer E. El-Diraby. Data analytics in asset management: Cost-effective prediction of the pavement condition index. *Journal of Infrastructure Systems*, 26(1):04019036, 2020. doi: 10.1061/(ASCE)IS.1943-555X.0000512.

**114** B.T. Polyak. Some methods of speeding up the convergence of iteration methods. *USSR Computational Mathematics and Mathematical Physics*, 4(5):1–17, 1964. ISSN 0041-5553. doi: 10.1016/0041-5553(64)90137-5. URL https://www.sciencedirect.com/science/article/pii/0041555364901375.

**115** R. Sutton and A. Barto. *Reinforcement Learning, An Introduction*. Independently Published, 2022. ISBN 979-8845864970.

**116** R.A. Fisher. The concepts of inverse probability and fiducial probability referring to unkown parameters. *Proceedings of the Royal Society, A* 139:343–348, 1933.

**117** R.A. Fisher. The use of multiple measurements in taxonomic problems. *Annals of Eugenics*, 7(2):179–188, 1936.

**118** Alec Radford and Karthik Narasimhan. *Improving language understand- ing by generative pre-training*, 2018.

**119** Alec Radford, Luke Metz, and Soumith Chintala. Unsupervised representation learning with deep convolutional generative adversarial networks. In Yoshua Bengio and Yann LeCun, editors, *4th International Conference on Learning Representations, ICLR 2016*, San Juan, Puerto Rico, May 2–4, 2016, *Conference Track Proceedings*, 2016. URL http://arxiv.org/abs/1511.06434.

**120** Jack W. Rae, Jonathan J. Hunt, Tim Harley, Ivo Danihelka, Andrew Senior, Greg Wayne, Alex Graves, and Timothy P. Lillicrap. Scaling memory-augmented neural networks with sparse reads and writes, 2016. URL https://arxiv.org/abs/1610.09027.

**121** Pranav Rajpurkar, Jian Zhang, Konstantin Lopyrev, and Percy Liang. SQuAD: 100,000+ questions for machine comprehension of text, 2016. URL https://arxiv.org/abs/1606.05250.

**122** Marc'Aurelio Ranzato, Fu Jie Huang, Y-Lan Boureau, and Yann LeCun. Unsupervised learning of invariant feature hierarchies with applications to object recognition. *2007 IEEE Conference on Computer Vision and Pattern Recognition*, 2007. doi: 10.1109/cvpr.2007.383157.

**123** A.N. Refenes and M. Azema-Barac. Neural network applications in financial asset management. *Neural Computing and Applications*, 2:13–39, 1994.

**124** M. Riedmiller and H. Braun. A direct adaptive method for faster backpropagation learning: The RPROP algorithm. In *IEEE Conference on Neural Networks*, 1993.

**125** Suzanne Rivoire, Mehul A. Shah, Parthasarathy Ranganathan, and Christos Kozyrakis. JouleSort: A balanced energy-efficiency benchmark. In *Proceedings of the 2007 ACM SIGMOD International Conference on Management of Data*, SIGMOD '07, pages 365–376, New York, NY, USA, 2007. Association for Computing Machinery. ISBN 9781595936868. doi: 10.1145/1247480.1247522.

**126** V.K. Rohatgi and A.K.M.E. Saleh. *An Introduction to Probability and Statistics.* Wiley Series in Probability and Statistics. Wiley, 2015. ISBN 9781118799642. URL https://books.google.co.uk/books?id=RCq9BgAAQBAJ.

**127** Raul Rojas. *Neural Networks - A Systematic Introduction.* Springer-Verlag, Berlin, 1996.

**128** Kevin Roose. The brilliance and weirdness of ChatGPT. *The New York Times,* pages Section B, page 1, 2022.

**129** F. Rosenblatt. Principles of neurodynamics: Perceptrons and the theory of brain mechanisms. Cornell Aeronautical Laboratory. Report no. VG-1196-G-8. Spartan Books, 1962. URL https://books.google.co.uk/books?id=7FhRAAAAMAAJ.

**130** Frank Rosenblatt. The perceptron—a perceiving and recognizing automaton. Cornell Aeronautical Laboratory, Report 85-460-1, 1957.

**131** S. Minsky and M. Papert. *Perceptrons: An Introduction to Computational Geometry.* MIT Press, 1969. ISBN 978-0-262-63022-1.

**132** Yousef Saad. *Iterative Methods for Sparse Linear Systems.* Applied Mathematics, 2nd edition. SIAM, 2003. ISBN 978-0-89871-534-7. doi: 10.1137/1.9780898718003. URL http://www-users.cs.umn.edu/~saad/IterMethBook2ndEd.pdf.

**133** Shibani Santurkar, Dimitris Tsipras, Andrew Ilyas, and Aleksander Madry. How does batch normalization help optimization? In *Proceedings of the 32nd International Conference on Neural Information Processing Systems,* NIPS'18, pages 2488–2498, Red Hook, NY, USA, 2018. Curran Associates Inc.

**134** Dominik Scherer, Andreas Müller, and Sven Behnke. Evaluation of pooling operations in convolutional architectures for object recognition. In Konstantinos Diamantaras, Wlodek Duch, and Lazaros S. Iliadis, editors, *Artificial Neural Networks – ICANN 2010,* pages 92–101, Berlin, Heidelberg, 2010. Springer-Verlag, Berlin, Heidelberg. ISBN 978-3-642-15825-4.

**135** John Searle. Minds, brains and programs. *Behavioral and Brain Sciences,* 3(3):417–424, 1980.

**136** Charles Sherrington. Experiments in examination of the peripheral distribution of the fibers of the posterior roots of some spinal nerves. *Proceedings of the Royal Society of London,* 190:45–186, 1898.

**137** Pannaga Shivaswamy and Ashok Chandrashekar. Bias-variance decomposition for ranking. In *Proceedings of the 14th ACM International Conference on Web Search and Data Mining,* WSDM '21, pages 472–480, New York, NY, USA, 2021. Association for Computing Machinery. ISBN 9781450382977. doi: 10.1145/3437963.3441772.

**138** Mohammad Shoeybi, Mostofa Patwary, Raul Puri, Patrick LeGresley, Jared Casper, and Bryan Catanzaro. Megatron-LM: Training multi-billion parameter language models using model parallelism. *CoRR,* abs/1909.08053, 2019. URL http://arxiv.org/abs/1909.08053.

**139** David Silver, Aja Huang, Christopher J. Maddison, Arthur Guez, Laurent Sifre, George van den Driessche, Julian Schrittwieser, Ioannis Antonoglou, Veda Panneershelvam, Marc Lanctot, Sander Diele-man, Dominik Grewe, John Nham,

Nal Kalchbrenner, Ilya Sutskever, Timothy Lillicrap, Madeleine Leach, Koray Kavukcuoglu, Thore Graepel, and Demis Hassabis. Mastering the game of go with deep neural networks and tree search. *Nature*, 529:484–503, 2016. URL http://www.nature.com/nature/journal/v529/n7587/full/nature16961.html.

**140** Karen Simonyan and Andrew Zisserman. Very deep convolutional networks for large-scale image recognition. In Yoshua Bengio and Yann Le-Cun, editors, *3rd International Conference on Learning Representations*, ICLR 2015, San Diego, CA, USA, May 7–9, 2015, *Conference Track Proceedings*, 2015. URL http://arxiv.org/abs/1409.1556.

**141** Shaden Smith, Mostofa Patwary, Brandon Norick, Patrick LeGresley, Samyam Rajbhandari, Jared Casper, Zhun Liu, Shrimai Prabhumoye, George Zerveas, Vijay Korthikanti, Elton Zheng, Rewon Child, Reza Yaz-dani Aminabadi, Julie Bernauer, Xia Song, Mohammad Shoeybi, Yux-iong He, Michael Houston, Saurabh Tiwary, and Bryan Catanzaro. Using deepspeed and megatron to train megatron-turing NLG 530B, A large-scale generative language model. *CoRR*, abs/2201.11990, 2022. URL https://arxiv.org/abs/2201.11990.

**142** Tyler M. Smith, Robert A. van de Geijn, Mikhail Smelyanskiy, Jeff R. Hammond, and Field G. Van Zee. Anatomy of high-performance many-threaded matrix multiplication. In *IPDPS*, pages 1049–1059. IEEE Computer Society, 2014. ISBN 978-1-4799-3799-8.

**143** Saleh Soltan, Shankar Ananthakrishnan, Jack FitzGerald, Rahul Gupta, Wael Hamza, Haidar Khan, Charith Peris, Stephen Rawls, Andy Rosenbaum, Anna Rumshisky, Chandana Satya Prakash, Mukund Sridhar, Fabian Triefenbach, Apurv Verma, Gokhan Tur, and Prem Natarajan. AlexaTM 20B: Few-shot learning using a large-scale multilingual Seq2Seq model. *arXiv*, 2022. URL https://www.amazon.science/publications/alexatm-20b-few-shot-learning-using-a-large-scale-multilingual-seq2seq-model.

**144** Nitish Srivastava, Geoffrey Hinton, Alex Krizhevsky, Ilya Sutskever, and Ruslan Salakhutdinov. Dropout: A simple way to prevent neural networks from overfitting. *Journal of Machine Learning Research*, 15(56):1929–1958, 2014. URL http://jmlr.org/papers/v15/srivastava14a.html.

**145** J. Stewart. *Calculus*. Available 2010 Titles Enhanced Web Assign Series. Cengage Learning, 2007. ISBN 9780495011606. URL https://books.google.co.uk/books?id=jBD0yTh64wAC.

**146** Chris Stokel-Walker. ChatGPT listed as author on research papers: Many scientists disapprove. *Nature*, 613:620–621, 2023.

**147** Sainbayar Sukhbaatar, Arthur Szlam, Jason Weston, and Rob Fergus. End-to-end memory networks. In C. Cortes, N. Lawrence, D. Lee, M. Sugiyama, and R. Garnett, editors, *Advances in Neural Information Processing Systems*, volume 28. Curran Associates, Inc., 2015. URL https://proceedings.neurips.cc/paper/2015/file/8fb21ee7a2207526da55a679f0332de2-Paper.pdf.

**148** Christian Szegedy, Wei Liu, Yangqing Jia, Pierre Sermanet, Scott Reed, Dragomir Anguelov, Dumitru Erhan, Vincent Vanhoucke, and Andrew Rabinovich. Going deeper with convolutions. In *2015 IEEE Conference on Computer Vision and Pattern Recognition (CVPR)*, pages 1–9, 2015. doi: 10.1109/CVPR.2015.7298594.

**149** Romal Thoppilan, Daniel De Freitas, Jamie Hall, Noam Shazeer, Apoorv Kulshreshtha, Heng-Tze Cheng, Alicia Jin, Taylor Bos, Leslie Baker, Yu Du, YaGuang Li, Hongrae Lee, Huaixiu Steven Zheng, Amin Ghafouri, Marcelo Menegali, Yanping Huang, Maxim Krikun, Dmitry Lepikhin, James Qin, Dehao Chen, Yuanzhong Xu, Zhifeng Chen, Adam Roberts, Maarten Bosma, Yanqi Zhou, Chung-Ching Chang, Igor Krivokon, Will Rusch, Marc Pickett, Kathleen S. Meier-Hellstern, Meredith Ringel Morris, Tulsee Doshi, Renelito Delos Santos, Toju Duke, Johnny Soraker, Ben Zevenbergen, Vinodkumar Prabhakaran, Mark Diaz, Ben Hutchinson, Kristen Olson, Alejandra Molina, Erin Hoffman-John, Josh Lee, Lora Aroyo, Ravi Rajakumar, Alena Butryna, Matthew Lamm, Viktoriya Kuzmina, Joe Fenton, Aaron Cohen, Rachel Bernstein, Ray Kurzweil, Blaise Aguera-Arcas, Claire Cui, Marian Croak, Ed H. Chi, and Quoc Le. LaMDA: Language models for dialog applications. *CoRR*, abs/2201.08239, 2022. URL https://arxiv.org/abs/2201.08239.

**150** T. Tieleman and Geoffrey Hinton. Lecture 6.5-rmsprop, 2012.

**151** New York Times. Electronic brain teaches itself. *New York Times*, pages Section E, page 9, 1958.

**152** Alan Turing. On computable numbers, with an application to the Entscheidungs problem. *Proceedings of the London Mathematical Society*, 41(1):230–265, 1937.

**153** Alan Turing. Computing machinery and intelligence. *Mind*, LIX:433–460, 1950.

**154** Jeffrey Ullman and John Hopcroft. *Introduction to Automata Theory, Languages, and Computation.* Pearson, 2006. ISBN 0321455363.

**155** Ashish Vaswani, Noam Shazeer, Niki Parmar, Jakob Uszkor-eit, Llion Jones, Aidan N. Gomez, Łukasz Kaiser, and Illia Polosukhin. Attention is all You Need. In I. Guyon, U. Von Luxburg, S. Bengio, H. Wallach, R. Fergus, S. Vishwanathan, and R. Garnett, editors, *Advances in Neural Information Processing Systems*, volume 30. Curran Associates, Inc., 2017. URL https://proceedings.neurips.cc/paper/2017/file/3f5ee243547dee91fbd053c1c4a845a.

**156** Oriol Vinyals and Daniel Povey. Krylov subspace descent for deep learning. In Neil D. Lawrence and Mark Girolami, editors, *Proceedings of the Fifteenth International Conference on Artificial Intelligence and Statistics*, volume 22 of *Proceedings of Machine Learning Research*, pages 1261–1268, La Palma, Canary Islands, 21–23 April 2012. PMLR. URL https://proceedings.mlr.press/v22/vinyals12.html.

**157** Li Wan, Matthew D. Zeiler, Sixin Zhang, Yann LeCun, and Rob Fergus. Regularization of neural networks using dropconnect. In *ICML (3)*, volume 28 of *JMLR Workshop and Conference Proceedings*, pages 1058–1066. JMLR.org, 2013.

**158** Alex Wang, Nikita Nangia Yada Pruksachatkun, Julian Michael Amanpreet Singh, Omer Levy Felix Hill, and Samuel Bowman. GLUE: A multi-task benchmark and analysis platform for natural language understanding. In *International Conference on Learning Representations*, 2019.

159 Alex Wang, Nikita Nangia, Yada Pruksachatkun, Julian Michael, Amanpreet Singh, Omer Levy, Felix Hill, and Samuel Bowman. SuperGLUE: A stickier benchmark for general-purpose language understanding systems. In *33rd Conference on Neural Information Processing Systems*, 2019.

160 Christopher John Cornish Hellaby Watkins. *Learning from Delayed Rewards*. King's College, Cambridge, United Kingdom, 1989.

161 Colin White, Mahmoud Safari, Rhea Sanjay Sukthanker, Binxin Ru, Thomas Elsken, Arber Zela, Debadeepta Dey, and Frank Hutter. Neural architecture search: Insights from 1000 papers. *ArXiv*, abs/2301.08727, 2023.

162 Hugh Wilson and Jack Cowan. Excitory and inhibitory interactions in localized populations of model neurons. *Biophysical Journal*, 12:1–24, 1972.

163 Rodney Winter and Bernard Widrow. MADALINE RULE II: A training algorithm for neural networks. In *IEEE International Conference on Neural Networks*, pages 401–408, 1988.

164 W. Pitts and W.S. McCulloch. How we know universals the perception of auditory and visual forms. *Bulletin of Mathematical Biology*, 9(3):127–147, 1947.

165 Jie Xu. A deep learning approach to building an intelligent video surveillance system. *Multimedia Tools and Applications*, 80:5495–5515, 2020.

166 Jingjing Xu, Xu Sun, Zhiyuan Zhang, Guangxiang Zhao, and Junyang Lin. Understanding and improving layer normalization. In *Advances in Neural Information Processing Systems*, volume 32. Curran Associates, Inc., 2019.

167 Santiago Ramón y Cajal. *Manual de Anatomía Patológica general*. N. Moya, 1906.

168 Matthew D. Zeiler and Rob Fergus. Visualizing and understanding convolutional networks. *CoRR*, abs/1311.2901, 2013.

169 Daniel Zhang, Erik Brynjolfsson Nestor Maslej, Terah Lyons John Etchemendy, Helen Ngo James Manyika, Michael Sellitto Juan Niebles, Yoav Shoham Ellie Sakhaee, and Raymond Perrault Jack Clark. The AI index 2022 annual report, 2022.

# Index

*Demystifying Deep Learning: An Introduction to the Mathematics of Neural Networks,*
First Edition. Douglas J. Santry.
© 2024 The Institute of Electrical and Electronics Engineers, Inc. Published 2024 by John Wiley & Sons, Inc.

Printed and bound by CPI Group (UK) Ltd, Croydon, CR0 4YY

16/04/2025

14658592-0001